GORBACHEV'S ECONOMIC DILEMMA: AN INSIDER'S VIEW

GORBACHEV'S ECONOMIC DILEMMA: AN INSIDER'S VIEW

Olimpiad Solomonovich Ioffe

Edited by David A. Rome

Merrill/Magnus Publishing Corporation
St. Paul

Copyright © 1989 by Merrill/Magnus Publishing Corporation

Merrill/Magnus Publishing Corporation
One Merrill Circle
St. Paul, Minnesota 55108

Library of Congress Cataloging in Publication Data

Ioffe, O.S. (Olimpiad Solomonovich), 1920-
    Gorbachev's economic dilemma.

    Includes bibliographical references.
    1. Soviet Union—Economic policy—1986-   . 2. Perestroika.
3. Gorbachev, Mikhail Sergeevich, 1931-   . 4. Trade regulation—
Soviet Union.
I. Rome, David A.   II. Title.
HC336.26.I58 1989   338.947′009′048   89-12154

ISBN 1-877927-02-3

10 9 8 7 6 5 4 3 2

Printed in the United States of America

CONTENTS

Preface

Thanks to the day-to-day coverage of internal events in the Soviet Union, the terms *glasnost'* and *perestroika* have become a part of the vocabulary of even the casual observer of Soviet affairs in the West. *Glasnost'* and *perestroika* have come to epitomize the notions of political and economic reform. Where China may have erred in emphasizing *perestroika* at the expense of political freedom, Mikhail Gorbachev had the right combination of both, or so many Westerners thought as Gorbachev's reforms were met with high expectations.

More recently, cautious pessimism has become the norm outside the Soviet Union, as it arguably has been inside the Soviet Union from the outset. There is considerable cause for pessimism just from reading the newspaper headlines. This week alone, there are reports of strikes in the coal fields, continuing ethnic unrest, and experiments with limited economic autonomy for the Baltic Republics. Meanwhile, *The New York Times* asks, "Why aren't American political leaders and policy experts more concerned for Mikhail Gorbachev's fate?"

Olimpiad Ioffe has reason to be concerned for Mikhail Gorbachev's fate. He is not a soothsayer, but he has spent a career analyzing, interpreting, and even writing Soviet civil and economic law and is a master at sorting out the theory from the actual practice, the appearance from the substance. He has found mostly appearance in Gorbachev's economic reforms.

Before applying to emigrate in the late 1970s, Olimpiad Ioffe was considered the Soviet Union's most prominent legal scholar. As Chairman of the Civil Law Department of the prestigious Leningrad State University, Ioffe had authored 32 books and over 150 articles that have been translated into twelve languages. He was also the principal drafter of the modern Russian Civil Code and the 1961 Fundamental Principles of Civil Legislation upon which much of Soviet civil law is based.

Like so many of the other hundreds of thousands of Soviet Jews who applied to emigrate in the 1970s and early 1980s, Olimpiad and his family were denied exit visas and became Refuseniks. Thanks only to special efforts by American legal scholars with whom Olimpiad had worked over the years were they able to leave in 1981. Olimpiad continued to teach and write about Soviet law at Harvard and Boston University before joining the faculty of the University of Connecticut School of Law in 1982.

It was at the University of Connecticut that I had the distinct fortune to hear Olimpiad lecture on the Soviet economy and legal system and the opportunity to work on his earlier books on Soviet law. Whereas his earlier books had broached the subjects of the inner workings of the Soviet economy and the interaction of the law and the economy, this book goes right to the heart of the matter in describing and analyzing what is happening—and what is not happening—in the Soviet economy despite what appear to be the best intentions of Mikhail Gorbachev.

Much of the commentary worldwide on Gorbachev's economic and political reforms takes them on their face. This book focuses on those reforms that have the potential for genuine impact and reveals their limitations in light of the fundamental components of the Soviet system.

There are two such fundamental components of the Soviet system: unlimited political power of the ruling elite and economic monopoly by the same elite as the source of its unlimited power. If either of these elements is eliminated, the Soviet system will have been replaced by another system. In Marxist-Leninist terms such a change is characterized as a revolution, not a reform. What Gorbachev strives to achieve is no revolution, despite some high profile parliamentary changes and decentralizing economic measures.

Economic reforms result not from the whims of the Soviet rulers but from the nature of the Soviet system, which is consistently cyclical. Because of the dependence of unlimited political power on the economic monopoly, the latter must be maintained centrally; but the inefficiency inherent in centralized administration of a monopolistic economy necessitates periodic decentralization. Olimpiad Ioffe's book teaches an important lesson based on the experiences of past Soviet reformers. If Gorbachev's economic reforms fail to survive even the publication of this book, then the reader can find answers to the questions "Why?" and "How?" in these pages.

To thank just a few of the many who contributed to the making of this book, Olimpiad and I would like to mention our wives and also our typist Louise Renock of the University of Connecticut School of Law. Special thanks goes to the publisher, Merrill/Magnus, for the editorial assistance and other contributions they have made to the project and for the speed with which they have brought this timely work to print.

David A. Rome
Hartford, Connecticut
August 1989

Introduction:
Understanding What Is
Really Happening in the
Soviet Union

Mikhail Gorbachev's initial plans for economic and political reforms followed closely on the heels of his ascension to the post of General Secretary of the Communist Party of the Soviet Union (CPSU) in March 1985, and his rhetoric suggested that these reforms had to be more far-reaching and substantial than those debated and begun during the brief tenures of Iurii Andropov and Konstantin Chernenko. In one of his first speeches in April 1985,[1] Gorbachev made no secret that his principal focus would be reform. He stated:

> [The significance of these projected reforms] can be summed up by the following words of Lenin: "Our tasks today are much clearer, more concrete and graphic to us than yesterday; we are not afraid to point out our mistakes openly so as to be able to remedy them. Now we will concentrate all the efforts of the Party on improving its organization, advancing standards and contents of its work, establishing closer ties with the masses, working out even more correct and accurate tactics and strategy of the working class."[2]

Any listener well-versed in Soviet history would realize that this speech by Lenin was delivered in the early 1920s when Lenin's New Economic Politics (NEP) had replaced War Communism as the principal plan for societal organization. Those two systems were not merely different but

1

diametrically opposed to each other. War Communism meant the complete abolition of private ownership and free trade based on goods-money exchange as well as the establishment of all-embracing state ownership administered through the rigidly centralized planned distribution of all products with neither monetary reimbursement nor compensation in kind. In contrast, NEP entailed restoration of private ownership to a great extent, broad development of the goods-money exchange, substantial mitigation of the planned distribution implemented by central governmental agencies, and the complete abolition of distribution in kind without any monetary payment or occasional reimbursement in another form. Thus, the difference was so striking that Western observers of that era almost unanimously came to the conclusion that the Soviet leadership had abandoned its revolutionary goals and returned to traditional forms of social order. History has proved how erroneous that conclusion was. NEP helped to save the new system from an economic collapse and, as a result, from a political demise. But when the fatal danger threatening the Soviet regime passed, the "liberties" of NEP were eliminated and the previously established dictatorship was first revised and afterwards essentially reinforced.

One would think that this mistake of assessing NEP as a complete replacement and defeat of War Communism would constrain Western observers from similar impetuosity with respect to other Soviet reforms. Such an assumption would be especially reasonable as applied to Gorbachev, because, in proclaiming his reform program, he has expressly referred to Lenin's declaration of NEP. To some extent this assumption has proved to be realistic. Voices of those forecasting renovation of the system have hardly been heard. Cautious optimism has been more prevalent than thoughtless euphoria.[3] However, strange as this is, there has also been no shortage of super-utopian prognoses. To avoid these extremes, one must know the genuine truth deduced not only from the speeches of Soviet rulers but also from formal innovations established by new legal provisions and, first and foremost, from actual modifications occurring in daily practice. This examination will demonstrate whether the new reforms affect the Soviet system itself or whether the system remains intact despite sincere intentions and efforts to reform it.

The first step taken by Gorbachev after his coming to power was the proclamation of a high-sounding program on alcoholism. By itself this step was neither original nor extraordinary. This correctly identified priority can be characterized both as an imitation of Nikita Khrushchev, who introduced a number of similar measures in the 1950s, and as a continuation of Andropov's political line of 1983, earmarked to strengthen labor discipline. It was the extent of specific actions implemented by Gorbachev that has surpassed those applied by Khrushchev and even by Andropov: the drastic decrease in production of liquor, severe restrictions on its sale, etc. Despite the opposite assertion widespread in the USSR, the state budget incurs no losses as a result of these approaches. Decreases in the production of alcohol have been accompanied by price increases in the same or even in higher proportions. At the same time, the shortage of vodka in the official state economy, having almost no impact on the level of consumption, has entailed a number of other negative phenomena, such as the disappearance of colognes which become a substitute for liquor, underground production and sale of moonshine in a volume unheard of in Soviet history, and a significant increase in the death rate as a result of consumption of certain toxic liquids as alcohol substitutes. The Soviet rulers have been compelled to go back on their words, mitigating numerous measures that had been proclaimed as unshakable in the beginning.[4] But, regardless of whether or not Gorbachev failed in his campaign against drunkenness, this campaign has little to do with an intention to modify the Soviet system.

Russian drunkenness is incomparably older than the Soviet system, and the struggle against the former cannot modify the latter simply because both phenomena are different in origin and in substance. One can, of course, contend that peculiarities of the Soviet system that suppress the freedom of individuals and deprive them of opportunities to develop their abilities according to their own solutions stimulate the spread of drunkenness. This assertion would be reasonable because in Russian history drunkenness has never reached the level attained under the Soviet regime. However, if the Soviet system can be interpreted as one of the sources of unprecedented drunkenness, the fight against drunkenness deals not with the system as a cause but only with consequences arising from this factor. Whichever approach is employed, it should be recognized that Gorbachev's measures against drunkenness do not represent his reforms of the Soviet system. Only those reforms affecting the ingredients of the system itself can acquire the appropriate significance.

The Soviet system consists of two essential ingredients: unlimited political power of the ruling elite and economic monopoly by the same elite as the source of its unlimited power. If either of these elements is eliminated, the Soviet system will have been replaced by another system. In Marxist-Leninist doctrine, such an event is called revolution, not

4

reform. If both these ingredients are only modified but not abolished, the Soviet system will be retained with certain new features attached to it. In Marxist-Leninist doctrine, such an event is called reform, not revolution.

Sometimes, Soviet leaders give the title of "a revolution from the top" to certain measures implemented by the government and imposed on the nation. For instance, Stalin called his bloody "collectivization" of agriculture in the late 1920s and early 1930s "a revolution" when, by means of cruel repressions and terror, collective farms were created "on the basis" of liquidating individual farming.[5] Gorbachev also applies the term *revolution* to his economic and other innovations.[6] But these cases represent peculiar uses of the words rather than precise observances of Marxist-Leninist dogma. From the Marxist-Leninist point of view, what Gorbachev strives to achieve is no revolution. It is a matter of reforms, and because reforms modify only certain features of a given system and not the system itself, Soviet leaders tirelessly repeat that their new program earmarked to improve the economic and political situation in the USSR must ensure these achievements within the limits of the Soviet system and not in contradiction to its substance and principles.[7]

Such are the official declarations. Do these declarations mirror present Soviet reality or distort it? Is Gorbachev's purpose to improve or to abandon the Soviet system? Will this system be only renovated or completely regenerated under the influence of Gorbachev's reforms? To answer these questions, both ingredients of the Soviet system must be considered in more detail and the fate prepared for each ingredient by the new processes taking place in the USSR must be ascertained.

The first ingredient of the Soviet system—unlimited political power—must have its specific personification. In striving to discover this personification, it is necessary to distinguish between ceremonial and working agencies of power in the USSR. For instance, the Supreme Soviet of the USSR, though proclaimed the organ of highest power formally,[8] is a purely ceremonial agency in fact: it only rubber-stamps laws developed and approved by more authoritative Soviet institutions. The Law on Modifications and Supplementations of the Constitution (the Fundamental Law) of the USSR, promulgated on December 1, 1988,[9] in appearance strives to change this situation, renovating Chapter 15, "The Congress of People's Deputies and the Supreme Soviet of the USSR." However, since the requirement of previous approval of all drafts of laws by the Politburo remains intact, these formal innovations can hardly strengthen the actual power of the legally highest agencies of the USSR. The first Congress of People's Deputies and the first meeting of the Supreme Soviet created by this Congress, as described by *Izvestia* in late May and early June 1989, were unusual for the USSR in form because of the active discussion, criticism and counter-criticism, and rare dissension in voting, etc. But all of the decisions approved by the Soviet rulers previously were maintained by the Congress and Supreme Soviet. From this viewpoint, everything remains unchanged.

In contrast, the USSR Council of Ministers is a working agency and as such it implements the real functions of political power. This power cannot be unlimited, however, because its volume depends on governmental jurisdiction.[10] The same conclusion is applicable to all other working agencies, including the KGB, which plays a very important role in the maintenance and strengthening of the Soviet regime but as a holder of restricted jurisdiction cannot exercise unlimited power. Political power can be considered unlimited when it is all-embracing and free of subordination to any other power or legal or other restriction. Actually, though not formally, such a position is occupied only by one organ — the Politburo.

There have been temporary or extraordinary deviations from this principle in Soviet history. For instance, after establishing his indisputable personal dictatorship, Stalin restrained the Politburo and became an individual bearer of unlimited power; and, in 1957, when a majority of the Politburo decided to oust Khrushchev, his adherents managed to abolish this decision at an extraordinary meeting of the CPSU Central Committee. These deviations aside, only the Politburo personifies the ruling elite which exercises unlimited political power in the USSR.

Regardless of the specific personification of unlimited political power, this ingredient of the Soviet system is by definition affected mainly by political reforms, though it is not neutral toward economic reforms. In this connection, it should be recognized that political life in the USSR has in fact acquired certain features unimaginable in previous times. But the question is whether these new phenomena demonstrate deep or merely shallow social processes.

Among all of the political modifications, the strict separation of functions implemented by agencies of the Party and the Soviets, as provided for by the Nineteenth Party Conference, seems the most important and promising.[11] The official interpretation that accompanies this substantial reconstruction maintains the leading role of the Communist Party, by requiring the first secretaries of all the Party agencies, from districts to union republics, to be chairmen of the appropriate local Soviets. Of course, the same combination is applicable to the offices of Secretary General of the Communist Party and President of the Soviet Union. Both must be elected pursuant to directives from the Nineteenth Conference. These directives have been transformed into generally binding norms in the new version of the Soviet Constitution. Under the circumstances, there is no need to argue that, referring to the separation of power in name, the Party Conference means merger of power, at least at the level of the ruling offices of the Party and the Soviets. Will this strengthen the Soviets in their relations with the Party or, on the contrary, will the Party be strengthened in its domination over the Soviets? Formulation of this question begs its own answer, and in light of the latter, numerous other questions can be easily answered.

For instance, what about the plan to replace the rule "one deputy, one nominee" with the rule "one deputy, no fewer than two nominees?"[12] This change is obviously precluded with respect to chairmen of Soviets or the President of the USSR, since those who must occupy such offices do not exist in a multitude: each local or republican Party committee is headed by one first secretary, and only one Secretary General can be at the head of the CPSU. But because the rule "one deputy, one nominee" is retained with respect to the key positions in the Soviet system, its leaders can afford certain deviations from this rule without any danger for the system itself. Furthermore, this danger does not exist, since according to 1988 constitutional and electoral innovations, one-third of the deputies of the Congress shall be elected by the Communist Party and societal organizations themselves, while the Supreme Soviet shall be elected by this Congress, not directly by the whole people. As a matter of course, even restricted application of the rule "one deputy, no fewer than two nominees" is a step toward democratization in comparison with the comprehensive force of the rule "one deputy, one nominee." But this democratization is cosmetic rather than substantial; it affects neither the nature of the Soviet system nor even specific forms revealing the latter.

The next very impressive innovation is *glasnost'*, a Russian word now well-known to foreigners in its meaning, although imprecisely translated by the English word *openness*. *Glasnost'* is considered as a miracle not only by Western observers but by Soviet people themselves, first and foremost by the Soviet progressive intelligentsia. A great number of works of art inaccessible to the broad masses for decades have been published or exhibited. Soviet media have begun to inform readers about daily events that have occurred without much of the previous censure. Pre-Gorbachev regimes have become the issue of broad criticism, except Lenin's era. Various nationalities in the USSR have learned things that contemptible leaders had strived to bury forever. Therefore, it would be unfair and even impossible to deny the positive impact of Gorbachev's *glasnost'*. But would it be reasonable to assess this phenomenon with exaggeration that borders on euphoria and to employ it as a sign of a revolution unprecedented in the USSR?

When in the early 1950s the newspaper *Leningradskaia Pravda* reported that a flood had occurred in South America while there was also an unreported and well-known flood in Leningrad, everybody could only laugh at being told that floods were incompatible with the Soviet system. Gorbachev has eliminated similar nonsense in a great number of specific cases, for example, when in 1988 Soviet media announced that a railroad disaster took place between Leningrad and Moscow, resulting in numerous deaths and casualties. Floods or railroad disasters can take place everywhere and do not compromise any nation of the world, including the USSR. Silence concerning similar events is weaker than rumors capable of disseminating the same information with all possible exaggerations and distortions. Hence, in allowing such information, Gorbachev has proved to be simply a reasonable person rather than a great reforming statesman.

The Chernobil disaster, however, caused Gorbachev to behave identically to his predecessors, because this disaster compromised the USSR as a system. As a result, there was silence in the beginning, certain revelations afterward, and relatively complete information that could be independently ascertained by Western technology in the final analysis.

Concealing works of art compromises the Soviet system even more than restricting information: the latter usually is nothing more than either nonsense or supervigilance, while the former reveals a political policy of deliberate vagueness and obscurity. In addition, works that Khrushchev had banned as politically dangerous, such as *Doctor Zhivago* by Boris Pasternak, have a childlike innocence compared to works published in the USSR by certain other writers afterward. When a production of *Boris Godunov* staged by the famous Iurii Lubimov was cancelled by Brezhnev's sycophants, it was done out of fear that the General Secretary would find a similarity between Godunov and himself. Gorbachev, in contrast, has no reason for such fear: even his most confirmed enemies could not make a convincing analogy between Gorbachev and the Russian tsar who resembles Brezhnev, thanks to Lubimov's interpretation. However, works of art, previously concealed, are being declassified not en masse but selectively, and each new release appears in bookstores only after a decision by a competent agency. Thus, several books by Vladimir Nabokov have been released while others are kept secret. Moreover, certain of Aleksandr Solzhenitsin's works announced by the magazine *Oktiabr'* have never appeared in this or any other magazine. Hence, the USSR under Gorbachev adopts not *glasnost'* as such but only restricted and checked *glasnost'* which, instead of damaging the Soviet system, mitigates the political losses resulting from previous concealment. For the Soviet Union, even such a *glasnost'* is a miracle. But assessing it from the viewpoint of a normal democracy, one must be astonished not so much by Soviet *glasnost'*, but by the astonishment this *glasnost'* so often provokes in observers.

The criticism of Gorbachev's predecessors in power deserves special attention. To reiterate, Lenin is exempt from this criticism. Although without Lenin one cannot understand the appearance of Stalin, who is broadly criticized, the Soviet regime needs its own icon, a role reserved for Lenin. Soviet sources also avoid criticizing Andropov and, with certain exceptions, Chernenko, mainly because their tenures in office were so short. Andropov has also never been criticized because Gorbachev was his protegé, in contrast to Chernenko, who is labeled now and again as one of Brezhnev's adherents. Khrushchev receives an ambivalent attitude from Soviet media: his reforms were the forerunners of those proclaimed by Gorbachev and are therefore worthy of praise, but as a person he was to a great extent a ridiculous character, so he is depicted with criticism to avoid the humiliation of having Gorbachev considered his natural heir.

In contrast, Stalin and Brezhnev have received much deserved merciless denunciation. In substance, both were very different: Stalin was a cruel dictator, Brezhnev was a mediocre ruler. They are bound by a subordination of all their thoughts to their personality: by Stalin—to personal power, by Brezhnev—to personal fame. Both were absolutely indifferent toward the people in the street, remembering them only as objects of dictatorship (Stalin) or as sources of glorification (Brezhnev).

By directing uninterrupted criticism against both, Gorbachev plays it safe. Remaining adherents of Stalin and Brezhnev cannot provide any defense to such criticism without being denounced. One such would-be defender, N. Andreeva, authored an article in *Sovetskaia Rossia* in March of 1988 attempting to protect Stalin and Brezhnev, but the attempt was rejected by *Pravda* in April of the same year. These adherents aside, in criticizing or stimulating the criticism directed against both leaders, Gorbachev makes a political capital with the overwhelming majority of Soviet nations.

It is important to bear in mind that several years have passed since Gorbachev came to power, yet nothing has improved in the realm of food and other supplies necessary for the Soviet population. Time passes, and soon the new leadership will be asked: Well, you have managed to criticize your predecessors eloquently, but what have you done for us? When will your reforms begin to work? Or is it that your predecessors were such evil geniuses that their debacles cannot be overcome by your kind and effective capacity? To postpone the imminent questions and the answers to these questions, the new leadership must extend the sharp criticism toward its political predecessors for as long as possible. In this regard, criticism directed against Gorbachev's predecessors does not jeopardize the Soviet system. It only strengthens the power of the new leadership.

But even this activity has its limits, and the criticism dangerous for the Soviet system is precluded by the plenary power retained by the new Soviet leadership.

From this point of view, what happened with Boris Eltsin in 1987 seems especially demonstrative. As head of the Moscow Party Committee and a nonvoting member of the Politburo, Eltsin occupied a high position in the Soviet hierarchy. In addition, he was one of Gorbachev's faithful adherents promoted to a responsible office by Gorbachev himself. Nevertheless, at a meeting of the CPSU Central Committee, Eltsin delivered a speech that resulted in him losing both positions—Secretary of the Moscow Party Committee and nonvoting member of the Politburo. Information concerning this demise was broadly published in the USSR with reference to the ill-fated speech. But the speech itself was not published, despite insistent requests, oral and written, addressed to high Soviet officials, including Gorbachev. As a matter of course, various rumors spread immediately, and Gorbachev's wife Raisa was hinted at as one of the principal targets of Eltsin's criticism. Seemingly, these rumors had to be abolished in the only possible way—by publication of Eltsin's speech. Nothing like that happened, despite Gorbachev's *glasnost'*, until March 1988, when the first issue of a new magazine *Izvestia Tsentral'nago Komiteta KPSS* published the speech. This issue is unavailable for foreign journalists. Certain high political interests prevented an appeal to *glasnost'* which therefore proved to be applicable only to the extent that it does not become harmful for the Soviet political regime and the unlimited political power exercised under this regime by the ruling Soviet elite.

In assessing the correlation between the exercise of unlimited political power and the proclaimed line of political democratization, the problem of popular demonstrations and so-called informal societies springing up throughout the USSR must be considered. Previously, demonstrations could take place only in connection with official holidays. Now this restriction is formally abolished, and with the permission of a local executive committee a demonstration can be organized for other reasons.[13] However, to date almost no permit has been issued by the Moscow executive committee, according to dissident sources, and this situation is hardly peculiar to Moscow. Unauthorized demonstrations have occurred now and again, but the powers-that-be have behaved differently depending on specific circumstances. After the turmoils connected with Nagornii Karabakh, whose Armenian inhabitants supported by the masses of the Armenian Republic protested against discrimination on the part of governing agencies of Azerbaijan, Soviet rulers decided that it was more reasonable to abstain from interfering in unauthorized demonstrations in August 1988 dedicated to the independence of Estonia, Latvia, and Lithuania. On the other hand, demonstrations in Moscow on August 21, 1988, the 20th anniversary of the Soviet invasion of Czechoslovakia, were dispersed by the police, while similar demonstrations in Prague were implemented under the supervision of the police but without its interference. Thus, with formal expansion of the right to demonstration, the government of the Soviet Union and its satellites have managed to maintain this right in appearance and yet protect the ruling elite from its exercise in fact.[14]

As to informal societies, this terminology results from the fact that, according to Soviet law, any society can be created on the basis of special permission, but now numerous societies have arisen without formal approval of the competent governmental agencies. Soviet rulers are tolerant of these societies whose development allows the contention that, despite the existence of only one political party— the CPSU, political pluralism as a condition for a genuine democracy is not unknown in the Soviet system. At the same time, the large number of newly-created informal societies are not homogeneous from the viewpoint of their political goals. They embody a whole rainbow of political nuances, from the most innocent to the chauvinist or even neo-fascist.

Is the official attitude toward all these societies the same or selective? The society *Pamiat'* (Memory) is probably the most illustrative in this regard. Arising as an entity to protect monuments of Russian history and culture, *Pamiat'* soon regenerated into a mouthpiece of Russian chauvinism bordering on fascism. A number of individuals and groups have protested against this activity, but their efforts have been futile. For instance, in the summer of 1988, *Pamiat'* held its meetings almost in the very center of Leningrad, demanding that the Soviet Union rid itself of Jews and other non-Russians (*inorodtsi*). These meetings were not formally permitted, but neither were they formally prohibited. A Party secretary from the appropriate Leningrad district appeared, failing to object to the racist speeches. Soviet media have published other denunciations of meetings labeled fascist gatherings.[15] But *Pamiat'* continues to function unrestricted and, needless to say, unprohibited. At the same time, individuals or groups seeking permission to denounce *Pamiat'* publicly through meetings and demonstrations are unconditionally refused. Why do the Soviet agencies apply such inequality and discrimination? If one believes the rumors, it is said that allegedly *Pamiat'* relies on the support of a certain well-placed person —Raisa Gorbachev, according to one version, or Fedor Ligachev, according to another assertion. This rumor can hardly be trusted, taking into account the proportion between comparatively restricted opportunities of the above-mentioned persons and the strength of protests broadly developed against *Pamiat'*. The point, probably, is that the unlimited political power implemented by the ruling elite in the USSR possesses a palpable trend toward Russification, and that which supports this trend must be protected in favor of the bearers of this power, while that which precludes such support must be rejected, in a gentle form but strongly and unconditionally.

Thus, despite all of the steps made to democratize the Soviet system, its first ingredient—unlimited political power of the ruling elite—remains unshakable. Within these limits Gorbachev's innovations are reforms, not revolutions, not even those implemented from above in contrast to genuine revolutions initiated from below. Now the second ingredient of the Soviet system—the economic monopoly of the same elite—must be considered similarly to conclude whether Gorbachev's reforms abolish this ingredient or only modify it.

If unlimited political power is the principal means of domination of the ruling elite, the economic monopoly of the same elite is the principal source of its domination. The KGB and other punitive agencies maintain the Soviet system by drastic reaction against those who violate the basis or components of this system. However, a population of almost 300 million cannot be kept in obedience exclusively as a result of punitive activities. Various forms of Soviet

16

propaganda also play a strengthening role with respect to the Soviet system. Propaganda, however, is even less capable than coercion of keeping in check the whole population of such a large country. The economic monopoly of the ruling elite is a substantially different phenomenon: it entails the economic dependence of each individual on the Soviet state and thus ensures comprehensive obedience of the former to the orders of the latter. This is why the economic monopoly must be qualified as the principal source of the unlimited power of the ruling elite.

This monopoly is, in principle, compatible only with centralized economic administration. The broader the administration of the economy exercised directly by the ruling elite, the stronger the political power kept in its grasp. Therefore, Lenin and his adherents started with War Communism — a system relying on utmost centralization. However, although dependable politically, absolute centralism does not work economically, depriving producers of all economic inducements to increase their productivity. As a result, the whole economy comes to the verge of collapse, and to prevent this disaster, Soviet leaders are compelled to supplement centralism by certain decentralization. This is why Lenin and his adherents replaced War Communism by NEP in the early 1920s. Unfortunately decentralization has its own shortcomings: mitigating the economic monopoly, it negatively affects the unlimited political power. Therefore, in the late 1920s, Stalin began to replace NEP by centralized administration and in the late 1930s no traces of NEP remained in the country. A similar theme can be traced throughout the subsequent economic development of the USSR. Hence, economic reforms result not from the whims of Soviet rulers but from the nature of the Soviet system. Because of the dependence of unlimited political power on the economic monopoly, the latter must be maintained in the centralized way; but because of the inefficiency of centralized administration of a monopolistic economy the latter requires periodic economic decentralization. Thus, the Soviet economy is subordinated to a cyclical development: from centralism to a certain decentralization and from decentralization back to centralism. If this development had always assured at least some upsurge, it could be called not cyclical but spiral. Sometimes the return from one cycle to the other, especially from decentralization to centralism, entails a decline, instead of an upsurge, which renders the adjective *cyclical* more precise than *spiral*.[16] But regardless of the term used, periodic transfer from centralism to decentralization is intrinsic to the Soviet system.

Gorbachev resorted to economic reforms owing not to his personal inclinations (even if such inclinations really characterize his personality) but to the fact that he came to power at a point in the economic development of the USSR that required expansion of decentralization at the expense of centralism. Only those who disregard this cyclical pattern of Soviet economic policy can consider the present line of decentralization irrevocable and earmarked for permanent strengthening. The view of those who continue to see this cyclical pattern is that sooner or later the cycle of decentralization will be supplanted by the cycle of centralism, unless there is a wholesale rejection of the Soviet system.

The terms *centralism* and *decentralization* are applicable to the Soviet economy insofar as one deals with the administration of the state economy. Within the limits of this economy, various low-level entities, such as enterprises and associations, participate in economic activities. Various central agencies, such as the State Committee of Planning (Gosplan) and economic ministries, exercise the function of economic administration. The more the activities of the former depend on orders issued by the latter, the stronger the centralism dominating in the economic system. The corollary is that the broader the opportunities for free solutions available to the lowest entities functioning independently from central agencies, the more powerful is the trend toward decentralization. Thus, economic reforms enlarging decentralization at the expense of centralism can reach different volumes: the very modest, such as those announced by Khrushchev in the early 1960s, to the quite substantial, such as those developed by Kosygin in 1965 but gradually abolished by Brezhnev in 1973-1974. If Gorbachev's reforms are made a reality without distortion, in strict accordance with the promulgated laws, they will be the broadest in Soviet history, except for the period of Lenin's NEP.

There are, however, signs of substantial deviations in practice from the laws in this regard. For example, the 1987 Law on the State Enterprise (Association)[17] establishes that instead of all-embracing centralized distribution of produced products, enterprises and associations will be bound only by state orders (*zakazi*), and beyond these orders, sales will be left to the discretion of producers. But as Soviet media report almost daily, the state orders issued by central agencies encompass the entire output of enterprises and associations, which are therefore left with nothing to dispose of freely. Regardless of the volume of reforms of this character, they do not diminish the size of the state economy in the USSR. Their only effect is redistribution of the appropriate functions between central and subordinate agencies. Under any such distribution, the economic monopoly of the Soviet state remains intact, and Gorbachev, like all of his predecessors who resorted to analogous reforms, has no intention of eliminating this second ingredient of the Soviet system.

It is not simply a matter of the economic monopoly of the Soviet state but the exercise of this monopoly by the ruling elite as the principal source of its unlimited political power. It is clear that redistribution of economic administrative functions in favor of the lower entities lessens the economic power of the ruling elite and therefore must indirectly affect its political power. Of course, mitigation is not equal to elimination, and consequently, redistributing reforms in the realm of economic administration cannot abolish the political monopoly of the ruling elite, just as political reforms are powerless to destroy the state's economic monopoly. But diminution of the economic monopoly of the ruling elite is seen by the elite as an unavoidable evil to be tolerated only as long as necessary to prevent a comprehensive crash. As soon as this danger passes, the forced redistribution of economic functions in favor of decentralization can be abolished by restoration of previous centralism. This is the way Gorbachev's predecessors behaved and so shall either Gorbachev himself or his successor behave, when the time comes to change the direction from decentralization to centralism. Personal peculiarities of Soviet leaders can forestall but not preclude these events, because the regularity of the cyclical development of the Soviet economy is stronger than the individual desires of Soviet leaders.

Along with the correlation between centralism and decentralization, significant only within the limits of the state economy, the correlation between state and nonstate economies also is substantial for the economic monopoly of the ruling elite. The former correlation has to do with the functional distribution affecting different governmental entities, but it does not affect quantitatively the state economy. The latter correlation has to do with the size of the state and nonstate economies, demonstrating the volume of the economic monopoly that is in the grasp of the Soviet state represented by its ruling elite. Interpreted literally, monopoly means that one entity alone is entitled to implement a certain activity, that is to exercise exclusive possession or control of something. Accordingly, economic monopoly means that its bearer must either possess or control the entire economy. Neither the Soviet state nor any other government can be the owner of the entire economy existing in a country. Even in the time of Stalin's rule, consumer goods acquired by individuals belonged to them, not to the state. However, combining ownership and control, the existence of governmental economic monopoly in the USSR can easily be found in the literal meaning, although the proportion between ownership and control varies.

The economic monopoly of the Soviet state was established very soon after the creation of the Soviet regime by means of the transfer to the state of all urban enterprises and land throughout the country. For tactical reasons the term *nationalization* as a synonym for the transformation of individual property into state ownership was employed at that time for all objects except land. Individual farming was not encompassed by state ownership, but it was under such close control that the state was entitled to withdraw any quantity of agricultural produce from the peasantry; therefore, the economic monopoly of the ruling elite in this respect was no weaker than the same monopoly exercised within the limits of state ownership. Such was the situation under War Communism (1917-1920).

The replacement of War Communism by NEP in the early 1920s diminished the size of state ownership by restoring private ownership to a certain extent. But it did not abolish the economic monopoly of the ruling elite. On the other hand, so-called *komandnie visoti* (commanding heights) of the economic system—large industrial and trade enterprises, banks, most types of transport, etc.— were retained by the state and this ensured the dependence of private ownership on the state economy. The creation and activities of private enterprises were under the control of the appropriate governmental agencies which could, if necessary, interfere in their activity by means of auditing and orders subject to unconditional execution. NEP also mitigated governmental control of individual farming because only certain quantities of agricultural produce in accordance with the rate of agricultural taxes could be claimed by the state from each peasant economy. In all other regards, governmental control continued to exist, and the state economic monopoly was retained, though in a different proportion between state ownership and state control than previously. Such was the situation under NEP (1921-1928).

The creation of collective farms in the rural areas and the abolition of private enterprise all over the country in the late 1920s and early 1930s not only restored but also substantially enlarged the state economic monopoly in terms of ownership rather than control: individual farming was replaced by collective farming which was in fact transformed into a part of the state economy, though formally it was considered as a collective economy separated from the state. At the same time, control retained its significance as a means of exercising the economic monopoly of the Soviet leadership. The 1936 Constitution established a restricted enumeration of objects of property that could belong to Soviet citizens as consumers, not producers, and government control over the strict observance of this enumeration prevented the expansion of individual ownership incompatible with the state economic monopoly. Such was the situation under Stalin's rule from the end of NEP until his death (1929-1953).

Khrushchev did not restore private ownership. However, because of the disastrous state of the Soviet agriculture, in 1954 he increased the size of plots of land that could be allocated to members of collective farms. This slightly enlarged the individual economy but did not, in principle, affect the significance of the state economy. Furthermore, Khrushchev himself soon abolished his innovation, erroneously thinking that Soviet agriculture had already been essentially improved and groundlessly fearing excessive enrichment of the Soviet peasantry. The economic monopoly of the Soviet state in the forms employed by Stalin was left intact by Khrushchev and incurred no change under Brezhnev, Andropov, and Chernenko. It is true that the so-called underground economy, originating during Stalin's reign, was broadly developed under his successors, especially under Brezhnev, when unheard of bribery was both stimulated by the underground economy and employed to stimulate this economy itself. However, the underground economy (private enterprise disguised by a lawful cover) is prohibited by law and, therefore, it cannot be considered as a component of the Soviet economic system. The denial of the state economic monopoly with reference to the underground economy is deprived of any logical sense. Although the very existence of the underground economy impinges on the state economic monopoly, because the former is a crime, it cannot be considered a competitor of the latter.

Under this analysis, during the regimes of Khrushchev and his successors, the economic monopoly was in the grasp of the ruling elite to the same extent that it had been during Stalin's rule. Such was the situation during the entire post-Stalin period before Gorbachev came to power (1953-1985).

Has Gorbachev abolished the economic monopoly of the Soviet ruling elite by means of his economic reforms? The substance of these reforms is the only issue of detailed analysis presented in the remainder of this book. It must suffice now to use certain general indications and certain specific examples to answer the question formulated above. Generally speaking, Gorbachev strives to define a new correlation between the state and nonstate economies, either borrowing methods from his predecessors or developing his own.

As to the practices borrowed from Gorbachev's predecessors, they all come down to the expansion of individual labor activities. This modifies the proportion between state and individual economies in favor of individual economies through the increase of the latter. The modification is not quantitatively substantial. Qualitatively it can be characterized as permission to implement types of individual activity that can meet needs unfulfillable by the state entities. At the same time, these new forms of individual activity depend on state supplies and are subject to government control which completely precludes their undermining the economic monopoly of the Soviet state.

In contrast, new methods developed by Gorbachev and affecting the proportion between state and nonstate economies are more numerous. First of all, the forms of cooperative activities are significantly enlarged, and as a result, numerous cooperatives created recently are without precedent in Soviet history from the viewpoint of their specific profiles and economic independence. Second, new forms of economic relations between economic entities and individuals or groups of individuals have been introduced—the contractual imposition of certain tasks by state entities on their brigades or by collective farms on members' families, etc. Third, long-term lease of land by individuals is allowed, and using this land for cultivation, the lessees may acquire tractors and other means of agricultural production, previously unavailable to individual economies. Acquisition of these means of production was allowed to individuals only during NEP and is a policy introduced again by Gorbachev's reforms. The same is true of foreign trade, which is now available not only to economic entities of the Ministry of Foreign Economic Connections. It is also true of the creation of the mixed socialist-capitalist enterprises on the condition that the foreign capital does not exceed 49 percent. Despite the newness of these methods, they do not abolish the economic monopoly of the Soviet state considered from the viewpoint of state ownership and state control. State ownership is not affected in its size as a result of the lease of land or the admission of foreign capital to the Soviet economy. Governmental control is sufficiently strong in all these cases owing to the terms of contracts for the lease of land, the majority share of Soviet capital in the mixed enterprises, and so forth.

Thus, it must be completely clear that, although drastic changes in the Soviet system do result from Gorbachev's economic reforms, nevertheless, these reforms are implemented within the Soviet system, whose limits must not be transgressed under any circumstances. This peculiarity of

Gorbachev's reforms, which seems advantageous for adherents of the Soviet system, including Gorbachev himself, must, however, be the most substantial cause unavoidably leading to the failure of all efforts employed by the Soviet leadership at the present time to eradicate the stagnation in economic development. The delusion of Gorbachev, which can become for him a personal tragedy and for the country a last opportunity, is that he strives to combine that which is incompatible—the economic monopoly as the source of unlimited political power with genuine goods-money production as the prerequisite for producers' incentives to prompt economic progress. Genuine goods-money production assumes the independence of producers, adjustment of the volume of production to the real demand, freedom of prices, unlimited monetary circulation, unrestricted maneuvering of material resources, etc. In contrast, the economic monopoly ensuring unlimited political power relies on subordination of producers to their rulers, adjustment of artificial demands to predetermined volumes of production, regulation of prices, limitation of monetary circulation, restrictions on the disposition of material resources, etc. Hence, combination of the former and the latter must be doomed. To argue such a general conclusion, even the most abstract juxtaposition of these different or, more precisely, opposite systems must suffice.

However, a generally formulated deduction cannot satisfy those who are interested in knowing Gorbachev's economic reforms in detail. These innovations must be assessed as either realistic or fantastic, applicable in practice or completely impracticable, efficient at least to some extent or entirely inefficient. To satisfy the demands of readers of this character, Gorbachev's economic reforms must be analyzed in light of different sectors of the Soviet economy and the interconnections between these sectors. The Soviet doctrine distinguishes among the state economy, the cooperative economy, and the individual economy. These economic sectors predetermine the issues of consideration in the first three chapters of this book. The fourth chapter is dedicated to interconnections between the enumerated sectors, taken sometimes together and sometimes consecutively. The principal deductions resulting from the analysis offered will find their place in the conclusion. It seems also useful to inform readers about the situation that existed in the pre-Gorbachev period, the period of Brezhnev (Andropov and Chernenko had no time for their own contributions of this character), before addressing the appropriate current reforms of Gorbachev.

CHAPTER

1

The State Economy

The state economy consists of a number of branches. Industry doubtlessly occupies the prominent place among these branches. Industry is also the principal focus of the latest economic innovations. The systems of trade or transportation have been either disregarded by economic reforms (this is especially striking with respect to all modes of transportation) or affected by reforming measures only as an inevitable result of transformations in the industrial area (this impact is especially visible in the realm of wholesale and, to some extent, retail trade). Some reforms have encompassed banking activities—banks have grown in number and their functions have acquired more of an economic than administrative character (bank control). But even the banking reforms reflect an outgrowth of modifications introduced for industry rather than a desire to reconstruct the banking system itself. Therefore, an analysis of Gorbachev's reforms addressed to the state economy can be reduced to those innovations implemented with respect to state industries.

A. Organization of State Industry

Industrial enterprises have typically occupied the low-est level of the state industrial structure and yet remained relatively independent of the higher agencies both economi-cally and legally. Only seldom have they been included in larger trusts (e.g., in the coal industry.) As a rule, industrial enterprises were directly subordinated to the appropriate economic ministry. Therefore, a decentralizing economic reform in 1965 attributed to Aleksei Kosygin (then Chair-man of the USSR Council of Ministers) was concentrated on enlarging the rights and strengthening the economic independence of industrial enterprises.[1] In replacing Kosygin's decentralization with centralism, Brezhnev, in the early 1970s,[2] did away with all but the largest enter-prises, replacing them with production associations as the fundamental link in the chain of Soviet industry. Enter-prises were incorporated into the newly created production associations under the title "production units" and, as a result, they lost their previous economic and legal indepen-dence. Formally, this independence was transferred from the enterprises to associations. In fact, however, this was not the case. Along with the production associations, Brezhnev created industrial associations as purely adminis-trative agencies, and as often as not, the production asso-ciations were subordinated to republican industrial asso-ciations, which in turn were subordinated to all-union industrial associations. Above all of these links were the economic ministries. However, the point was not so much the increase in the number of links embodying the indus-trial system, but rather the transfer of purely economic functions (the execution of contracts, orders concerning construction works, etc.) from the production association,

30

an economic entity, to the industrial association as an administrative agency. As a result, administrative agencies began to deal with economic activities, while the economic activities of economic entities were substantially restricted. It is difficult to imagine a more centralized form of industrial administration than the form established by Brezhnev.

Gorbachev abolished a number of Brezhnev's centralizing innovations.[3] He liquidated the industrial associations and consequently returned all of the economic functions that could be centralized by higher administrative agencies to production associations. As a result of this reform, direct subordination of production associations to economic ministries, without any intermediate links, was restored. It is true that Gorbachev has complicated the centralized economic administration system somewhat, having created bureaus and other agencies of the USSR Council of Ministers to regulate the activities of different groups of economic ministries. The creation of such agencies reveals a centralizing, not decentralizing, trend. However, in contrast to the measures adopted in 1973-1974, these new governmental links appear at a level higher than the economic ministries, and as a result, they do not hamper direct connections between economic ministries and production associations. From this point of view, the introduction of a new organizational system has been as a whole a substantial step toward decentralization.

At the same time, Gorbachev has proved to be less decisive with respect to transformation of enterprises into production units (structural units, according to the 1987 law dedicated not only to production but to all state enterprises and associations). This original change made in 1973-1974 was organizational in form and economic in substance. When industrial enterprises were independent, they could directly take part in goods-money exchange. Despite the limitations of such exchanges, they do stimulate a producer interested in fulfilling all of its contractual duties toward its obligees, including delivery of high quality products on time, expeditious payment of receipts, quantitative and qualitative verification, etc. In other words, an independent enterprise is a commodity producer in the Soviet interpretation with all of the consequences following from this capacity. However, the enterprises lost their capacity as commodity producers as soon as they were transformed into a part of a production association under the name "production unit." A production unit cannot leave the gate of a production association and establish direct economic relations between itself and other entities. As a result, goods-money relations were closed to enterprises and declined throughout the country. This was the most palpable negative impact on the Soviet economy entailed by Brezhnev's centralization.

One of Gorbachev's premises is that economic entities "should be given the right independently to sell to one another what they produce over and above the plan, as well as raw materials, equipment, etc., which they do not use."[4] In translating this call from common language into economic terminology, it signifies that goods-money relationships must be developed so long as they do not contradict the imperative planned tasks. It would seem that under this premise the first task of Gorbachev's economic policy had to be to abolish the transformation of enterprises into production units deprived of the capacity to take part in goods-money relationships and to restore their previous status before Brezhnev's centralizing measures, at least to re-establish those legal conditions that had been introduced for them by Kosygin's 1965 reform. However, Gorbachev did not take this path.

He expanded the rights of the structural units created on the basis of the former enterprises. Sometimes this expansion creates for them an opportunity to take part directly in goods-money relationships. According to the 1987 law, as a general rule, a structural unit may conclude economic contracts with other entities on behalf of the association. At the same time, however, the association may grant a structural unit the right to conclude economic contracts on behalf of the structural unit itself and bear independent responsibility for those contracts within the limits of the property allocated to it.

All of these provisions of the 1987 law demonstrate that Gorbachev strives to do his best to permit goods-money exchange by enterprises previously deprived of this right as a result of their transformation into production units. But his purpose is achieved in a very cumbersome way: a production unit, though a part of a production association as an economic entity, can execute certain contracts on its own behalf and on the basis of its own responsibility. No jurist could reasonably explain this situation; it creates insurmountable difficulties for Soviet jurists themselves who, by definition, must suggest a satisfactory interpretation but cannot do so within the limits of elementary juridical logic. The problem becomes even more complicated because of an indication in the 1987 law that if a structural unit's property is insufficient to meet the unit's separate financial responsibility, the latter must be borne by the association. If a structural unit may execute a contract on its own behalf, it functions as an independent entity. Then, why would the association be responsible for its debts? Conversely, if the association is responsible for a contract executed by its structural unit, how can this unit establish contractual relationships on its own behalf? To formulate the same question more generally, if production units execute contracts on their own behalf, even backed by the subsidiary liability of a production association, why cannot production units be recognized as independent enterprises rather than retain their previous status as internal departments of another economic entity?

The point is that, except during War Communism, Soviet leaders have always maintained an ambivalent attitude toward commodity production and goods-money exchange. On the one hand, they subconsciously understand that without goods-money exchange an economy cannot develop under the present circumstances. But on the other hand, they have been afraid that goods-money exchange based at least on the relative independence of participants can destroy the Soviet system. Thus, Lenin introduced commodity production to replace War Communism in 1921, but at the same time he warned that this was a forced retreat which had to be abandoned as soon as the danger threatening the Soviet system was overcome. Stalin almost completely abolished commodity production before World War II, retaining only certain features of goods-money exchange. Yet in 1952 he published his work, *The Economic Problems of Socialism in the USSR*, in which commodity production was substantially rehabilitated as an unavoidable satellite of socialism and certain Soviet economists of that era were accused of underestimating the merit of socialist goods-money relationships. Approval was retained by Khrushchev, and Kosygin strove to strengthen the significance of goods-money relationships with the 1965 reform. It was the events of 1968 in Czechoslovakia, especially the slogan calling for the creation of so-called market socialism, that entailed a radical turn in the views of the Soviet rulers. Frightened by these events, they were ready to deny the compatibility of socialism with any market device. However, because the socialist economy did not work without its own market, Brezhnev came to the conclusion that it was not enterprises but substantially stronger entities that had to transact goods-money activities. Owing to this reasoning, the production associations were invented, and enterprises, except the largest ones with rights identical to those of associations, were transformed into production units as internal departments of the broader and supposedly stronger economic entities.

Gorbachev appears to value commodity production more than any of his predecessors. His 1987 law on state enterprises and associations for the first time emphasizes that receipts obtained by economic entities from the marketing of their products must recoup their material expenses. Profits or income must be the general indicator of economic performance of associations and enterprises, insofar as enterprises are retained in the Soviet economy.[5] Through this attitude, Gorbachev strengthened the economic and legal positions of the former enterprises he inherited as production units. His main goal was to open slightly the gate of goods-money exchange hermetically closed for production units by Brezhnev's 1973-1974 legislation. The fear of a market economy that obsessed his predecessor perhaps has not been conquered completely by Gorbachev. He actually stopped at a halfway point, simultaneously recognizing a restricted right of production units to participate in goods-money relationships but avoiding the restoration of the same units to their previous capacity

35

as independent industrial enterprises. Even on the organizational level, Gorbachev has not created all of the opportunities requisite for normal development of the Soviet economy. With respect to industrial enterprises, he has somewhat mitigated an extremely centralized structure resulting from Brezhnev's drastic steps. But under Gorbachev, industrial enterprises have not attained even the degree of economic independence granted to them by Kosygin's reforms of 1965. This proves that contemporary economic innovations, at least within the limits of Soviet industry, give no basis for the propagandistic euphoria developed in the USSR and not infrequently picked up by Western observers. An economic reconstruction is, of course, under way but to a lesser degree than is sometimes descriptively outlined.

From this point of view, it is interesting to look at the characterization by Gorbachev's closest allies of the 1965 reform as a measure to strengthen industrial enterprises. One of Gorbachev's most authoritative advisers, Abel Aganbeguian, published a book in 1987,[6] claiming that the 1965 reform was approved by a decree of the CPSU Central Committee and the USSR Council of Ministers, that this reform endowed the industrial enterprise with broad rights economically justified, and it was because the decree did not provide the necessary guarantees to protect these rights that various conservative departments, including Gosplan, the Ministry of Finance, etc., managed to deprive the enterprises of their newly acquired rights reducing the 1965 reform to zero.[7]

Aganbeguian distorts reality in explaining the failure of the 1965 reform by referring to the absence of legal guarantees that allegedly gave various governmental agencies the opportunity to neutralize that which had been declared for the top of the Party and the Government. No single subordinate Soviet agency could be brave enough to implement measures abolishing directives of the ruling elite. If Gosplan, the Ministry of Finance, and certain other agencies indeed issued numerous "instructions" and "indications" that soon left almost nothing of the 1965 reform, this could occur only as a result of a secret order from the top that preferred to retreat silently from its own publicly announced decision than formally abolish it. Aganbeguian must know that, as any other Soviet scholar or even someone in the street could explain, Brezhnev's 1973-1974 legislation, which not only diminished the rights of industrial enterprises but liquidated them, could appear only because of preparatory work gradually implemented against the 1965 reform almost immediately after its promulgation.

Right or wrong in his interpretation of the causes of the failure of the 1965 reform, Aganbeguian at any rate demonstrates his adherence to that scheme's orientation. He shares the idea of strengthening enterprises and regrets only the fate of the 1965 reform attributable by him to the observance of legal guarantees. Then why does he not suggest that Gorbachev restore enterprises completely to their position before Brezhnev transformed them into production units? Where is the consistency between complaining about the demise of the 1965 reform and yet supporting current reforms that fail to reach the earlier level?

Putting aside the fact that it is far easier to criticize Kosygin's foes than Gorbachev's decisions, a more revealing answer is quite clear. The present generation of Soviet reformists have not rid themselves of the traditional Soviet ambivalence toward commodity production and goods-money exchange. They are against restrictions on these phenomena resulting from extremely centralized trends but, at the same time, they cannot accept what seems to be exaggerated and excessive decentralization. This is why in his treatment of enterprises Gorbachev stopped somewhere between Brezhnev and Kosygin, while Aganbeguian, protecting Kosygin, in fact prefers Gorbachev's middle position.

One might assume that this issue is only one of the problems under discussion at the upper echelon of the Soviet government and therefore, the indecisiveness of Gorbachev in this regard is an isolated case and not a general flaw. Such an assumption cannot be accepted. In defining the guidelines for reorganizing economic mechanisms, Gorbachev combined in his speech at the 27th CPSU Congress two tasks: heightening the efficiency of centralized guidance of the economy and enlarging the framework of the autonomy of economic entities.[8] Retaining the centralizing trend together with decentralization in all cases, including transformation of industrial enterprises into production units, does not result from mistake or oversight. It reflects instead a clear political line maintained by Soviet rulers.

Meanwhile, Aganbeguian contends that "self-management" must be the most important feature of the new economic reforms. He says that until now "administrative methods of ruling based on the unquestioning subordination to Gosplan were applied. . . . We intend to eradicate this system and to refuse unconditional directives and the forced plan."[9] According to the author, economic entities must themselves regulate their activities and in this respect be independent. However, even taking this declaration at face value, it can be applied only to production and other associations. As to enterprises, they are not economic entities, becoming production or structural units of production and other associations. Thus, "self-management" as the principal feature of Gorbachev's reforms, to whatever extent it must be introduced, will function only at a high level of the Soviet economy, on the level of production and other associations. In contrast, the lower but more important level—the enterprise level—will remain unchanged, and Gorbachev's reforms in their principal feature have no chance to affect these structural elements of the Soviet economy.

Along with self-management, the 1987 law formulates two other principles of organization of state production entities: full economic accountability and self-financing. Self-financing is a new term for Soviet law, while economic accountability has been known worldwide by the Russian word *khozraschet*, a method of economic activity that assumes reimbursement of all expenses for the income of an economic entity itself, without governmental subsidy applied to any part of the economic entity's debts. Because previously this rule was not applicable to a great number of cases and any economic entity facing financial difficulties could be bailed out by government subsidies, precluding its bankruptcy, the 1965 reform, aiming to modify this situation, replaced the word *khozraschet* with the title *full khozraschet* or *khozraschet* without interference or subsidies of any kind. This replacement in its original meaning was restored by the 1987 law.

Khozraschet as a specific method of economic management was introduced by Lenin as a component of NEP of no less significance than the limited restoration of private ownership. In its undistorted form, however, *khozraschet* has never been applied previously in Soviet economic history. Before the present reform, there were three different forms of property organization of economic entities in the USSR.

One group of Soviet economic entities functioned on the basis of so-called budget-estimate financing. This meant that all of the expenses of these entities were reimbursed by the state budget within the limits of a confirmed estimate and all products produced by them were transferred free of charge to consumers in accordance with the indicators provided by the centralized distribution. This practice was, for instance, employed by a majority of military producers.

A second group of Soviet economic entities operated on the basis of a combination of *khozraschet* and governmental subsidies. A centralized plan defined which expenses had to be reimbursed by an entity's own income and the extent to which budget financing could be used for the same purpose. These entities were called *planovoubitochnie* (those whose unavoidable losses were provided for by the plan up front and had to be compensated by the appropriate amount of budget financing). This category included numerous enterprises that produced consumer necessities. Retail prices for these goods were set below cost, because otherwise they would be inaccessible to Soviet consumers. By establishing retail prices much lower than cost, the Soviet leadership made up for producer's deficits by redistributing profits accumulated by the state budget. It was not only producers of consumer necessities but also a number of heavy industry entities, such as metallurgical plants, that enjoyed a high priority in the realm of curtailed *khozraschet* and additional budget subsidies.

The third group of Soviet economic entities operated under *khozraschet* precluding any government subsidy. But even in this case, one could not call it full *khozraschet* because if any such entity became insolvent, the government resorted to financial measures to rescue the entity from liquidation. Bankruptcy as an economic phenomenon did occur frequently with Soviet enterprises as a result of failure to fulfill the plan, producing defective goods, shortages of raw materials, decreases in demand, etc. As a legal phenomenon, however, there was no bankruptcy because the government never allowed a state economic entity to be liquidated with reference to bankruptcy as the legal reason for such an extreme measure.

As a result, *khozraschet*, designed to stimulate Soviet production, could not do so regardless of whether government subsidies were available. An entity's work could be good or bad, but each worker and each official received his or her salary guaranteed by the state in cases where the entity could not meet these obligations. When plans were unfulfilled, workers and officials could lose their bonuses, but the bonuses were so insignificant in proportion to guaranteed salaries that little attention was paid to this result.

Soviet *khozraschet* also suffers from other, more substantial and serious shortcomings. The income of economic entities is based on the prices for their output. The higher the prices, the easier it is to achieve the goals of *khozraschet*. In the USSR, prices are established not as a result of the correlation between supply and demand, but by central agencies that plan prices either directly or on the basis of data submitted by producers. Under these circumstances, how can it be determined that prices are realistic or pure fantasy, corresponding to the actual economic state of affairs or indifferent to it? This author has had the opportunity, in addition to extensive reading on the topic, to speak directly with planners of prices in the USSR and no reliable or even comprehensible calculation has been revealed. In past conversations, reference was usually made to previous prices or to these prices and certain increases or decreases, etc. The most sincere planners with whom the author spoke admitted that they simply pull new prices out of the air. Under such a procedure for establishing prices, one can never say whether *khozraschet* ensured the requisite result or the result appeared owing to circumstances that had nothing to do with *khozraschet*. The Soviet system by definition deprives *khozraschet* of its effectiveness as supposedly the most important economic stimulus, and its various forms of organization can by themselves change nothing.

Gorbachev, however, strives to improve the efficiency of *khozraschet* within the limits of the Soviet system. His principal step in this direction is the declaration of full *khozraschet* with respect to all Soviet economic entities, including industrial ones, that is, production associations and the few remaining enterprises that have retained their independence and have avoided transformation into production units. In this context, the word *enterprises* will be employed either as a general term, encompassing associations, or in the proper meaning of the word along with the term *associations*.

The introduction of full *khozraschet* for all enterprises signifies that neither enterprises financed by the state budget nor those subsidized by it will exist anymore. If an enterprise needs additional money, it can receive bank credits, whose extension is regulated more reasonably now than previously by the 1987 law and by special decrees of the CPSU Central Committee and the USSR Council of Ministers.[10] The new legislation does not use the term *bankruptcy*, an institution hardly as comprehensive as *khozraschet* in the USSR. Otherwise, the entire Soviet economy would be destroyed quickly by the declaration of bankruptcy, bearing in mind that according to the *New York Times* on September 21, 1988, it is estimated officially that about one in eight industrial enterprises operates at a loss, and an additional one in eight is marginal. Nevertheless, the above mentioned 1987 decree concerning banking allows banks together with the Ministry of Finance to submit to the appropriate agencies proposals to liquidate or reorganize enterprises that over a long period fail to make their payments to the state budget, banks, and their suppliers. In 1987 the Soviet government did allow a failed construction entity in Leningrad to disband and its 2,000 employees were hired by other local builders. On September 17, 1988, the newspaper *Sotsialisticheskaia Industria* published a list of thirty-one state enterprises, including a major tractor factory in Kharkov, that could be liquidated if they failed to improve their financial situations. The future will reveal whether this is a psychological threat or a truly implementable measure. At any rate, the 1987 law dealing with the liquidation of enterprises establishes that an enterprise can be liquidated "given lengthy unprofitability and insolvency." It is not inconceivable that this is a euphemistic title for bankruptcy. Nevertheless, even high-level Soviet agencies cannot explain how declarations of bankruptcy will be implemented. For instance, commenting on the actual bankruptcy of one state enterprise, the Ministry of Finance of the USSR points out that "now conditions of reorganization and liquidation of enterprises are not established. It is not known who can initiate liquidation and who is entitled to adopt a final decision."[11] This is a problem of the future, not of the present time.

The substance of full *khozraschet* in its contemporary interpretation is that it must:

(1) be comprehensive, encompassing all enterprises;

(2) ensure the complete compensation of all expenses by the enterprise itself relying on its own income and bank credits; and

(3) entail the liquidation of an enterprise as a result of its lengthy unprofitability and insolvency.

In form, this structure for full *khozraschet* seems quite reasonable and can evoke no criticism.[12] However, its practicability engenders numerous questions, two of which deserve special attention.

The first question concerns those enterprises previously financed or subsidized by the state budget. The first group's product can be priced below cost. In the second group, this discrepancy between price and cost was the rule without exception. Application of full *khozraschet* to enterprises of both groups means that from now on their products' prices must be based on cost plus a profit. Legislation on the new economic reforms foresees this necessity. A decree of the CPSU Central Committee and the USSR Council of Ministers of July 17, 1987, "On the Main Directions in the Restructuring of the Pricing System under the Conditions of the New Economic Mechanism" provides in Article 1: "The main task in the restructuring is considered to be the creation of a qualitatively new price system oriented on the intensification of social production, extensive use of economic methods in management, and strengthening cost accounting and self-financing in order to accelerate the country's socioeconomic development."[13] In short, prices must be increased, at least in the first and second groups of enterprises, where full *khozraschet* was not previously employed. But if salaries remain at the same levels, increasing prices will preclude the acquisition of even the bare consumer necessities by the overwhelming majority of the Soviet populace. Hence, salaries must be increased too and in an equal proportion. Moreover, workers and officials will need the increase in salaries all over the country and throughout the economy, including the enterprises that have always worked on the basis of full *khozraschet*. Finally, prices must be increased as much as salaries. But the increase in salaries requires tremendous additional resources.

Where can the Soviet state find these resources in order to increase salaries to the level predetermined by the all-embracing application of full *khozraschet*? Only by increasing labor productivity can these demands be satisfied. This objective, however, is certain to lead to other undesirable consequences, such as unemployment, which has always been considered by Soviet propaganda as a disease of capitalism and unknown to socialism. According to I. Zemtsov, a former assistant to Geidar Aliev, a Soviet leader ousted in 1987, the program of modernization of production announced by Gorbachev will deprive approximately 19 to 20 million workers and officials of their jobs in the near future.[14] This proves that full *khozraschet* promises not just economic prosperity. It holds in store for millions of Soviet citizens an economic misfortune beyond what they have experienced under the previous system of economic management, despite all its shortcomings recognized by the new Soviet leadership.

The second question is connected with the prerequisites for full *khozraschet* as such. In order to implement genuine full *khozraschet*, wholesale and retail prices must be defined to ensure equivalence between producers' costs supplemented by a reasonable profit and the amount consumers pay for acquired merchandise. In a free market, the correlation between supply and demand will reach an equilibrium price level in accordance with this requirement. But what about the Soviet economy which has no prospect of developing a free market in the foreseeable future? The above mentioned "Main Directions in the Restructuring of the Price System"[15] takes into consideration this general problem, providing in Article 3:

> In order to bring the price system into line with the requirements of the new economic mechanism and strengthen the effect of prices and tariffs on increased efficiency in social production, a review must be undertaken as soon as possible of the entire system of prices and tariffs, making it possible on the basis of these prices and tariffs to draw up the plan of economic and social development for the 13th Five-Year Plan and insure the comprehensive use of the principles of full *khozraschet* and self-financing in all sectors of the national economy.

It must be recognized that in an abstract form the task is formulated correctly, and the authors of this decree understand rather well what must be done with prices in order to ensure the introduction and efficiency of full *khozraschet*. But how do the same authors suggest implementing their general directive? The answer can be found in Article 10 of the same decree which states:

> In connection with the development of economic management methods and in line with the new economic mechanism, it is deemed necessary to apply the following prices and tariffs:

- prices and tariffs set on a centralized basis;
- contract prices and tariffs;
- prices and tariffs set independently by enterprises and organizations.

The decree does not and cannot predict the correlation in volume of production of these three methods of defining prices and tariffs. At any rate, in all of the cases where delivery must depend on state orders, prices and tariffs will be set on a centralized basis, and since these orders encompass almost the full volume of produced products, prices and tariffs established centrally will be either all-embracing or obviously dominant. But it is also important to assess the compatibility of these economic management methods with full *khozraschet*.

In fact, the decree under discussion deals not with three but with two methods of defining prices and tariffs: centralized and decentralized. Within the limits of the decentralized method, the decree distinguishes between prices defined by agreement of both parties and those unilaterally established by one party, producing the product, providing the service, etc. Because unilaterally established prices and tariffs are not binding for the customer, this acceptance of another party's terms can be qualified as consent, and as a result, an agreement serves as the basis for prices and tariffs in both cases as opposed to the centralized method.

Agreement (or acceptance) as a method of defining prices and tariffs could correspond to the requirements of full *khozraschet* if the seller were entitled to take into consideration the demand of all of the consumers of its goods. Under these circumstances, the interaction between supply and demand would determine prices in the final analysis, and the producer would receive compensation for its production efforts based on the objective necessity for those efforts. But because produced products are available only to Soviet entities, not to Soviet individuals served by the retail trade system, and because only demands provided for by the plan under the system of planned distribution can be addressed, these demands cannot encompass all of the requirements of a given product in Soviet society. Hence, as a rule, prices and tariffs defined by this method must be lower than the demand of all of society addressed to the appropriate producers would warrant, and as a result, the compensation necessary for full *khozraschet* cannot be ensured by the method of defining prices under consideration. In addition, this method cannot affect prices paid by producers themselves for materials, equipment, labor, etc., if they are established centrally or unilaterally by a seller without any discount. This method of defining prices is fundamentally incompatible with full *khozraschet*.

The centralized method contradicts full *khozraschet* even more than the decentralized method. The centralized method is actually the way the system operated before Gorbachev's reforms, and its economic defects have already been criticized. Retaining this method, Gorbachev, in fact, has changed nothing, except for supplementing it with some decentralization. But to assess the real significance of the latter innovation, the proportionate applications of the two different or even opposite methods must be understood. Judging from the present practice of using nearly all-encompassing state orders for the legal basis of deliveries of produced products, the proportion favors the centralized methods. At the same time, defects generally intrinsic to the centralized method of establishing prices acquire a menacing character as soon as they are connected with full *khozraschet.*

Centralized prices cannot by definition correctly reflect the value of the producer's efforts. This task can be resolved only by the correlation between supply and demand expressed freely and comprehensively. But the appropriate central agencies establishing prices cannot take this correlation into account because it remains completely unknown under the Soviet system. Therefore, centralized prices will be inevitably erroneous, either exceeding the actual value of an enterprise's productivity or underestimating its achievements. In the former case, an enterprise will collect more profit than it deserves at the expense of its contractual partners who are compelled to pay more than they should pay in accordance with the principle of full *khozraschet.* In the latter case, an enterprise will have losses, thus undermining full *khozraschet,* not because it operates improperly but as a result of the mistake of a central agency establishing prices for this enterprise's product.

To avoid these inevitable consequences of centralized prices, all prices established by central agencies for billions of items must be properly coordinated. This task seems absolutely unmanageable because of two circumstances. On the one hand, to coordinate prices for billions of items because of a planner's mistake at least in one case, one must be able to quantify this mistake. However, such knowledge can only be reached by comparing a normative price established by a central agency and a real price resulting from the interplay between supply and demand. In the USSR such data do not exist, so there is nothing to compare. If this data existed, the real price would be known and could be set without error. On the other hand, even if central agencies could, at least approximately, ascertain the degree of a possible error as the basis of the comprehensive coordination of all centralized prices, this would not render the requisite coordination practicable. Bearing in mind the number of products subject to centralized prices, even a sophisticated American computer model could hardly ensure the appropriate result. For the USSR, where computerization is at a much lower level, achieving such a goal would be a dream.

It is very significant that the problem of prices is discussed by Soviet media not so much in light of *khozraschet*, but rather with reference to demand that does not meet the appropriate supply. This in turn threatens price increases and further deterioration of the economic situation. "Demand without Supply," proclaims one newspaper; "actually, demand is not satisfied with respect to all fundamental types of products," echoes another.[16] Moreover, the USSR Council of Ministers adopts a decree "On Measures of Elimination of Defects in the Existing Practice of Formation of Prices."[17] There is not a single word about *khozraschet*. Attention is paid only to measures preventing increases in prices when supply is exceeded by demand.

Thus, full *khozraschet* as one of two principles of the present reforms of the Soviet economy is both impracticable, because of defects in the system of pricing intrinsic to this economy, and disastrous, because it must entail mass unemployment resulting from increases in salaries in accordance with the necessary level of increased prices.

The second principle of organization of state production entities—self-financing—is to some extent similar to full *khozraschet*. Generally speaking, it signifies that an enterprise must finance its own activity, using extracted income and repaying its bank credits. However, in fact, the term *self-financing* is employed by legislated economic reforms only with respect to capital construction.

Before the 1965 reform, an enterprise could construct new buildings only if these construction projects were included in the centralized plan. However, planned construction projects were financed not by the enterprise but by the state budget. The enterprise took part in the creation of a fund for capital investment through periodic monetary installments. But these installments became budget resources immediately after their transfer, and construction projects could never be ensured by the requisite financing without additional resources allocated by the state budget. Therefore, this system was called a system of budget financing.

Self-financing in the realm of capital construction was introduced for the first time by the 1965 reform. It established that an enterprise itself had to finance construction projects if the costs could be paid through bank credits to be repaid within a five-year period. However, this innovation was intertwined with the fate of the 1965 reform itself. Eliminating Kosygin's reforms as a whole, Brezhnev's centralization abolished the unique case of self-financing provided for by the 1965 legislation. Thus, capital investments, always more centralized than other economic activities in the USSR, enjoyed a restricted decentralization for only a short time during the 1965 reform. In a year or two, this program was abolished by secret instructions without public amendment of the 1965 legislation. As a result, centralization of capital investments was restored to the degree that had characterized it from the outset of Stalin's dictatorship, and self-financing could no longer be employed, even in the modest limits established by the 1965 reform.

Gorbachev, proclaiming self-financing as one of the principles of the economic activity of enterprises, has ordered it to be employed also in the realm of capital investments. The 1987 law distinguishes between two types of capital construction: those capital projects implemented by the enterprise itself and those provided for by state orders. In the former case, financing must be ensured by the enterprise either by using its own income or through the extension of bank credits that must be repaid afterward. Because bank credits can be received only on the basis of a one-year or five-year plan,[18] this innovation actually restores Kosygin's reform that allowed self-financing only within the limits of construction projects reimbursable within a five-year period. As established by the legislation on new reforms, all construction projects implemented in accordance with the centralized plan must be financed by the state budget. In these cases, self-financing is no more applicable than it had been previously. This fact only proves that, in contrast to the transformation of Soviet enterprises into production units where Gorbachev stopped half-way between Kosygin and Brezhnev, in the realm of capital construction, Gorbachev went as far as Kosygin, leaving behind Brezhnev's retrograde steps.

What does this mean for the economic development of the Soviet Union? If an economic entity is interested in enlarging the volume of its production, it will insist on implementing self-financed construction projects. But, as discussed, full *khozraschet* is impracticable in the USSR and therefore there are no economic incentives to stimulate Soviet economic entities to initiate self-financed construction projects. Each such project will eventually increase a planned task of production or other activities and each such increase will deter an economic entity from similar initiatives in the future. As a result, self-financing established to a certain extent in the realm of capital investments cannot create the incentives attributed to it by Gorbachev's propaganda. Those who know how the Soviet mechanism works can predict the procedure that will be employed to compel economic managers to initiate construction projects based on the principle of self-financing, which is necessary not so much to these managers as to their rulers. In the typical case, the appropriate manager will be called to a district committee of the CPSU where it will be suggested to him that he take the requisite initiative. Can he protect himself against orders stemming from a Party agency? He cannot, despite the legal guarantees ensured by the 1987 law. It is true that according to Article 9 of the 1987 law, "if a ministry, agency or other higher body issues an act which does not correspond to its competence or in violation of the requirements of the law, an enterprise is entitled to file for state arbitration, declaring the said act to be fully or partially invalid." The same article provides, "losses incurred by an enterprise as a result of compliance with instructions from a higher body which has violated the rights of the enterprise, and also as a result of improper fulfillment by a higher body of its obligations toward the enterprise shall be compensated by this body. Disputes over compensation of losses are decided by state *arbitrazh*." Avoiding the psychological issues (e.g., a subordinate's practical ability to initiate a dispute against a higher agency) and the purely financial ones (e.g., how a higher agency would find the monetary resources to compensate damages caused to a subordinate entity), the most important fact is that these real or, more likely, fictitious guarantees of protection are allocated to enterprises in relationships between them and higher governmental agencies. As to the more authoritative and genuinely powerful Party bodies, no remedies against their arbitrariness are provided in the legislation of Gorbachev's reforms. Party agencies are beyond any court's jurisdiction and cannot be affected by a legal coercion designed to protect impinged economic entities.

Thus, this analysis proves that neither principle of the organization of enterprises in the realm of the Soviet economy meets the purposes of Gorbachev's reforms because of the impracticability of these principles under the dominant Soviet economic and political systems. In his speech at the 27th Congress of the CPSU, Gorbachev emphasized: "Today, the prime task of the Party and the entire people is to reverse resolutely the unfavorable tendencies in the development of the economy, to impart to it the necessary dynamism and to give scope to the initiative and creativity of the masses, to truly revolutionary change."[19] As has been demonstrated, this "truly revolutionary change" follows neither from full *khozraschet* nor from self-financing, as they can be employed in Soviet practice under the given circumstances. But even if their irremovable defects did not exist, full *khozraschet* and self-financing could not ensure by themselves the desirable results. It is no less important to ascertain how the property basis of these principles must be organized, which planning forms can be qualified as the most efficient, and which forms for the correlation between plan and contract seem optimal in the view of the present reforms.

B. The Property Basis of State Industry

Beginning with the 1936 Constitution, Stalin's Constitution, according to the previous official terminology, state ownership has been defined as "the wealth of the whole people."[20] But Soviet economic entities, including industrial enterprises, also need property and they must have certain legally protected rights with respect to this property. Otherwise, they could not work as relatively independent participants in economic life in the USSR. What are those rights? It has been difficult to consider them as components of the right of ownership because of at least two circumstances. On the one hand, almost all of the state's ownership is distributed among state economic and other entities. Only money in the state budget and land as an object of exclusive state ownership in the USSR either remain undistributed as, for example, money in the state budget, or in possession, but not owned by the users, for example, users of land, whether they are individuals, collective, or state entities. Under these circumstances, qualifying state entities as owners would eliminate state ownership or, at best, reduce state ownership to such objects as land and undistributed funds in the state budget. Neither politically nor even economically can such a conception be acceptable to the Soviet leadership. On the other hand, the right of ownership consists of the rights to possess, use, and dispose of owned objects. State entities have never before exercised those three rights with respect to all property objects allocated to them by the state. They could either possess and use certain objects (e.g., means of production) but not exercise the right of disposition, or possess and dispose of certain other objects (e.g., produced products) but not use them for their own purposes. Hence, the volume of the property rights of state entities was restricted in comparison with the right of ownership.

Several exceptions aside, Soviet scholars have avoided calling those rights *ownership*. First the legal doctrine[21] and then the legislature[22] preferred to identify them not as ownership but as operative management. This phrase, not very clear by itself, has been interpreted by law and doctrine in two respects:

(1) operative management is not administrative management, because its exercise belongs to the jurisdiction of the lowest links of the Soviet economy, not to the higher agencies; and

(2) ownership depends in its volume only on law and on being, consequently, broader than administrative management, which must be exercised in accordance not only with law but also with the purposes of the activity of each state entity (such as a machine-building plant or a confectionery factory), planning tasks established by the competent state agencies (such as the Gosplan mandate to produce a certain quantity of specific goods), and the purposes of a specific property fund (such as fundamental or circulating assets, etc.).

Until the most recent time, such interpretation of the property rights of state economic entities evoked no objection. Moreover, in 1981 the Presidium of the USSR Supreme Soviet included in the Fundamental Principles of Civil Legislation Article 26-1, exclusively dedicated to the definition of operative management.[23] The definition extended the concept of operative management, but left its content intact. Operative management is derived from state ownership (or ownership of the state and certain nonstate entities), and subordination of the former to the latter, economically and legally, strengthened the centralism that characterizes the structure of the Soviet economy, especially in its state sector.

The 1987 Law on the State Enterprise (Association), the principal statutory act of Gorbachev's economic reforms, does not use the term *operative management*, a fact that has evoked a certain confusion in the Soviet legal doctrine. One group of scholars contends that "operative management" must be eliminated from the Soviet legal vocabulary, while another group thinks that this concept remains the most adequate description of the actual situation.[24] There are scholars that suggest qualifying ownership as both the state's and the state entities' property right. They contend that this ownership has an administrative nature in the former case and civil law character in the latter.[25] Bearing in mind that Gorbachev himself advocates revision of the concept of socialist (including state) ownership,[26] various ideas from Soviet legal and economic doctrine in this regard can be expected. Especially peculiar is the fact that the 1987 law contains no general definition of the property rights of state enterprises. The terminology in this law differs depending on the specific property fund provided for by the appropriate norm. As a matter of course, for those interested in the substance of the present reforms, it is not the terminology but the actual situation that is of first and foremost importance.

The property of state enterprises is not homogeneous from economic and legal points of view. It is distributed among various funds (fundamental and circulating assets, repair funds, incentive funds, and so forth), and each fund is specifically regulated as the basis of property rights allocated to a state entity as its holder. Since not a single fund has been connected with the sum of rights equal to ownership, the property rights of state enterprises have had to be qualified not as ownership but otherwise, for instance, as operative management. Throughout the history of the Soviet economy, there were cases where enterprises' property rights concerning certain property funds were extended to the point that those rights were very similar to ownership. For example, under the 1965 reform, incentive funds could not be withdrawn from state enterprises by higher agencies and had to remain at the disposal of enterprises without any time limitation. Therefore, certain economists and jurists of that time were tempted to consider state enterprises as owners of incentive funds. Disregard the fact that higher governmental agencies did not consider themselves actually restricted by this legal provision and, if necessary, withdrew the incentive funds of enterprises without reference to any law. Suppose that the above-mentioned provision of the 1965 reform were highly respected and unfailingly observed. What then? Did this transform the state enterprise into the owner of its incentive funds? Although incentive funds formally could not be withdrawn, the enterprise itself was entitled to use them, not at its discretion (as an owner) but in accordance with predetermined purposes (as a nonowner). In addition, the Soviet state is the owner of all state enterprises. How then could enterprises also be owners? Incentive funds were genuinely protected by law against interference by higher agencies in any form, including withdrawal. However, as a representative of the state, the competent agency could withdraw the entire enterprise, with all its funds, including incentive funds. Bearing all these facts in mind, it would be naive to consider a state enterprise as an owner of any property allocated to it by the Soviet state.

As will be demonstrated, Gorbachev enlarged the property rights of state entities. But no matter how great this enlargement in any specific case, the Soviet state remains the owner, in contrast to state enterprises that do not acquire the right of ownership even under the broadest legal provisions defining their property rights. Article 11 of the 1977 Soviet Constitution, proclaiming the Soviet state the owner of state enterprises, retains its force, despite promulgation of the 1987 Law on the State Enterprise (Association). Moreover, this new law treats enterprises as objects of state ownership, not as owners independent of the state. For instance, Article 23 provides, "an enterprise can be liquidated, if the need for its further operation has disappeared." But who is empowered to come to such a conclusion? Of course, the state as the owner can decide whether it shall continue to invest its property in the form of a specific enterprise. Consequently, the very attempt to qualify any of the property rights of the state enterprise as the right of ownership seems completely senseless. At the same time, to come to a conclusion about the innovations concerning the property of state enterprises, this question must be studied separately with respect to each property fund provided for by the 1987 law.

According to Article 4, "fundamental and circulating assets, as well as other material values and financial resources, make up the material and technical base and means of the enterprise. The enterprise exercises the rights of possessing, using and disposing of this property." In appearance, this formula can be perceived as a general definition of the property rights of state enterprises. In fact, however, it has no such significance, because possession,

use, and disposition can be components of different rights
—ownership and nonownership—while this, the most
important characterization, is dropped by the rule under
discussion. This article is important mainly as the only one
that mentions the fundamental and circulating assets of
enterprises. Neither here nor elsewhere in the 1987 law is
the legal regime established for the fundamental assets mentioned. But according to subpart 3 of Article 4, "the circulating assets of the enterprise are in its full command and
not subject to withdrawal." Hence, the fundamental assets
are not provided by similar privileges guaranteed to state
enterprises. This gives an opportunity to assess
Gorbachev's innovations with respect to both property
funds.

Since these privileges are connected only with the circulating assets and cannot be applied to the fundamental
assets, Gorbachev's reforms have not affected the rules governing fundamental assets. This means that the state enterprise possesses these assets and may use them in accordance
with its purposes. As to the right of disposition, the enterprise actually does not exercise it, except for renting out
equipment temporarily (less than one year) unused by the
enterprise.[27] Dealing with the circulating assets, the 1987
law employs a broader provision than exists in practice
("the full command of the enterprise"), and simultaneously
restricts its own formula, obliging the enterprise in Article 4
"to ensure the safety, rational utilization and accelerated
circulation of the circulating assets." But what if this duty is
violated; what if, for example, an enterprise irrationally
uses its circulating assets? Will the higher agency interfere
to improve the situation? Of course it will, and it even must
do so according to Article 9 of the 1987 law. This law also
precludes withdrawal of the circulating assets in contrast to

previous legislation entitling the higher agencies to redistribute surpluses of such assets at the end of an economic year, or even during an economic year if surpluses appear not as a result of highly efficient production but because of decreases in a planned task ordered by the same higher agency. However, what if the enterprise cannot use its surplus in the next economic year or if a surplus appears as a result of a change in a planned task during an economic year implemented by the enterprise itself or by those agencies entitled to address state orders to the enterprise? The 1987 law does not answer these questions. But if the circulating assets must be left intact even under such circumstances, this will lead to their immobilization for the whole national economy, and instead of economic improvement, substantial damage will be caused. It can be predicted, therefore, that economic necessity will compel the introduction of the appropriate corrections into legal provisions concerning circulating assets, because now these provisions represent more of a propagandistic than a realistic approach. In addition, under all circumstances, and despite "the full command of the enterprise," the circulating assets must be used in accordance with their purpose only as circulating assets. Any other use of these material resources is prohibited. Thus, the state enterprise is not endowed with all of the rights which must stem from "the full command" allocated to it with respect to circulating assets.

The state enterprise is also obliged to create and replenish other property funds: the wage fund, the material incentive fund, the fund for the development of production, science and technology, the social development fund, and a repair fund. Creation of these funds is obligatory, whereas creation of a financial reserve or a fund for currency deduction depends on the enterprise's own discretion. The 1987 law provides for different methods for the creation of property funds; however, the choice made by the enterprise is subject to the approval of a higher agency as well as to established norms (*normativi*). The transfer of resources from one fund to another is still prohibited, except for resources of the incentive fund, which can be transferred to the social development fund and the fund for the development of production, science and technology.[28] Only the fund earmarked for bonuses to be paid to workers and officials for their individual efforts can be diminished by the transfer to certain other funds. All of the other funds are now subject to the same severe provisions that preceded the new economic reforms.

In defining the property rights of state enterprises, the 1987 law could not manage to avoid exaggerated demagogy that, unfortunately, renders certain provisions of this law completely unclear. The most important example is connected with the correlation between an enterprise and its labor collective. On the one hand, this law definitely distinguishes between these two phenomena. Nevertheless, Article 1 under the title "The state enterprise (association) and its tasks" establishes in subpart 2: "At a state enterprise the labor collective, using public property as a master, builds up and multiplies the people's wealth and sees to it that the interests of society, the collective and each worker are combined." What does it mean that property rights belong to the state enterprise but the labor collective is the master of this property? Why is it the master if, according to Article 7 of the 1987 law, the consent of the labor collective is required only for the solution of certain property problems by the manager of the enterprise? In addition, the term *master* has no strict legal significance, and although employed by the law, there is no explanation of the labor collective in its capacity as the master. The same law introduces another new phrase—*khozraschet* income[29] of the collective. This income seems very peculiar from the viewpoint of its creation as well as in light of the definition of its holders.

The procedure for creating *khozraschet* income is twice described in the 1987 law. A general definition in subpart 2 of Article 2 states: "Part of the profit (income) must be used by the enterprise to fulfill its obligations with regard to the budget, banks and the higher body. Another part is placed at the full disposal of the enterprise and, together with means of labor remuneration, forms *khozraschet* income of the collective. . . . " In contrast, subpart 1 of Article 3 of the same law obliges the enterprise to create or replenish at the expense of profit (income) all funds of the enterprise in accordance with generally binding norms (*normativi*), and only the residual profit and the wage fund can be considered as a collective's *khozraschet* income. It is clear, however, that if this income "is placed at the full disposal of the enterprise," it cannot belong to the worker collective and cannot be called a collective's *khozraschet* income. At the same time, whoever is the rightholder in this case, if *khozraschet* income is at its full disposal, the rightholder itself must decide which property funds must be created and in what amount. In contrast, if the creation of certain property funds at the expense of profit (income) is a duty of the enterprise predetermined by centralized norms (*normativi*), neither the enterprise nor the labor collective can be considered as the unrestricted master of this income. Such an obvious contradiction of the 1987 law only demonstrates that in the realm of property rights allocated to state enterprises the legislature strives to say more than it gives.

Gorbachev's reforms concerning the property rights of state enterprises are far from revolutionary measures in comparison with legislation previously enacted. Modifications are introduced, but because of their lack of significance they do not deserve to be described as revolutionary, in the classical sense of that word. Actually, two innovations are comparatively important:

(1) prohibition on withdrawal of resources from the circulating fund; and

(2) creation of the labor collective's right not only to determine utilization of the funds for production developments, science and technology, material incentive, and social development, as previously, but also to channel the resources in incentive funds into certain other property funds.

However, as discussed, the innovation concerning the status of the circulating fund is not indisputable as to its economic efficiency viewed in the context of the national economy. As to the second innovation, it is more likely to inflict a blow to the interests of individual workers than protect those interests, bearing in mind the degree of the dependence on enterprise managers of trade unions and other societal entities.

As a matter of course, the concept of the residual profit that remains after all payments are made and all obligatory property funds are created deserves special attention since it is placed "at the full disposal of the enterprise." It cannot be predicted whether such a profit will remain at all, and if it will, its amount—substantial or insignificant—will also continue to be uncertain. Abstractly speaking, the residual profit can be used in connection with two purposes: enlargement of the volume of production and increase in the compensation of workers at the enterprise. Both purposes are very important because increasing productivity and the standard of living are the main goals of the new economic reforms, according to official declarations made by Soviet leaders and ruling agencies. But even if efficiencies in these innovations reveal themselves in the future, a long time will pass before such an impact will be felt.

The Soviet economy is an economy of shortcomings, as the economist Igor Birman has expressed.[30] Before any residual profit appears, Soviet enterprises will suffer from shortcomings of monetary and other resources necessary to create obligatory property funds and to fulfill monetary duties toward the state budget, banks, and their superior entities. No one can predict how long it will take until results are achieved; even the most optimistic of Gorbachev's advisors do not express encouraging prognoses. For instance, Aganbeguian distinguishes between three states of Soviet economic development. He gloomily describes the pre-Gorbachev stage, is enthusiastic insofar as he deals with the achievements of the Gorbachev stage, but even this optimist predicts that palpable consequences of the present reforms will be felt in 2017—at the hundred-year anniversary of the Soviet regime.[31] The specific year was, of course, chosen owing to this anniversary and therefore cannot be seriously accepted. But the long postponement of desirable results is a general trend for Soviet adherents of Gorbachev's reforms. There is no reason to emphasize modest innovations addressed to the property rights of Soviet enterprises as revolutionary measures.

In assessing the economic significance of present reforms, it is important to first try to predict their eventual economic impact on the enlargement of production and increase in the living standard. It is a positive sign, of course, that instead of being appointed by a higher body, now "managers are elected on a competitive basis at enterprises,"[32] even despite the reservation that "if the candidate elected by the labor collective is not endorsed by the higher body, new elections are to be held."[33] The Soviet election system, previously regarded worldwide as a senseless ritual, began to acquire certain new features, as demonstrated by the 1989 election of people's deputies. If the same system is employed in the case under discussion, the new elections should create an opportunity for the best managers to be selected. It is also encouraging that along with the election of an enterprise's manager, the general meeting of the labor collective will consider and endorse plans for the economic and social development of the enterprise as well as collective labor agreements between the trade union and management.[34] All of these innovations, though democratizing an enterprise's administration, in fact or more merely in appearance, are not directly connected with increasing productivity and raising the living standard. Does the new reform legislation do anything to stimulate these most important indices of economic activity?

Only two factors mentioned in their discussion so far can play such a role. The first factor is connected with the expansion of the property rights of Soviet enterprises. But as has been shown, this expansion is so modest and so restricted that it is unreliable as a significant stimulus for productivity. The circulating assets can be protected against withdrawal, but if one cannot acquire by these means the necessary materials or equipment because they are in short supply, the level of productivity will be stagnant and accumulated monetary resources will be immobilized.

The monetary resources of the incentive fund can be transferred to other property funds. This will definitely diminish bonuses that are to be paid to successful workers and officials, while the higher achievements in the realm of productivity under comprehensive shortages of materials and equipment will be as dubious as before.

The second factor important for the reforms is connected with increasing the standard of living depending on the system of wages. Article 14 of the 1987 law is directly dedicated to this issue, and its analysis facilitates the formulation of a correct answer to this question. According to the 1987 law, the wage fund is the principal source for remuneration of labor. This fund must be set up at each enterprise "according to the normative." Thus, the entire amount of this fund depends on the *normativi* established, not on the discretion of the enterprise itself or its labor collective body. As the 1987 law provides, the enterprise, with account for production specifics and the tasks facing it, independently breaks down the wage fund according to individual categories of personnel. The enterprise also determines the total number of staff, and their vocational and qualification composition, and approves lists of staff members. All these functions can be exercised only "within the wage fund," whose size depends not on the discretion of the enterprise but on *normativi* confirmed at the top of the economic system. As a result, the capacity of enterprises to maneuver the wage is not free: they are limited by the size of the wage fund.

The 1987 law considers reasonable use of labor compensation as an important means of promoting the growth of labor productivity. In principle, this idea is doubtlessly true. But its implementation is restricted by the size of the wage fund, on the one hand, and the volume of the incentive fund, on the other. It is not easy for the enterprise to follow an unrestricted declaration of the 1987 law announcing that "the wages of every worker shall be determined by the end results of his work and his personal work contribution, with no maximum limit set on them." How can an enterprise disregard the maximum limit if its resources are limited by the size of the wage and incentive funds? From a demagogical point of view, the provision eliminating "the maximum limit" has appeal; but in reality, it reveals itself as a fiction rather than as a legal rule capable of implementation.

There is another peculiar contradiction concerning wages and bonuses as economic stimuli for increasing productivity in the Soviet economy. Wages and bonuses are paid in money, but their real value depends on the products in kind that can be bought by money. Soviet media persistently report information concerning commodity supply of the Soviet populace. Judging from assertions of eyewitnesses, the more *perestroika* is developed, the less food and other commodities are to be found in the state retail system. On September 12, 1988, Soviet television depicted the arrival of Gorbachev in the northern city of Krasnoyarsk. Large crowds were waiting for his arrival, but instead of applause, he was met with cries of: "Visit our shops; they are literally empty . . . Visit our apartment buildings; there is no hot water, major repairs have not been made for decades, and new housing construction has been completely stopped." Gorbachev's face on that telecast must have revealed his bewilderment. He was bereft of a reasonable explanation for the indignant crowd and resorted to standard excuses about the mistakes of local bureaucracy and standard assurances about the central government's concern about these problems. Bearing in mind that the absolute increase of wages in the form of bonuses is very modest (several rubles per month or a hundred rubles per year), workers have no real stimuli to overexert themselves for the sake of insignificant increases in wages that will not improve their buying power with respect to scarce or nonexistent goods.

Gradually this fact is becoming prevalent in public opinions expressed in Soviet media. An article published by *Izvestia* under the title "Wages in Kind: Why Are They Forgotten?" evokes special interest.[35] Wages of this form were employed only during War Communism, when money had lost its value and could buy nothing. War Communism aside, collective farmers have traditionally received remuneration in kind for a part or all of their labor. This remuneration is so meager, however, that it is drastically disproportionate to collective farmers' labor. The author of the aforementioned article suggests restoring wages in kind in all branches of the Soviet economy, at least as a part of the remuneration of individual labor. According to the article, this method will be more stimulating than monetary bonuses because a worker or an official will directly receive from an employer that which is difficult or impossible to find in retail shops. This reasoning, although persuasive by itself, has one very substantial defect: forms of wages do not create merchandise in kind. If shortages of goods are an integral part of the economic system in its present status, these shortages cannot be eliminated by replacement, even in part, of monetary remuneration of labor by the direct distribution of goods. The author's reasoning is circular: to increase productivity, he suggests introducing a certain proportion of in-kind remuneration, but to introduce this form of wages, the appropriate increase in production must be achieved.

The Soviet Union has already experimented with wages in the form of monetary bonuses paid at the expense of special incentive funds. This system of economic stimuli was introduced by the 1965 reform. Although the actual gain of each worker or official did not exceed several rubles per month, overall demand was increased to such a degree that Soviet supply, very poor before the 1965 reform, faced the danger of a complete collapse as a result of this innovation. The threat of an irreparable crash of the retail trade system was one of the principal causes of the abrogation of the 1965 reform, along with the political competition between Kosygin and Brezhnev. Kosygin had no arguments to protect his incentive funds in the struggle with Brezhnev, who referred to the imminent collapse of the Soviet system of supply, and these funds were transformed into sources for road construction rather than payment of bonuses. The 1965 reform failed, despite the good intentions of its proponents.

Now the Soviet Union faces the same problem. In this respect Gorbachev is not original: he reinvented the wheel or as the Russian saying goes, "He discovered America," by increasing wages to stimulate productivity. Abstractly speaking, this is the only reasonable approach, but because of the peculiarities of the Soviet economy, this approach can ensure nothing. It would be necessary to modify the system to achieve the results desired by Gorbachev. But he cannot and has no intention of doing so, regardless of his secret desires. His reforms considered within the limits of the property rights of state enterprises are doomed. The extent to which this result will affect the personal fate of Gorbachev as a political leader seems less interesting than the fate of his reforms as a comprehensive economic program.

C. Planning

The most centralized planning of production and distribution in Soviet history coincided with the last stage of Stalin's rule. In both cases, similar systems of planning were in force. Only a very small portion of production and distribution, encompassing the least significant objects, remained within the jurisdiction of producers and wholesale purchasers. Beyond these limits, there was the following procedure.

Before the end of each economic year, all enterprises/producers submitted information through their ministries to Gosplan concerning their production capacities for the next economic year. This information bound neither the ministries nor Gosplan. It only provided Gosplan with data to be taken into account in developing a production plan. After the draft of the plan was ready, it had to be approved, except for very insignificant kinds of products, by the Council of Ministers and then promulgated as a law by the USSR Supreme Soviet. Then, Gosplan distributed production tasks among economic ministries, and the latter distributed them among subordinated enterprises. Nonfulfillment or underfulfillment of a planned task entailed economic sanctions for workers of the entity subject to the plan, along with the personal responsibility of managers and sometimes other officials.

Development of the plan of distribution required, in principle, the same procedure. Each economic entity as an eventual consumer of planned products submitted the amount of its demand to its economic ministry which afterwards transferred the demands of all of its enterprises to Gosplan with respect to the most substantial products and to the State Committee of Supply (Gossnab) for all other items distributed by the plan. This information was binding for neither Gosplan nor Gossnab. It served only as the basis of subsequent calculation. A plan of distribution developed by any of these agencies—Gosplan or Gossnab—entered into force as such, except for certain important objects and indicators that required governmental approval. Relying on the plan of distribution, Gosplan or Gossnab informed the ministries/producers and the ministries/consumers about the quota allocated to each of them. Afterward, this quota was distributed by the appropriate ministries among subordinated enterprises obliged to execute contracts indicated by the plan. They could not deviate from the plan of distribution in any direction—either by increase or decrease. They also could not avoid executing contracts provided for by the plan of distribution, even if their demand changed as a result of new circumstances (e.g., modification of the technological process). Moreover, the plan of distribution provided almost all of the terms of eventual contracts, and the parties had in fact nothing to negotiate during their precontractual dealings. If one party indicated by the plan of distribution attempted to avoid executing a contract or tried to establish contractual terms deviating from the plan, a special agency, state *arbitrazh*, compelled it to follow the plan and obliged it to pay fines for violations of the so-called contractual discipline. Under these circumstances, execution of contracts provided for by the plan was a pure formality which could not be seriously taken into consideration by economic entities preferring to perform planned tasks without contracts. But the Soviet leadership considered the execution of planned contracts to be very important, despite their purely formal significance. By means of these contracts, the parties expressed their resoluteness to perform the plan, and this resoluteness was more substantial than formal. Therefore, on April 21, 1949, the USSR Council of Ministers promulgated a decree signed by Stalin under the title "On Execution of Economic Contracts,"[36] that obliged economic managers to execute economic contracts provided for by the plan under the threat of personal responsibility of those who disregarded this binding directive.

These provisions retained their force until 1961-1962, when Khrushchev introduced two substantial, though diametrically opposed innovations to law in force. A decree of the USSR Council of Ministers dated June 30, 1962, established that a purchaser could refuse to execute a planned contract of delivery either completely or in part, on notice to the deliverer and the planning agency within ten days after the planned task was brought to the purchaser's attention.[37] Even after those ten days, *arbitrazh* practice liberated the purchaser from its duty if it was proven that it did not need, completely or in part, the items allocated to it by the plan. But the 1959 legislation on the issue of supply conversely diminished the number of planned indicators and appropriately enlarged the contractual freedom of parties to define their reciprocal obligations.[38] Nevertheless, in principle, planning of distribution, to say nothing about planning of production, remained strongly imperative and extremely detailed. Economic contracts based on detailed plans could be executed not as a result of negotiations between their parties but by their silence during a certain period after receipt of documents describing the planned tasks,[39] a procedure which frankly recognized that under Soviet economic relations the contract is a ceremonial institution.

The first decisive step genuinely earmarked to mitigate this strict centralized planning and to create conditions necessary for economic entities' own initiatives was made by the 1965 reform.[40] Innovations inserted into state planning by this reform can be reduced to the following:

(1) each enterprise received at the eve of the economic year planned targets issued by a higher planning agency, in which the indicator of profit is the leading one and planned tasks are expressed in kind only by a general description of objects of production and several features specifying these objects;

(2) on the basis of planned targets the producers must employ marketing techniques in order to ascertain the demand for their product;

(3) the results of market research must be expressed in the form of contracts executed between producers and consumers;

(4) relying on these data, the producers develop their plan of production;

(5) the production plan enters into force after confirmation by the higher planning agencies; and

(6) if the plan confirmed differs from the plan suggested, all the executed contracts must be modified in accordance with the former and deviating from the latter.

Soon after promulgation of the 1965 reform, it was discovered that this reform did not work, or more precisely, it worked contrary to the hopes and expectations of its proponents. The all-embracing shortages characterizing the Soviet economy led to a peculiar result: the profit indicated by the plan could be easily extracted, no matter what the entity produced, because everything offered to consumers was bought owing to the comprehensive lag of supply in comparison with demand; however, the objects the government considered to be important from political and similar points of view ceased to be accessible in appropriate amounts because enterprises strove to produce that which generated the planned profit the easiest.

Uralmoshzavod in Sverdlovsk is one of the most striking examples. It is a huge plant consisting of more than one hundred workshops equal to large enterprises. Each of these enterprises strove to produce what ensured extraction of the planned profit in the easiest way. As a result, the workshops of Uralmoshzavod not only fulfilled but overfulfilled their plans. The workshops, though overfulfilling their plans, did so in an uncoordinated way, precluding assembly of other constituent parts. When the items produced by the hundred different workshops reached the assembly shop, the assemblers could only produce about 60 percent of their planned output. This situation could not be retained for long.

The most important lesson of the 1965 reform for the Soviet leadership was that the profit indicator that sufficed under all other economic systems did not work under the economic system of the USSR. They decided, therefore, to deter gradually from this odious reform. For several years, planned indicators in kind surrounded profit indicators in a permanently growing number, and finally not the profit but other indices began to dominate in both production and distribution plans. The 1965 reform eventually withered away. The previous system of planning was actually restored in the Brezhnev's centralization process.

Certain features of the 1965 decentralization were retained despite the centralizing measures of 1973-1974. The new legislation for supply of the Soviet economy promulgated in 1981[41] accepted the principle of contracts executed before the development of the plan of supply with respect to consumer goods. According to this principle, the plan cannot exceed the contracts executed. But from the economic point of view, this changed nothing. The supply of consumer goods still had not reached the level of demand, and therefore only in extraordinary cases could consumers require less than planning agencies were ready to allocate. As a result, those features of the 1965 decentralizing reform that were retained by Brezhnev must be disregarded. In fact, the Soviet economy returned to tough centralized planning and did not undergo substantial changes until Gorbachev's reforms. The problem is the extent to which these reforms are realistic and coordinated among themselves.

In 1987 the Central Committee of the CPSU and the USSR Council of Ministers promulgated two decrees concerning the two most important agencies of central planning—Gosplan and Gossnab.[42] Article 1 of the decree concerning Gosplan states that "a resolute switch from predominantly administrative to predominantly economic methods is to be effected in the organization of all planning work." This resolute switch, according to Article 6 of the same decree, signifies that the central planning agencies will:

(a) define the control figures reflecting the social need for the goods produced by a given enterprise and specify minimum production efficiency levels;

(b) determine state orders to guarantee the satisfaction of priority needs of each enterprise;

(c) establish long-term five-year economic norms (*normativi*) to ensure close coordination between statewide interests and the interests of *khozraschet* enterprises; and

(d) fix quotas to define centralized state capital investment in accordance with a confirmed list of enterprises and their projects.

Article 1 of the decree concerning Gossnab states: "It is
necessary to radically change the forms and methods of
organizing material and technical supply to create conditions for effective activity of enterprises on the basis of
khozraschet. . . . " This radical change, according to Article
2 of the same decree, signifies that the central planning
agencies must distinguish between two forms of supply:

(a) wholesale trade in means of production and
(b) centralized distribution of material resources:

Wholesale trade in means of production as a promising
and progressive form of material and technical supply
is carried out according to orders from consumers without quotas and funds. . . . A centralized policy is used
for distributing products that are of primary significance for the formation of the rates and proportions of
public productions, the solution to key problems in the
development of the economy, and the improvement of
public well-being.

At first glance, the restructuring of production and supply planning provided by both decrees retains within the
grasp of the central agency only the general administration
of economic activity (e.g., by means of the control figures or
the definition of the quotas of centralized supply), along
with ensuring the most important governmental interests
(e.g., those embodied in state orders or within the limits of
centralized distribution of material resources). In all other
respects, enterprises are independent. This impression is

strengthened by the 1987 Law on the State Enterprise (Association), especially by provisions such as 10(3) ("An enterprise independently drafts and endorses the five-year plan"); 10(4) ("Yearly plans are drafted and endorsed by an enterprise independently"); 15(1) ("Through wholesale trade the enterprise purchases material resources without limits" and "through centralized distribution [this exception to the general rule] the enterprise is assigned separate material resources within the limits"); and 10(4) ("Agreements for the production and delivery of consumer goods are concluded as a result of a free sale of goods on wholesale markets").

A reading of these legal provisions produces astonishment. Will it really be so? Is this not a fairy tale? Try to imagine consumer goods, mostly inaccessible for decades, being freely bought without distribution in the country where it is impossible to buy anything except bread in locations outside Moscow; enterprises, permanently subordinated in all details to instructions received from the top, can independently handle their activity paying attention only to general indications issued by the higher agencies; instead of searching with all possible efforts for material resources necessary for production activity, a manager can receive everything necessary—not more but also not less. Is it believable? Careful examination of the statutory provisions expressing Gorbachev's economic reforms reveals their own self-destruction. Appeal to Soviet reality and the striking destruction will be substantially strengthened.

Dealing with independent five-year and yearly planning exercised by the enterprise, it is important to take into consideration "initial data" that must be utilized in the planning process by the enterprise in accordance with Article 10(3) of the 1987 law. Among these data, control figures are preeminent. They were first mentioned by the 1965 reform, and in this case Gorbachev only borrows an idea developed by Kosygin. The 1987 law does its best to mitigate the ruling force of the control figures: "They [allegedly] are not of a directive nature and must not restrict the labor collective in drafting the plan" (Article 10). It is important to examine Article 4(a) of the 1987 decree on Gosplan that defines the social need for the appropriate goods as follows: "the control figures include an indicator for the production of goods (work, or services) in terms of cost (estimates) for the conclusion of contracts, profit (income), foreign currency earnings, and the most important general indicators relating to scientific and technical progress and to the development of social life." Both the 1987 decree and the 1987 law emphasize the same premise: the control figures "must not fetter a labor collective during the elaboration of the plan, but must give it wide scope in the adoption of decisions and the selection of partners of economic contracts." The issue of partners of economic contracts will be discussed later. For now, it is significant to point out that the control figures express "the social need" for the appropriate goods. The enterprise's plan cannot vary from the proportion of goods enumerated by the control figures. Nor can indicators in these figures that specify planned output be disregarded or modified by the enterprise. Its initiative may be exercised only in the production of more goods than the control figures require or in the specification of details omitted by the control figures. It is clear that the independence of enterprises in the realm of planning seems broader in the general declarations than it does when the specific provisions are examined.

Second among the "initial data" to be taken into account by the enterprise in the planning process are state orders. Gorbachev, seemingly, has not forgotten that one of the principal causes of the failure of the 1965 reform stemmed from the profit indicator being the only significant means of assessing enterprise efficiency. As a result of this miscalculation, enterprises extracted their planned profit but they did not produce the appropriate product in kind according to the Soviet leadership's needs. State orders introduced by Gorbachev should prevent these undesired consequences. Article 6(b) of the decree dedicated to Gosplan provides:

> State orders guarantee the satisfaction of priority social need and are issued to enterprises for the purpose of commissioning production capacities and projects in the social sphere funded out of centralized state capital, and also for ensuring the delivery of certain types of goods needed above all to resolve social tasks of state importance, implement scientific and technical programs, strengthen the country's defense capacity, ensure its economic independence, or guarantee agricultural deliveries.

The fact that these enumerated tasks are to be fulfilled through state orders leaves no doubt that they are absolutely binding for their addresses and that within these limits an enterprise has no freedom to plan its activity within its own discretion. To judge the extent to which these new institutions will affect independent planning implemented by state enterprises, the volume of production encompassed by the state orders must be considered. On July 20, 1988, the USSR Council of Ministers summarized the performance of the state plan established for the first half of the 1988 economic year.[43] Based on information from the meeting, it appears that during the period under discussion, almost the entire output of the Soviet economy was produced on the basis of state orders, and consequently no place remained for enterprises' independent planning. The USSR Council of Ministers informed all Soviet economic entities that development of plans for 1989 will require from them more activity because "under the forming of the plan of the next year state orders will have restricted significance."[44] It is hardly possible to explain this optimistic prediction for enterprises' independence in the realm of planning in 1989 if one takes into account that according to the same information, "the production of national income increased, in comparison with the first half of 1987, at 5% under the goal of 6.6% established for 1988. Fourteen percent of associations and enterprises failed to meet their contractual obligations, including delivery of 2.2 billion rubles worth of products."[45] If under state orders encompassing almost the entire national output of Soviet industry such a lag could not be overcome, then how will it be eliminated by restricting the employment of state orders? Where are the material prerequisites of this restriction to be found in the achievements of the Soviet economy?

After state orders, the 1987 decree dedicated to Gosplan refers to long-term (five-year) economic *normativi* that will ensure close coordination between statewide interests and the interests of *khozraschet* enterprises. Two facts attract attention in this regard. First, since the long-term norms must be established by the central agencies and are binding on all enterprises and associations, it is not the enterprises' and associations' independence in the realm of planning but subordination to the unchangeable central-ized norms that is the most important requirement of the new economic reforms. Second, how can the enterprises avoid being fettered in their economic decisions when the economic state of affairs is constantly changing yet the eco-nomic norms are invariable for no less than five years? As a matter of fact, in introducing the stable norms the adher-ents of the new reforms meant to avoid the previous vicious practice from which frequent plan changes from the top caused disorder on the bottom. But they disregarded a sub-stantial defect of stable norms that deprives economic enti-ties of opportunities to implement economic maneuvering during the term of these norms. At any rate, the right of independent planning allocated to state enterprises must depend on the stable norms established by the central agencies.

The final indicator provided for by the 1987 decree on Gosplan refers to quotas defining the ceiling for centralized capital investments by the state that must be established for each state enterprise. This indicator actually specifies the principle of self-financing declared by Gorbachev's eco-nomic reforms. As discussed above, previously all capital investments were planned and financed centrally. The enterprises paid periodic monetary installments to the state budget for the purpose of capital construction. But these installments immediately became a part of the state budget. The enterprises themselves took no part in the planning of capital construction, which included in the centralized plan, was financed by the state budget. The economic reforms under way substantially change this situation. The previous procedure retains its force only with respect to construction projects encompassed by centralized quotas and special lists that enumerate the enterprises that can function as customers for construction projects. These enterprises are obliged to include the appropriate quotas in their plans, consequently possessing no rights to independent planning in this area. Such rights belong to them only with respect to construction exceeding the centralized quotas and implemented by them as a result of their own initiative and on the basis of their own finances. In this regard, their rights to plan capital construction are doubtlessly expanded.

The problem, however, is the extent to which new legal opportunities are ensured by enterprises' economic resources. Enumerating the property funds of the enterprise, the 1987 law does not mention the capital investment fund. Specific resources, directly earmarked for capital construction, do not exist in the enterprises. The repair fund can be used, as its name suggests, for the purpose of repairs, not new construction. The social development fund is earmarked for housing construction, at least in part. Housing construction, though important, does not belong to the realm of production construction and therefore cannot characterize the degree of the enterprise's independence in the realm of production planning. The fund for the development of production, science, and technology can be employed for numerous purposes, including financing of renewal and expansion of the fundamental assets that represent a form of capital construction. But because there is a great number of purposes for this fund, it hardly ensures much capital construction. It is true that the enterprise has the right to channel a part of the material incentive fund to the fund for the development of production, science, and technology. Such a measure will, of course, increase the volume of capital construction implemented in accordance with the principle of self-financing. But this will be made at the expense of the material incentive fund, which is hardly reasonable, bearing in mind that the new reforms try to transform the material incentives into the principal stimuli for economic progress in the USSR.

Only one source of eventual noncentralized capital construction remains as an issue of serious discussion — the so-called *khozraschet* profit of the state enterprise. Will this profit suffice after all of the deductions provided for by law to ensure, along with other demands of the enterprise, sufficient capital construction? According to the information stemming from the meeting of the USSR Council of Ministers referred to above, the Soviet government has established that "the financial situation of many enterprises remains unsteady."[46] There is no reason to assume that a state enterprise will be able to use its expanded rights to plan capital construction in the foreseeable future.

An attentive analysis shows that in the most vulnerable point of the Soviet economy — extremely centralized planning — Gorbachev's reforms have changed less than widely believed, relying more on the general declarations than on the genuine substance of the declared innovations. Although numerous changes have taken place, in principle, the planning remains as centralized as it has been for decades in reality. Only certain secondary planning functions are transferred from the top to the bottom.

Along with the transfer of certain planning functions to the enterprises, the enterprises' rights in this area can also be enlarged by abrogation of certain types of planning. With respect to the system of material and technical supply, this approach is employed by the 1987 decree concerning Gossnab. According to Article 2 of the decree, "material and technical supply includes: wholesale trade in means of production and centralized distribution of material resources."

Wholesale trade in means of production "must be carried out according to the orders from consumers without quotas or funds."[47] In contrast, "a centralized policy is used for distributing products that are of primary significance for the formation of the rates and proportions of public production, the solution to key problems in the development of the economy, and the improvement of public well-being."[48] In other words, wholesale trade in means of production must be implemented without centralized planning, exclusively on the basis of free agreements between sellers and purchasers, while suppliers of material resources must be subordinated to the centralized planning relying upon state orders and the appropriate quotas and funds that will be accordingly allocated to the consumer entities. These provisions clarify all of the distinctions between the previous system and the new system of planning addressed to material and technical supply. That which is encompassed by state orders remains in the realm of centralized planning, and in this regard the rights of the state enterprises are unchanged, despite the new economic reforms. In comparison, that which is transferred through wholesale trade entails the execution of free contracts disconnected from centralized planning, and in this regard the new economic reforms expand the rights of the state enterprises. But this formal expansion must be realistically assessed. As the meeting of the USSR Council of Ministers certifies, during the first half of 1988 the state orders expressing centralized planning encompassed almost the entire amount of the output produced by state enterprises, and therefore nothing remained for free wholesale trade in means of production. Soviet economic reality has proved to be less generous than the authors of the Soviet economic reforms would indicate.

As to the distribution of consumer goods, Article 10(4) of the 1987 Law on the State Enterprise (Association) establishes that "agreements for the production and delivery of consumer goods are concluded as a result of free sale of goods on wholesale markets. . . . " To implement such a legally confirmed program, the country must have an abundance of food. The opposite idea leads nowhere: an abundance of food cannot result from free contracts employed for their distribution. The Soviet leaders recognizes this fact as much as do their theoretical foes. Nevertheless, they resort to a legal declaration that is knowingly impracticable. On the one hand, this declaration contradicts the provision of Article 6(b) of the 1987 decree concerning Gosplan, that establishes that state orders must, among other tasks, guarantee agricultural delivery, the most important part of consumer supply. How can agricultural produce be purchased by free contracts between economic entities if state orders assume allocation of quotas and funds as the necessary planning prerequisites for the execution of any economic contract? On the other hand, the aforementioned meeting of the USSR Council of Ministers emphasized that "consumer goods have been produced less than the plan provided."[49] If the volume of produced consumer goods does not reach the level outlined by the plan of production, how can these goods be sold and acquired by economic entities without a plan of distribution?

The deplorable situation of food supply in the USSR is no secret: at the 27th Congress and 19th Conference of the CPSU this well-known fact was expressly recognized by Gorbachev and other Soviet leaders. They understand that if food markets are not satiated, the nations of the USSR will support neither *perestroika,* nor *uskorenie* (acceleration)—nor any other economic inventions of the new leaders. These leaders tirelessly reiterate that the food problem will be resolved first and foremost. The legal promise to introduce unplanned distribution of consumer goods is one of the forms of the insistent demagogy. But demagogy is not production. It is possible to resort to a fictitious declaration of a modified system of planning, but implementation of production requires genuine changes to this system. The facts prove that the USSR is not yet sufficiently mature to completely reject or substantially modify the centralized methods of economic administration. Therefore, a great number of innovations allegedly inserted into the Soviet system of economic planning are inexplicable in one part and impracticable in the other.

D. Contracts

A traditional concept in the law of continental European countries considers the contract as a free agreement executed to create the appropriate legal consequences. The same definition dominated in the USSR before the introduction of centralized administration of the Soviet economy. In the early 1930s a new institution of contracts arose. Applicable only to relationships between Soviet entities, this institution was called planned contracts. Under Stalin's rule, planned contracts acquired certain peculiar features unknown to other, unplanned contracts. Along with the application only between Soviet entities, not Soviet individuals either as one or as both parties, these features were as follows:

(a) at first, the appropriate plan (of distribution, of construction, of transportation of goods, etc.) had to be confirmed and only then could the corresponding contracts be executed;

(b) a contract was invalid if it did not rely upon the necessary planned prerequisites, for example, if it were executed before the plan had been confirmed or between parties not indicated by the plan;

(c) contractual terms contradicting the planned indicators were invalid in whole or in part and had to be modified in accordance with the plan;

(d) contracting parties were entitled to establish their own terms only to develop the planned indicators or to fill gaps in the plan, but these terms had to correspond to the principles of a given plan or its specific provisions; and

(e) entities indicated by a plan were not only entitled but obliged to execute the planned contracts. If execution of a contract was hampered by one of the parties or it did not occur because both parties could not reach the requisite agreement, a special agency —*arbitrazh*—heard the case and announced a contract executed in accordance with terms formulated by *arbitrazh* itself.

At different stages of Stalin's rule, certain details in the correlation between plan and contract changed. During the prewar and wartime eras, a planned task could be performed by both of its addressees, for example, the deliverer and the purchaser, on the basis of the plan without execution of a contract. After the war, execution of contracts provided for by the plan was obligatory, and before execution addressees of a planned task were prohibited from asking for or fulfilling performance. In some cases parties could not add anything to the planned indicators, and in other cases they could develop some initiatives. All these details aside, the general principles confirmed at that time were clear: the plan was the basis of planned contracts. Although Khrushchev somewhat mitigated the dependence of contracts on plans,[50] he left the general principle intact.

An attempt to modify this principle by reversing the role of plan and contract, so that the contract and not the plan was preeminent, was undertaken by the 1965 reform. According to this reform, enterprises were obliged at first to execute economic contracts with their partners, and only then, relying on contractual data, did the competent planning agencies have to confirm the plan. If innovations dictated by the 1965 reform were reduced to these commands, it is arguable that Kosygin inverted a principle of Stalin: instead of having the plan dominate the contract, the contract had to be the basis for the plan. But there were also two other rules established which rendered Kosygin's radicalism less radical than it might seem at first glance. One rule provided that the process of executing contracts had to be preceded by the establishment of control figures by planning agencies for all enterprises, whose task it was to execute as many contracts as necessary to fill the control figures. The other rule obliged all contractual parties to adjust their contracts to the plan as soon as the plan was confirmed. As a result, the principle of subordination of contracts to plans was not inverted by the 1965 reform. Although in a new form, this principle retained its force. Owing to the formal changes, the role of contract was strengthened in comparison with its significance during the prereform period.

The failure of the 1965 reform, resulting from numerous circumstances, also predetermined the fate of the new correlation between plan and contract. Remainders of this new form could be found in the realm of supply of consumer goods. In general, the correlation between plan and contract that had existed before 1965 was restored several years after 1965. Gorbachev has not eliminated this restored relationship. At the same time, he has not disregarded the experience of the 1965 reform. His economic policy in this respect has proved to be more complicated.

The above-mentioned law of 1987 and the decrees of the same year dedicated to Gosplan and Gossnab distinguish among three forms of contractual relationships. The first form is connected with state orders. Issued by higher agencies and addressed to state enterprises, state orders are binding on the producer that delivers its product to the appropriate customer and on the customer that personifies the state orders as a consumer. National economic material balances and plans for the distribution of products necessary to ensure that state orders are developed by Gosplan and Gossnab. On this basis, producers and consumers must execute their contracts. The rule establishing the domination of plans over contracts is expressed in this case as consistently as possible, without any deviation from the functioning of this principle in the pre-Gorbachev time. Moreover, the right of the customer to refuse to execute a contract completely or in part as provided for by legislation on delivery is modified in connection with state orders and other cases of distribution based on planned limits. The new Statute on Supply of Products of Production/Technical Designation, confirmed by the USSR Council of Ministers on July 25, 1988,[51] retaining this right with respect to annual plans, does not mention it for the contracts executed in accordance with five-year plans. This signifies that within the limits of five-year planned distribution, the principle that "the plan is the basis for contract" functions stronger than before Gorbachev's reforms, acquiring the force it possessed under Stalin.

The second form represents wholesale trade in means of production. This form existed to some extent before Gorbachev's reforms. Wholesale department stores created to sell surplus means of production did so in relationships with Soviet entities. There were limits (quotas) or funds allocated to each entity, however, and no contract of wholesale trade could exceed these limitations. Wholesale department stores actually entered into planned contracts, although planning in this case differed from that generally employed in distribution. Gorbachev's reforms strive to transform this institution into unplanned contracts, providing that wholesale trade in means of production must be carried out according to orders from customers without limits (quotas) and funds. However, the control figures as a general prerequisite of economic activity also encompass wholesale trade in means of production, and because these figures are the initial component of planning, the appropriate contracts cannot be declared as completely free from planning regulation.

At the same time, the problem of practicality in unplanned wholesale trade in means of production must also be discussed. The 1987 decree on Gossnab characterizes wholesale trade in means of production with every reason as a promising and progressive form of material and technical supply. But to successfully implement this form, means of production must be produced at least in the volume corresponding to the economy's demand. If such demand cannot be satisfied, consumers will, of course, submit their orders but the wholesale department stores will be unable to completely satisfy their demand. As a result, either certain consumers will remain without requisite means of production or each will receive less than necessary. Given a prevailing shortage of material resources, free trade resembles utopia more than a reality. Any utopia is dangerous for the economy, which the authors of the contemporary reforms in the USSR do not forget even for a minute. This is why they declare free trade in means of production in legal provisions and simultaneously occupy all of these means by state orders, leaving, in fact, nothing to create even minimal material resources for unplanned supply, for distribution implementable without subordination of contracts to plans.

The third form must be applied only to consumer goods. All of the contracts between economic entities with respect to consumer goods must be executed without quotas or funds either directly between an entity-producer and an entity-consumer or between the same entities at wholesale markets which are periodically organized in the USSR. These contracts must be completely unplanned, disregarding the facts that production of consumer goods is also preceded by the development of control figures and that agricultural produce belongs in great part to those objects encompassed by state orders. Dealing with consumer goods, the 1987 law restores one of the most important ideas of the 1965 reform. As Article 10(4) indicates, free agreements on delivery of consumer goods must be "the basis for planning the line-up and raising the quality of goods and indices determining the production and social development of an enterprise." In other words, similar to the 1965 reform, contracts must be the basis of planning within the limits of the economic innovations of the 1980s. However, if Soviet planning could take and indeed did take

into consideration the entire demand expressed by contracts, the problem of the correlation between plan and
contract—one of the sharpest problems of the Soviet economy—would not exist. The contract would be the only
document defining the rights and duties of contractual parties. The plan would perform the function of a purely internal document for producers that, mirroring consumer
demand, would have to contain indicators of the production activities of producers. Under these circumstances, the
principle, "contracts are the basis of planning," is the only
acceptable one. Planning could be implemented within
each enterprise, while central agencies could restrict their
planning activity through certain general directives.

But in the USSR, at least at the given level of economic
development, such a correlation between plan and contract
is precluded by the shortage of goods. The 1965 reform
almost expressly recognized this fact: it proclaimed the subordination of plan to contract as the all-embracing system
with the exception of contracts previously executed which
had to be adjusted to plans confirmed afterward. In contrast, the authors of the latest reforms seemingly disregard
the same fact: they have excluded from subordination to
contracts only the planning of state orders, but all other
contracts are disconnected from the plan and need not be
modified after the plan is confirmed. Such a declaration is
groundless: where will the Soviet Union find a source of
food sufficient to assure supply in accordance with its
extremely generous promises? At any rate, such a source
does not currently exist, and until it is created, the promises
will remain on paper, while the actual situation will be,
most probably, regulated similarly to the 1965 provisions:
execution of contracts; confirmation of the plan; modification of contracts in accordance with the plan.

Dealing with the problem of Soviet planning and Soviet contracts, Western reviewers frequently pay no attention to the real causes that are permanently sharpening this problem. A number of these reviewers suggest: abolish or mitigate centralized planning, strengthen the proper initiative of economic entities by disconnecting or loosening the dependence of contracts on plans, and the results will be miraculous. Gorbachev tries to accommodate his reforms to these recommendations, but he can go no farther than formally expressed promises and actually rejected ways. It should be understood that it is not the fallacious correlation between plans and contracts dominating in the USSR but the impossibility of establishing a reasonable correlation implementable in this country that is the genuine cause of the devastating failures of the Soviet economy.

No one can contend that plans and contracts (or the certain correlations between them) are economically naive. A contract is an agreement creating an opportunity to take into consideration parties' demands in all detail. Is this institution futile? Of course not. Only by relying upon it can an economy be handled reasonably and efficiently. However, the Soviet system precludes execution of such contracts not only because of the all-embracing shortage of goods, but also because of the demands of the system as a whole that take precedence over the individual requirements of different economic entities. If the military build-up, or the priority of supply in the ruling elite precludes satisfaction of various entities' demands, then the most necessary contracts will be annihilated, and the worst planning indicators will acquire binding force.

A plan is an instrument of reasonable regulation of economic activities employed in anticipation of the future. Is this institution harmful? Of course not. Only by relying on it can needs be contemplated and satisfied. The Soviet system, pushed by shortage on the one hand and by demands of the ruling elite on the other hand, precludes the development of plans whose purpose is only to adjust the economy to the future. These plans must be detailed to satisfy requirements of the whole system personified by the ruling elite and to prevent distribution of meager food supplies that will leave numerous regions without bare necessities. Therefore planning must be centralized and, as a rule, cannot be completely transferred from the center to local entities, either governmental or economic. As a result of the same circumstances, planning must be detailed and, as a rule, cannot be comprehensively reduced to general directives, either abstract or even specific.

To expect from Soviet reforms, viewed in their substance not in their letter, something more means to hope that a system can produce results that are incompatible with the system itself. Why then does the Soviet system employ economic contracts at all? Is it not simpler to rely on centralized plans and abolish contractual institutions altogether? As discussed above, for a certain time such a practice existed in the USSR. However, contractual institutions were later restored for numerous reasons.

First, despite the all-embracing shortage of products prevailing in the USSR, production of some items does meet consumer demand or even surpasses it. For instance, consumer sewing machines, scarce during many postwar years, are now produced in abundance. Under these circumstances, the plan for their production probably must be decreased, but it would be senseless to plan centrally the distribution of these items. They are sold by producers to wholesale enterprises on the basis of unplanned contracts —that is, those that do not rely on planned distribution.

The Soviet economy also produces certain objects in insufficient amounts, but these objects (e.g., hunting equipment) are assessed as so unimportant to economic supply and demand that their planned distribution has never been employed and their sale has always been based on unplanned contracts. Replacement of contracts by plan cannot be comprehensive because unplanned contracts also exist in the USSR.

Second, as a rule, the centralized plan cannot foresee everything required for performance of an economic operation. For instance, the indicator of quantity exists in each plan distributing footwear. These objects have a number of varying attributes: size, color, footwear for men, women, and children, for winter and for summer, etc. No single plan can be developed in a way necessary to reflect all these indicators. Such a task must be imposed on the addressees indicated by the plan, and these addressees must come to the appropriate agreement, taking into consideration producers' opportunities and consumers' demand. It is apparent that in a great number of cases, the plan would be impracticable without contracts. Contracts supplement the plan, specify it, adjust it to the concrete circumstances of a given economic performance, and therefore serve as an indispensable legal instrument even in the centralized Soviet economy.

Third, there exist in the Soviet practice plans of distribution developed with such detail that actually nothing remains for negotiation between contracting parties. This method of planning is employed in the distribution of oil. Nevertheless, the law in force, as discussed above, requires the execution of contracts even under these circumstances, at least by the simplest procedure: silence of the deliverer

and the customer for ten days after the receipt of the appropriate planning documents signifies that the contract is executed on the terms expressed by the planned indicators.
Consequently, even those contracts reduced to pure formality are qualified as necessary for the centralized economy in
the USSR. Why? The point is that plans often contain
substantial mistakes: the producer is obliged to deliver
more than it produces or to promise the supply of an assortment that contradicts its technological process, or the consumer is given the planned right to acquire certain objects
that are not necessary for its activity or that exceed its
demand. These planning mistakes can be ascertained by the
addressees of a plan if they are obliged to execute a contract
in any form: beginning with mere silence and ending with
genuine negotiation. If a mistake of planning is ascertained,
the parties will refuse to execute a planned contract, and
this will compel the appropriate planning agency—either
directly or as a result of the intervention of *arbitrazh*—to
correct erroneously planned indicators and thus to prevent
inevitable economic failures under fallacious plans. Similarly, if the planned addressees have executed a planned
contract, even through silence, it means that the plan is
correct and the parties themselves approve it, expressing
their joint decision in an executed contract to perform what
the plan dictates by its indicators.

All of these arguments demonstrate that the Soviet
economy cannot function without centralized planning,
that this planning must be supplemented by economic contracts, that economic contracts must be subordinated to
plans, and that within the limits compatible with the plans,
the parties executing economic contracts can be entitled to
develop and supplement the planned indicators. Such is the

system, and, without exceeding its limits, one can maneuver between centralization and decentralization, either strengthening planning or strengthening the role of contracts, depending on specific features of a given stage of the cyclical development of the Soviet economy during various periods of the history of this country.

Gorbachev tirelessly vows that his reforms, including changes in the correlation between plan and contract, have significance within the system and are earmarked to improve this system, not to modify it. His approach to the correlation between plan and contract does not corroborate his promise, at least insofar as the new legal provisions are considered separately from the economic reality. These provisions are aimed to combine the centralized planning as an indispensable component of the Soviet economy and unplanned contracts of the free market as a phenomenon alien to this economy. But such a combination does not work. Preferring free contracts to planned agreements, one must eliminate centralized planning—that is, destroy the Soviet system, which according to Gorbachev's assertions, is not his purpose. In contrast, preferring centralized planning to initiatives of economic entities, free contracts must be eliminated—that is, the obsolete nonworking economic mechanism must be retained, which according to Gorbachev's assertions, will perpetuate the economic stagnation. The incompatibility of the above-mentioned combination with within-the-system reforms is obviously clear to the new Soviet leader. But at the same time he understands that if such a combination is not proclaimed, no one will take his economic reforms seriously. Therefore, a very peculiar trick has been performed. Legal provisions combine incompatibles: centralized planning represented by

state orders with free contracts disconnected from centralized planning for products not provided for by state orders.
From the viewpoint of economic reality, in contrast to the
same legal provisions, state orders as a means of centrally
planned distribution encompass almost all produced products and that which actually remains for free contracts does
not exceed the types and quantity of objects whose supply
has characteristically been met independently of centralized planning in the past. As a result, the previous correlation between plan and contract, renovated in the words of
the new laws, is left intact by facts of practice. This is why all
hopes connected with Gorbachev's economic reforms seem
futile. Indirectly, this conclusion was not precluded by
Gorbachev himself. As *The New York Times* informs,
Gorbachev told Soviet editors in a meeting that his campaign to reshape the country is faltering, undermined by a
gap between plans and deeds. He said, "We are going
slowly, we are losing time, and this means we are losing the
game."[52]

As demonstrated above, two factors of Soviet reality
predetermine the necessity of centralized planning and thus
preclude the orderly transformation from planned to
unplanned contracts: shortages of goods that can arise, and
sometimes do arise, not only in so-called socialist countries;
and specific requirements of the ruling elite that are peculiar features of so-called socialist regimes. The self-interest
of the ruling elite that results in notorious individual privileges such as special stores and "closed" restaurants can
certainly be moderated. However, the leadership should
keep in mind the fact that Khrushchev's austerity campaign
contributed to his ouster. In contrast, that which is necessary to strengthen the unlimited political power of the
ruling elite, for instance, military build-up or space

exploration, must be protected under all circumstances. These priorities require centralized planning, and no free contracts can be introduced to replace the obligatory established contractual relations.

As to the shortage of goods, adherents of the new reforms with Gorbachev at the head are actually entrapped by a hopelessly vicious circle. As has been shown, this shortage is not a uniquely socialist phenomenon and if scarcity were eliminated, planned distribution of goods could be replaced by unplanned contracts without any retreat from the system of socialism. But to introduce unplanned contracts for food and other commodities, their production must be increased to exceed demand. Such a result becomes achievable only by means of the perfect system of economic incentives addressed to producers and first of all by abolishing subordination to the centralized plan. However until the appropriate level of production of food and other commodities is reached, centralized distribution cannot be abolished. Otherwise shortages will be even more unbearable than under centrally planned distribution. Disregarding these circumstances, the 1987 law establishes the system of free contracts for supply of the wholesale trade system with consumer goods. Despite these most favorable legal commands, shelves in Soviet retail shops are empty because the produced consumer goods do not suffice, and in numerous Soviet cities certain foods are subject to rationing, although at the wholesale level they are to be acquired by free (unplanned) contracts.

A complicated situation has arisen in the USSR as a result of a contradiction between the reforms declared and their implementability under the given political and economic systems, and the situation presses the Soviet leadership to find an acceptable way out. To retain these systems

intact, it would seem that one must strive to slowly overcome the shortages of consumer goods and then gradually,
in accordance with achieved results, mitigate centralized
planning to the extent to which it is entailed by shortages
themselves. This option has proved to be very uncertain
economically and extremely dangerous politically. It is
uncertain economically because, as has been shown by the
reference to the 1988 meeting of the USSR Council of
Ministers, planned indicators concerning the growth of production were not reached during the first half of 1988 and it
is the production of consumer goods that lags farthest
behind. This signifies that either the requisite growth is
unachievable under the existing system or certain substantial steps forward require decades to be implemented. Judging from the above references to Aganbeguian, the latter
perspective is semi-officially assessed as the most realistic.
Such a perspective is politically dangerous. Soviet citizens
will be very disappointed in the new leadership that
promises to improve their living standard and at the same
time requires the span of a generation to make a reality of
this promise. The disappointment of the citizenry is hardly
enough to develop into a mass revolt in the USSR. During
the whole history of this country—from the establishment
of the Soviet regime up to the present time—only isolated
mutinies have occurred and the Soviet rulers have repeat-
edly demonstrated their capacity to cope with these explo-
sions. There is no doubt, judging, for instance, from the
events in Nagornii Karabakh, that this capacity has not
been lost by the Soviet rulers. The important factor is that
different wings of the Soviet summit are involved in incessant political in-fighting. In developing these battles,
Gorbachev's political foes use any opportunity, and the

failure of Gorbachev's economic reforms should doubt-lessly become a trump card in the grasp of those who strive to seize political control. If they win, the decentralized stage of the cyclical development of the USSR will be replaced by the stage of centralization, and, as a matter of course, the economic reforms now under way will be either gradually or promptly neutralized in accordance with new political goals.

Gorbachev and his collaborators understand this rather well. They incessantly resort to various measures, and one decree is published after another, but no substantial change seems palpable. This appears to be irrefutable evidence of the fact that the system itself does not work, and as a result, any approach to its economic structure produces failure instead of success.

Yet along with the state economy, there are cooperative and individual economies in the USSR. The individual economies have always been phenomena separated from, though dependent on, the state economy. As to cooperative economies, they are either disguised forms of state owner-ship (e.g., the property of collective farms) or transformed individual properties (e.g., the property of the garden socie-ties). In speaking about an economy other than that of the Soviet state, one can mean only individual economies and those cooperative economies that in fact represent trans-formed individual property. Both of these economic types attract the attention of Gorbachev who is probably aware that his goals are unachievable within the limits of the state economy. Therefore, his other efforts must be discussed first with respect to cooperative organizations and then in connection with individual economies.

CHAPTER

2

The Cooperative Economy

In contrast to state enterprises, which were unknown in prerevolutionary Russia, cooperative entities, including consumer and sale cooperatives, existed long before the 1917 coup. There is a long history of discussion in the Soviet doctrine concerning the economic and legal nature of cooperative entities. The Soviet civil codes of the 1920s considered cooperative organizations as private entities, although they hesitated to maintain this point of view unconditionally.[1] Later, especially beginning with Stalin's politics of collectivization—the coercive creation of collective farms—all types of cooperative entities were proclaimed socialist organizations.

A. Organization of Cooperative Entities

During Stalin's rule, the only cooperatives were collective farms and consumer cooperatives. Khrushchev added several other types, including housing cooperatives, *dacha*

103

cooperatives, garden cooperatives, and garage cooperatives. The so-called trade cooperatives (for tailors, shoe-
makers, etc.) developed under Stalin's rule were abolished
by Khrushchev throughout the country, except for the Baltic republics.

Putting aside official declarations and taking into
account the actual situation, before Gorbachev there were
effectively two types of cooperatives in the USSR.

The first type was represented by collective farms
(cooperatives of peasants implementing agricultural activities)[2] and consumer cooperatives (functioning in rural areas
to provide the rural population with supplies of commodities and to implement the selling of collective farm produce
to urban populations, although inhabitants of Soviet cities
could not be members of consumer cooperatives).[3] Proclaimed in words to be independent entities separated from
the Soviet state, they were considered in fact as ordinary
state entities. According to their charters, they had to create
and replenish certain property funds, perform planned
tasks established by the central agencies of planning, bear
responsibility for violations of so-called state discipline,
and so forth. The model charters of these cooperatives provided for certain forms of self-regulation: elections of ruling
bodies, development and confirmation of production and
other plans, and similar activities. However, these democratic rights existed only in the legal provisions. In practice,
the local Party committees decided everything, and general
meetings or conferences of collective farms or consumer
cooperatives only rubberstamped that which had been predetermined at the top.

The second type of cooperatives was represented by the
housing cooperatives, *dacha* cooperatives, garden cooperatives, etc. All these entities depended to varying degrees on

the state. To say nothing about the fact that each could be created only with permission of the appropriate governmental agency, in their daily activity they were under untiring governmental control. No new member could be admitted to a housing cooperative without approval from the local executive committee; no vacancy in a garden cooperative could be filled without agreement from the entity whose workers had created this cooperative, etc. Cooperatives of the second type retained features of organizations created by and consisting of individuals. These cooperatives, though construed as collective bodies, permitted heirs to succeed and inherit after the death of one of their members, and voluntary or involuntary termination of cooperative membership was accompanied by the receipt of a property share to which each member was entitled.

Gorbachev did not abolish this the most substantial distinction between the two types of cooperative organizations. He supplements cooperatives of the second type (representing transformed individual property) with sale of apartments to tenants in state apartment buildings. According to the government decree of December 2, 1988, each tenant becomes an owner of his apartment, all tenants create a society (a cooperative) as a collective owner of an apartment building, but this building must be administered by a state housing agency in accordance with a contract executed with a cooperative of owners. This innovation, very profitable for the Soviet state, proves that Gorbachev's activities with respect to cooperative property is even more contradictory than with respect to organizational forms of the state economy.

Dealing with the cooperatives of the first group—those which in fact are state entities under the mask of independent cooperative organizations—Gorbachev actually recognized the *de facto* situation and transformed it into a *de jure* situation. He created the State Committee on Agriculture and Industry (Gosagroprom)[4] as a government agency with control over all collective farms, consumer cooperatives, and all of the state enterprises connected with agricultural production (those producing fertilizer, processing agricultural produce, supplying agricultural entities with the requisite equipment, etc.). Gorbachev formally confirmed the subordination of these cooperatives to the Soviet government that previously implemented these functions without formal acknowledgement.

The Law on Cooperation in the USSR promulgated on May 28, 1988,[5] dealing with cooperatives of all types, and especially the new Model Charter of Collective Farms, which entered into force in 1988[6] addressed only to collective farms, do their best to represent collective farms and consumer cooperatives as the most independent and self-ruling nonstate organizations. According to these statutory acts, collective farms and consumer cooperatives create their organs, develop their plans, and run their daily activities entirely by themselves without any interference from the outside. As Article 10(2) of the Law on Cooperation emphasizes, "interference of state agencies . . . into the economic and other activities of a cooperative is prohibited. In the case where an agency of state administration . . . issues an act exceeding its competence . . . , the cooperative is entitled to appeal to the court or *arbitrazh* requiring the complete or partial invalidation of this act." This provision leaves a positive impression, especially bearing in mind that nothing similar ever appeared in

106

Soviet legislation. The problem, however, was the uncertain volume of the competence of the appropriate governmental agencies and how this volume restricted the application of this promising legal regulation. The competence of Gosagroprom as it was connected with collective farms and consumer cooperatives seemed very demonstrative in this regard. The above-mentioned decree dedicated to the creation of this body established:

> Gosagroprom is the central agency of state administration of the agricultural-industrial complex of the country, and it bears, along with the Councils of Ministers of the Union Republics, full responsibility for increasing production, the performance of plans of procurement of agricultural produce and ensuring its safekeeping, high-quality processing and substantial enlargement of the assortment of consumer goods. For these purposes, Gosagroprom has the appropriate rights and powers in the area of planning, financing and supplying the agricultural-industrial complex with material/technical resources. The decisions adopted by USSR Gosagroprom within the limits of its competence are binding upon and must be performed by all ministers and departments, institutions, associations, enterprises and organizations.[7]

Under this broadly outlined authority it could hardly have been possible to accuse Gosagroprom of unlawful interference into activities of collective farms or consumer cooperatives. Article 10(2), promising in appearance, had lost its attractiveness, proving to be merely one more provision included in Soviet law but deprived of actual significance. In addition, while the Law on Cooperation, encompassing all types of cooperatives, avoids using a single word revealing their subordination to the Soviet state, the 1988 Model Charter of the Collective Farm is less punctilious in this regard. Describing, for instance, the process of planning collective farms' activities and emphasizing that this process must be implemented by collective farms themselves, Article 15 of the Model Charter indicates that in developing its plan, each collective farm is obliged to proceed keeping in mind the need to "implement its duties toward the state." But, as was known, sale of agricultural produce to the state procurement agencies in the proportion established by Gosagroprom and for prices below cost was the principal duty of collective farms in their relationships with the state. In establishing this duty, the Soviet state in the person of Gosagroprom predetermined, at least in general, the directions of collective farm production and the correlation between different branches of this production. It should not be forgotten that state orders, previously discussed, must encompass the agricultural produce of collective farms, and as acts of centralized planning, they are binding for the collective farms despite all of the declarations concerning their independence.

The awkwardness of the situation resulting from the declaration of the independence of collective farms, on the one hand, and the creation of Gosagroprom and its local agencies, on the other hand, was probably felt by the Soviet leadership. In early 1989 Soviet media began to criticize local agencies of Gosagroprom—RAPO. For instance, on January 11, 1989, *Izvestia*, publishing an article entitled "One Can Live without RAPO," reports that collective farms of numerous districts leave RAPO as a governmental agency and create their own district unions to fulfill the same functions. A plenary meeting of the CPSU Central

Committee that took place in March 1989 went farther in this direction, suggesting replacement of all RAPOs throughout the country by unions created by collective farms, reorganization on the same pattern of provincial and republican administration of collective farms, abolition of Gosagroprom, and creation of a State commission of the Council of Ministers of the USSR on food and procurement.[8] To assess whether these changes are substantial or merely verbal, consider Gorbachev's words in this connection at the same plenary meeting:

> We maintain, of course, the discipline of procurement. But this discipline must be a discipline of reciprocal contractual obligations . . . , [and] after performance of duties based on state procurement the producer shall sell its other produce according to its own discretion.[9]

This discipline, according to Gorbachev, must be retained for the entire transitional period because after its expiration collective farms will themselves be interested in selling necessary agricultural produce to the state. What this transitional period means is explained in Chapter Four in the discussion of interconnections between collective farms and other economies. At the present stage of analysis, however, one can contend that the centralized administration of agriculture remains intact, despite democratization in appearance.

As to consumer cooperatives, the situation is the same in principle, despite adoption of their new chapters in 1989.[10] In substance, though by euphemistic words, these charters confirm the subordination of consumer cooperatives to the centralized planning, to the Soviet state discipline, financial orders, etc. It seems implausible that the

1988 Law on Cooperation changes the legal status of consumer cooperatives, despite the more democratic language of this law. Subordinated to state agencies to the same extent as collective farms, consumer cooperatives, similar to collective farms, continue to be state enterprises in fact disguised by a cooperative mask in appearance.

From the viewpoint of the centralized administration prevailing over certain forms of decentralization, Gorbachev's reforms do not substantially modify the actual status of collective farms and consumer cooperatives. He has also retained previously established interconnections between collective farms and consumer cooperatives. The collective farms can sell their produce to individuals through the consumer cooperatives after performance of all duties toward the state. This system is very profitable, bearing in mind that consumer cooperatives are entitled to establish their own prices, in contrast to state retail shops which are bound by prices introduced in the centralized manner. In visiting homogeneous shops of state and cooperative trade, one comes across astonishing phenomena. For instance, meat is priced, on the average, at two rubles per pound in state shops and eight rubles per pound in cooperative shops; however, the state shops' shelves are empty, while in cooperative shops meat is almost always available. This peculiar approach facilitates mitigation of the food problem in the USSR, but the problem itself retains its sharpness. To resolve it, Gorbachev has appealed to cooperatives of a certain group—those that represent not disguised state economy but transformed individual property. As demonstrated above, on the basis of the state economy Gorbachev's reforms have reached nothing so far nor will they be likely to do so in the future. This fact probably pushed Gorbachev to the conclusion that his efforts addressed to the state economy disguised by the cooperative form were also doomed to failure. He had to decide to employ the nonstate economy also represented by cooperatives, but those that personify a modified individual ownership instead of the state property formally connected with cooperatives. In contrast to collective farms or consumer cooperatives, which at best can be used only in the realm of food supply, other cooperatives appealed to by the new economic reforms can facilitate resolution of the problem of services provided to the populace, whose actual status is even worse than that of the food supply.

As a consequence, Article 1 of the Law on Cooperation provides that "the cooperative is entitled to implement all types of activities except those prohibited by legislation of the USSR or union republics." The law in force does not enumerate all types of activities prohibited to cooperatives; relying on certain legal provisions and taking into consideration Soviet practice, one can independently fill certain gaps. For example, Article 11 of the USSR Constitution establishes that the basic means of production in industry, construction, agriculture, etc. shall belong to the state. This must signify that all types of activities connected with such means of production are unavailable to cooperatives, except for collective farms which, according to Article 12 of the same Constitution, have as their principal task cultivation of land, or even industrial or construction activity if these are not connected with the creation of large enterprises. Probably, within these limits, a cooperative has been able to buy a state plant together with all its debts, considering this acquisition potentially profitable.[11]

As to practice, the situation is more complicated. For instance, publishing offices are not mentioned among those entities that cannot be created by cooperatives. Neverthe-less, the attempts of Soviet writers Fazil Iskander, Anatoly Ribakov, and Veniamin Kaverin to create a publishing cooperative failed, as dissident sources inform, while a Leningrad cooperative "Spektr," according to the same sources, managed to create its own publishing office. Regardless of whether a special prohibition is established, the creation of cooperative publishing offices is hardly a prospective business because of the political danger con-nected with enlarged opportunities for publication. But such extraordinary businesses aside, in the realm of service to the populace cooperatives are actually capable of meet-ing many needs: opening restaurants and cafés, implement-ing different kinds of repair work, providing babysitters, buying merchandise in accordance with customers' orders, washing cars, painting pictures, etc. Some of the purposes intended by recently organized cooperatives are astonish-ing, but they impressively illustrate the swing of these orga-nizations under the Soviet economic reforms of the present time. For instance, Soviet media inform the reader[12] that the cooperative "Genesis" has been organized by a district committee of the CPSU in Irkutsk. This cooperative offers its services connected with the transfer from administrative to economic forms of activities, consultation in the realm of administrative activities, psychological assessment of cad-res, study of fundamental principles of management, analy-sis of social and economic strategies of collectives, social research, etc. The drafters of the Soviet legislation on coop-eratives certainly did not envision these extraordinary types of services. Their intent was to enlist cooperatives in resolving basic food and service problems. The actual legal limits on the creation of cooperatives have proved to be broader than the legislature could have predicted.

Developed in multifarious forms, cooperatives of this group (i.e., those representing modified individual owner-ship) have done the most to justify the substantial hopes that the Soviet leaders have connected with their reforms. This occurs because the cooperatives under discussion do not belong to the Soviet economy in its proper meaning, and, as a result economic inefficiency is not intrinsic to them. The latter circumstance has its dark side: law in force simultaneously stimulates and hampers the development of these cooperatives.

Looking first at cooperative membership, a striking contradiction is easily ascertained between Article 12(1) and Article 46(2) of the Law on Cooperation. According to Article 12(1), each Soviet citizen of sixteen years can be a member of a cooperative, while Article 46(2) establishes that workers who lose their jobs at state entities, pensioners, invalids, housewives, and students are given preference in joining cooperatives. From the viewpoint of practice, this means that workers who quit their jobs at state entities cannot acquire cooperative membership. As a result, the law precludes migration of labor from the state economy to cooperative organizations, and the development of cooper-atives depends on attracting nonworking individuals. As to workers at state entities, they can take part in the coopera-tive production process only when they are free from their principal job.[13] These provisions create barriers for devel-opment of cooperative organizations.

The next barrier is connected with the procedure of formation of cooperatives. As Article 11 of the Law on Cooperation establishes, to create a cooperative, individu-als must develop its charter and register this charter with the local executive committee. Formally, the local execu-tive committee may refuse to register the charter only if it contradicts law in force. In contrast to other unlawful actions of governmental agencies whose implementation entails judicial disputes, legal appeals from refusal to register a charter are considered only by higher administrative agencies. In fact, this deprives the cooperatives of legal guarantees in the process of their creation and actually entitles the administrative agencies to regulate the development of cooperatives of different profiles in accordance with governmental demands, not the desire of individuals to apply their labor in a specific cooperative organized by themselves.

A substantial barrier has been created by a government decree of December 29, 1988, which restricts the activities of the new type of cooperatives.[14] Certain forms of activities, including production of medicines and reproduction of films, are completely unavailable to cooperatives. There are also forms of activities, including medical assistance and production of perfume, that can be implemented only on the basis of contracts between cooperatives and state entities. The enumerations contained in this decree are in some instances so flabbergasting that even Soviet media ironically ask, "What is allowed, what is prohibited and why?"[15]

A very peculiar psychological atmosphere has surrounded the inclination of certain individuals to open a new cooperative. For instance, the Minister of Finance of the USSR, B.I. Gostev, was asked by a journalist about his attitude toward cooperatives. He answered:

> I am not against cooperatives. But one must reasonably assess everything. Do not forget that people are going there first of all because of money. One woman expressed a quite reasonable opinion not long ago at a meeting of a group of deputies . . . "Why," she said,

"did you create such opportunities to members of cooperatives?.... You allow them to buy meat in shops and to sell it for ten-times higher prices."

When the journalist retorted that cooperatives should buy meat only at markets, the Minister was outraged:

What? Have you found at least one cooperative which buys something at the market? My wife herself saw a salesman of a shop cutting meat for a cooperative. And I declare with full responsibility that in practice everybody does so: they buy meat at a price a little higher than two rubles ... and sell it in the form of shashlik at a price of twenty-five rubles. ... Where do you see honest workers receiving a salary of a thousand rubles? Why do you not protect workers receiving only two hundred rubles?[16]

One reader of the magazine in which the Minister's interview was published answered him with the following words:

There are different opinions concerning cooperatives. Of course, they will come across various problems. ... But one must not declare the failure of this business as a result of an initiative of persons in positions of authority who view cooperatives with mistrust and suspicion.[17]

However, it is not only certain authorities who try to compromise cooperatives. The difficulty is that the prices of cooperative services exceed the economic capacity of the majority of the Soviet populace. Their services can be afforded only by the rich, who strive to do their best to protect cooperatives from sharp criticism. Bearing in mind these customers stimulating creation of new cooperatives, *Izvestia*[18] joyfully exclaims: "Cooperatives experience boom." As to the large masses of Soviet citizens, they are hostile toward cooperatives' members as those who have managed to become capitalists of the Soviet pattern.[19] Such a hostility not only entails negative consequences; another fact is more important. Despite the positive significance of the new Soviet cooperatives, their creation is far from a solution to the two critical problems: food supply and provision of services. The latter have not lost their sharpness even a bit, and therefore the new cooperative forms do not evoke any general delight.

In contrast to consumer cooperatives organized as a unified system all over the country—beginning with *sel'po* in villages and Tsentrosoiuz in Moscow—the new types of cooperatives are provided by law as numerous entities separated from one another. However, in a great number of cities these cooperatives are included in the city's or districts' *soiuz* (union) of cooperatives. Formally such a new organizational form arises as a result of the proper initiative of the cooperatives themselves. In fact, this initiative results from the appropriate instruction of the Party agencies that employ *soiuz*'es as methods of centralized administration of dispersed cooperative entities. It must also not be forgotten that if these cooperatives are created, they need to lease governmental premises distributed by local executive committees. The supplies necessary for production activities of cooperatives that agree to perform state orders also depends on the state,[20] and this is convenient for cooperatives that otherwise must provide themselves with necessary materials bought in the free market. They use the last opportunity, too, dealing more with agents of the unlawful underground economy which has at its disposal broader resources than individual sellers acting lawfully. This is why the underground economy substantially enlarged its limits after the creation of the new cooperatives. To the extent to which these cooperatives receive supplies from governmental entities to perform accepted state orders, they depend on the state and actually function under the confirmed governmental control. This control is strengthened by the duty of each cooperative to submit an annual declaration about the size of its extracted income.[21] In addition, these cooperatives, independently developing their plans, must take into consideration the accepted state orders in the process of planning.[22] According to the law, acceptance of the state orders depends on the free decision of a cooperative. In fact it is difficult to imagine a situation in which a central governmental agency addresses a state order to a cooperative and this order is refused by a cooperative's board or chairman. The independence of the cooperative's planning functions resembles fantasy more than reality, at least to the extent to which this planning concerns state orders.

State orders aside, the new types of cooperatives can indeed plan their activity in accordance with market demand. Centralized planning tasks are inapplicable under these circumstances, and therefore all of the failures resulting from the centralized administration of the Soviet economy become impossible within these limits with respect to the new cooperatives. It must be clear, however, that in this case too, economic efficiency can be reached not because of Gorbachev's reforms as such but as a result of their application to an economic realm that does not represent the proper Soviet economy.

Along with the cooperatives created by individuals, the Law on Cooperation (Article 11) allows cooperatives to be organized by state, cooperative, and social entities. In any case, individuals make up the members of the cooperatives. But the cooperatives are called independent only if they have been created by individuals. Cooperatives organized by enterprises or other entities are ruled by them and consequently do not acquire the appropriate independence. The purpose of cooperatives thus organized is to use the waste or excess of the principal production of an enterprise or to serve the principal entity in another way. On the other hand, creation of these cooperatives opens the gate to additional work and income for workers of the principal entity who are entitled to combine both their activities, using free time from their main jobs to participate in the cooperative production and receive payment for their participation. From this point of view, cooperatives that are derivative from other entities play a positive role. They can also contribute to the production of commonly used commodities or in providing commonly required services. In substance these cooperatives more closely resemble departments of enterprises or other entities that act as their creators. They cannot enjoy economic freedom to the extent available to so-called independent cooperatives, and as a result they cannot be relied upon as organizational forms capable of substantially facilitating the solution of tasks that stem from the contemporary economic reforms in the USSR. This is why the Soviet media, which overflow with materials elucidating cooperative activities, very seldom appeal to those cooperatives subordinated to an enterprise or another entity. Gorbachev's principal innovation in this area is connected with the independent cooperatives of the new type sponsored by individuals themselves.

B. The Property Basis of the Cooperative Economy

In the late 1920s and early 1930s, Stalin implemented his all-embracing collectivization of Soviet agriculture—the creation of collective farms by coercive methods. This compulsive socialization meant for peasants that they had to transfer to the collective farm ownership all objects of individual property connected with agricultural activity (farm equipment, cows and horses, etc.). Though criticizing Stalin for his coercive methods, Gorbachev continues to consider collectivization as a positive measure of the socialist character.[23] At first, Soviet law considered the collective farms as owners of the socialized property, entitling each collective farmer to receive back his share in monetary form if he terminated his membership in a collective farm. But this provision was a dead letter from the very outset because it was impossible to leave a collective farm. In contrast to urban inhabitants, collective farmers had no passports and without passports they could not change their place of residence. The right to receive one's share in a collective farm could not be exercised because the right to quit a collective farm did not actually exist.

Later on, when collective farms became almost the exclusive functioning form of agricultural activity, along with the relatively few state farms, children of collective farmers who reached age sixteen were automatically considered as members of the collective farms without socialization of their property or any property dues imposed on them. As a result, the right to receive back a property share disappeared *per se*. This right is also not provided for by the 1988 Charter of the Collective Farm. It is true that the new charter allows one to withdraw collective farm membership, and collective farmers have internal passports now as do urban inhabitants. Yet they cannot leave their collective farms because a specific feature of a number of their passports precludes change of their place of residence without the consent of their collective farms, as has always been the rule concerning the "freedom of movement" of collective farmers. Under all circumstances, the socialized property transferred to collective farms cannot be qualified as transformed individual property. Formally it belongs to the collective farms, whose property basis consists now not of the property socialized more than fifty years ago and therefore completely consumed, but of income collected by the collective farms themselves during the decades of their existence. Who is the actual owner of this property?

Recall the discussion dedicated to Soviet laws that distinguish between the right of ownership with respect to the Soviet state and the right of operative administration with respect to state entities. This distinction is retained by law in force, despite theoretical disputes that have arisen as a result of new legislation and certain ideas expressed by Soviet leaders. As has been emphasized, the former right is unrestricted, in contrast to the latter right, which must be exercised in accordance with commands issued by the owner in different forms (planned tasks, differentiation of various property funds, establishment of specific purposes for each fund, etc.). Is not the same model applicable to collective farms' property? Relying on the legislation that was in force before Gorbachev changed the charter of the collective farm, the requisite answer can be easily found. Each collective farm was obliged to perform the state plan of procurement of agricultural produce, to create numerous property funds, and to use each fund only in accordance with its purpose. Restricted in their property rights to such an extent, collective farms were not owners. They exercised the right of operative administration. Because the volume of this administration depended on commands issued by the Soviet state, the state was the actual owner of property formally declared the property of collective farms.

Did Gorbachev modify this situation by the 1988 Charter of the Collective Farm? In words, yes, at least to a certain extent. In substance, no, or more precisely, not very substantially. The new charter establishes that the collective farm "independently develops and confirms at the general meeting of collective farmers its production plan."[24] But at the same time the collective farm is obliged, in developing its plan, to take into account "performance of its obligations toward the state."[25] This signifies, in fact, that the forms of the use of collective farm property in the production process are determined and thus restricted by the state plan of procurement of agricultural produce. Furthermore, the new charter entitles the collective farm to define independently the size of the norms of deductions from its income into different property funds.[26] The number and character of each fund are dictated to collective farms, which must neither deviate from their predetermined purposes nor transfer a portion of one fund to another.[27] Thus previous restrictions on the property rights of collective farms are retained without change. This means that under Gorbachev the state maintains its ownership of the property of collective farms while collective farms are provided only with the right of operative administration of this property.

A similar situation exists with consumer cooperatives with respect to their activity in rural areas. Beginning in 1935, member-based consumer cooperatives have functioned only in rural areas. To become a member of a cooperative, an inhabitant of a village had to pay an entrance fee that could not be returned after termination of his membership. No other individual property was involved in the creation of the property basis of consumer cooperatives, which relied not so much on entrance fees, an insignificant amount, as on income extracted by the trade activity of these cooperatives. Thus consumer cooperatives could not be considered to represent transformed individual ownership. Each link of these cooperatives was qualified an owner by the appropriate legal provisions. However, cooperatives were obliged to fulfill state planning tasks distributed by Tsentrosoiuz and permanently maintain property funds in an amount and for purposes provided for by their charters.[28] In fact, their property rights constituted not the right of ownership but the right of operative administration similar to the property rights of state entities. Because commands concerning the limits of the cooperative right of operative administration were formulated by the Soviet state—either directly or through Tsentrosoiuz—the state was the actual owner of the property of the consumer cooperatives.

The 1988 Law on Cooperation changes nothing in terms of these principles addressed to consumer cooperatives in rural areas. Referring to this law, it must be recognized that now, as previously, the property of consumer cooperatives in their capacity as rural trade organizations is a disguised form of the property of the Soviet state. Certain changes, however, are implemented by the 1988 law with respect to activities of consumer cooperatives in the urban areas. Previously, consumer cooperatives could not have urban residents as members, but cooperative shops did exist in Soviet cities to sell agricultural produce at higher prices than in the state shops where such produce was almost constantly in deficit. This function can also be implemented by consumer cooperatives in accordance with the 1988 law. The same law introduces one substantial innovation with respect to consumer cooperatives functioning in Soviet cities.[29] As discussed above, Gorbachev's reforms entailed the creation of new cooperatives of various profiles representing transformed individual, not state, property. These cooperatives can organize their own city or district *soiuz*'es. The 1988 law ensures them another opportunity: they can become collective members of the system of consumer cooperatives.[30] As a result, inhabitants of cities as members of the new type of cooperatives indirectly become connected with the membership of the consumer cooperatives. Such an indirect membership does not modify the character of the property of the new type of cooperatives: it remains transformed individual property, and if an individual's membership is terminated, this member's share must be returned in monetary form.[31] Since, however, these new cooperatives enter into the system of the consumer cooperatives, the latter, acting in urban areas, represent to the respective degree not disguised state ownership but transformed individual ownership. As a result, the consumer cooperatives taken as a whole combine in unequal proportion the purely Soviet economy with a certain component that exceeds the proper limits of the Soviet economic system.

As to those cooperatives that, representing a modified individual ownership before Gorbachev's reforms (housing cooperatives, garden societies, garage cooperatives, etc.), facilitated solutions of the sharpest problems of Soviet life and guaranteed the desirable governmental control, their substance remains actually untouched by Gorbachev's reforms. Several governmental and the CPSU decrees were adopted in order to stimulate development of housing cooperatives' building projects, but these decrees had nothing to do with the substance of the cooperatives themselves, especially with the characterization of the property basis of their activity. Now as previously, such a cooperative form must be considered as a modification of individual property in the USSR.

This modifying form is new by itself, facilitating development of private initiatives if not to the extent known in the period of NEP, then to a level never allowed by the Soviet leadership after the transfer from NEP to the politics of economic centralization. The property basis of the newly created cooperatives must therefore be analyzed in detail, which might seem unnecessary with respect to other cooperatives.

The 1988 Law on Cooperation does not define the minimum number of individuals who can create the new type of cooperative. It only provides that these cooperatives can function in the realm of industry, construction, transportation, trade, food supplies, in the area of paid services and other branches of production, and in areas of social/cultural life. According to the 1988 Law, the cooperatives can be created and function for the purpose of production, procurement, processing, and sale of agricultural produce or goods of production-technical designation, for production of goods for the common consumer, collection and processing of secondary raw materials and excess of main production, for repair and maintenance of technology, production, road and housing construction, for retail trade and everyday service, for organization of cultural leisure time, medical and legal assistance, transport, scientific and design works, for sports and other services, as well as for activities in the realm of fishing and production of fishing produce, procurement of timber, for extraction of minerals, other natural resources, and for activities in other areas of the Soviet economy.[32] As is obvious, one cannot define the realms of the permissible activities of the new cooperatives more broadly than has Gorbachev and his 1988 Law.

Accordingly, individuals deciding to employ an opportunity created by this law in the appropriate areas must themselves define the amount of money necessary to implement a certain activity and the number of persons to be enlisted to create a cooperative provided with the requisite property. The cooperatives of this type can be created by few or numerous persons, by a family or an extended family, or by strangers. All of the combinations are allowed since not a single one is prohibited or listed exhaustively. The only things necessary to create a cooperative under the 1988 law are:

(1) the cooperative may not be connected with an area closed to cooperative activity;

(2) eventual members of a cooperative must develop their charter and submit it for appropriate registration; and

(3) each member must make his monetary or other contributions in an amount provided by the cooperative's charter.[33]

Along with these dues, the 1988 Law on Cooperation also considers as the property of a cooperative the product produced, income received as a result of the sale of this product or implementation of another activity, and money received in consequence of the sale of bonds and extension of bank credits.[34] As the 1988 Law emphasizes, formation of the cooperative's property can result from the assistance of other state, cooperative, and social organizations or even of individuals who are not members of that cooperative entity.[35]

Each cooperative must create its own property funds. In contrast to collective farms and consumer cooperatives, the law defines neither the number of these funds nor their purposes, to say nothing of the absence of a prohibition on channeling resources from one fund to another. These problems can be resolved only by a cooperative itself, without any interference from the outside.[36] Only so-called centralized funds—that is, those created for all the cooperatives of the appropriate type for purposes such as insurance, construction, etc.—are binding for each specific cooperative. However, as Article 20 of the 1988 law establishes, the norms for the installments that must be transferred to these funds can be defined only by a general meeting of the representatives of all the appropriate cooperatives, and consequently, even in this case the property right is exercised by the cooperative itself as an actual owner, not by other agencies imposing their decisions as binding on the various groups of cooperative entities.

Transformation of the individual property represented by the cooperatives under discussion affects the legal consequences of the termination of cooperative membership or the liquidation of a specific cooperative. As demonstrated above, a member of a collective farm or a consumer cooperative receives nothing back if he terminates membership. This is quite logical since the property of collective farms and consumer cooperatives embodies a transformed state property, not the property of the individual members. This rule must now be implemented by another legal provision concerning liquidation of a specific collective farm or a consumer cooperative. In this case, too, the individual members receive nothing. For instance, Article 36(3) of the Law on Cooperation provides that the property remaining after liquidation of a collective farm must be transferred to other cooperative or state entities dealing with agriculture. According to Article 48 of the same law, the entrance fees cannot be returned to a member of a consumer cooperative if he terminates membership. It says instead that the appropriate portion of the profit distributed among the members of a consumer cooperative must also be allocated to those who relinquish membership. But this can occur only if a cooperative decides to distribute its profit. This has never taken place—the total profit is used to replenish the property funds of a consumer cooperative and, if necessary, to enlarge its activity. In cases where a consumer cooperative is liquidated, its remaining property must be transferred to the higher cooperative agency and employed for purposes connected with activities of other consumer cooperatives.

As to the new type of cooperatives called for by the Law on Cooperation, "Cooperatives in the Area of Production and Service," the Soviet legislature, resolving the same problems, takes into consideration the fact that these cooperatives represent transformed individual property based on the principle of membership.[37] In ending membership in a cooperative of this type, an individual receives back his share in cash. Deductions from the appropriate amount can be made only within the limits of losses incurred by a cooperative and distributed among its members in accordance with the relevant provisions established by the cooperative charter. If a cooperative is liquidated, all its buildings, equipment, machinery, materials, and other goods must be sold to other entities, or to individuals if allowed by law. Proceeds from this sale and other money at the disposal of the cooperative at the time of its liquidation must first be used for payment of labor of hired workers and fulfillment of obligations toward the state budget, banks, and other creditors. The property remaining after these payments is distributed among members of a cooperative either equally, in the proportion corresponding to the members' shares, or in accordance with terms established by the charter of a specific cooperative.

Although these facts prove that the cooperatives under discussion represent individual property in a modified form, the Law on Cooperation does not expressly formulate such a conclusion. At the same time, it takes these peculiarities into account in certain specific legal provisions. The preamble to the law speaks about cooperatives of all types as a socialist sector of the Soviet economy. The same law, however, dealing with cooperatives in the realms of production and services, provides special measures solely to prevent employment of these cooperatives for purposes incompatible with the economic system of the USSR. For instance, the majority of Western observers analyzing the new type of Soviet cooperatives contends that in this way the Soviet leadership restores private enterprise. Meanwhile, Article 40(2) establishes that "the state shall apply measures preventing cases where cooperatives are employed for private enterprise activity accompanied by the use of hired labor under the disguise of the creation of a cooperative." Thus, the Soviet legislation not only precludes consideration of the new type of cooperatives as private enterprises but simultaneously attempts to preclude such transformation in actual practice. In Article 41(4), the local Soviets are obliged to stimulate an increase in the number of cooperatives in the territories administered by each Soviet. At the same time this article warns local Soviets to counteract the monopolistic trends of certain cooperatives, their attempts to artificially increase prices and decrease production of items or provision of services that are under high demand, etc. It must be clear that because of the deplorable status of the Soviet economy the creation and development of these types of cooperatives are permitted; such a necessity does not eliminate an official approach to these cooperatives as economic components alien to the Soviet system.

This ambiguous official attitude toward the new type of cooperatives entails even more palpable ambiguity in public opinion as represented by the Soviet media. For instance, the magazine *Ogonek*, one of the most popular mouthpieces of Soviet *glasnost'*, published an article under the title *"Tsivilizovannii Kooperator"*[38] (A Civilized Cooperativist). Consider the obvious uncertainty of its author. He maintains the development of new cooperatives, criticizing those governmental officials who strive to create obstacles to this development. He writes:

> Understanding of the political significance of cooperation and assertiveness earmarked to help it are visibly growing weak, once one goes below the regional department [of finances in the city of Vladimir which is not far from Moscow] on the hierarchical ladder. The departmental manager of the regional executive committee is indignant that one cooperative . . . has been allowed to deal with the job placement of the populace. . . . He is inexorable, exclaiming: "This must be prohibited." . . . There is not a single independent cooperative in Vladimir. All of them are attached in a binding procedure to an enterprise or an organization. . . . But

the cooperatives implement activities of different types which have nothing in common with their curator entities.[39]

In these cases the author does not conceal his sympathy to the cooperatives and his disapproval of actions of local officials. Reading another fragment from his article gives an entirely different impression. After describing a conversation between two women very critical of cooperatives, the author continues:

> There is no doubt that certain cooperatives are organized only to clean up and to close up shop. But one must give due respect to the cleverness of the managers of such cooperatives—the "butterflies." They understand that so far they are very few in number and capable of being monopolists and, mercilessly jacking up prices, and becoming rich in filling the void.[40]

Although with a shade of approval toward the business acumen of the managers of such cooperatives, the author somewhat frankly calls for vigilance and the prevention of the cooperative whose goals are if not unlawful, then at any rate incompatible with the propagated principles of the official ideology.

As emphasized above, the appropriate Soviet agencies can check and thus regulate the development of the cooperative through the official procedures that require that cooperatives register their charters. They can consequently be foreclosed through this simple process of registration. Similar opportunities are at the disposal of the same agencies in the realm of a cooperative's property. Though in the new type of cooperatives their property is transformed individual property, it cannot be separated from state control because of numerous circumstances.

First, the cooperatives under discussion simply could not exist or function with only their own property. They need to have premises for their activity and plots of land where these premises are situated. A cooperative must either rent state premises situated on state land or receive from the state a plot of land on which to construct its own buildings. As a result, the property of the new cooperatives is connected with the state's property, and the very existence of the former depends on availability of the use of the latter.

Second, the new type of cooperatives and their members must pay taxes in an amount defined by the state in accordance with the amount of collective or individual profit. At first these taxes were introduced in an amount that itself sufficed to paralyze anyone's desire to enter into cooperatives. Only later was the tax rate reasonably diminished. But who can guarantee its stability? The decision depends on the legislature, and if the Soviet leadership decides that the new type of cooperatives have been developed more than necessary, a single increase in taxes will suffice to alleviate this undesired phenomenon.

Third, each cooperative and each of its members must declare income to financial agencies within the timelimit provided by a governmental decision.[41] As a matter of course, these financial agencies are entitled to verify any of the declarations submitted. This verification can take different forms, including government audit of the financial, or more precisely, economic activity of each cooperative. The threat of such an audit must keep the cooperatives in check from exceeding the limits established for them. As a result, the actual freedom of the new cooperative movements is more restricted than can be imagined considering official slogans and propagandistic cries.

In supplementing these three factors by certain others — extension of bank credits, governmental supply of items unavailable at free markets where cooperatives might procure them, etc. — prospects for the development of the new cooperatives proclaimed in the USSR are less optimistic than one would think.

The question arises: "Why?" Decades of centralized economy based on state property, including its disguised forms — the property of collective farms and consumer cooperatives — demonstrate that this economy cannot be efficient because by definition it leaves no space for economic incentives addressed to the individual participants in collective production. In contrast, the new type of cooperatives, retaining dependence on the state economy and permitting governmental control, are inseparable from the requisite economic incentives because they represent transformed individual property. Using the broadly disseminated Soviet terminology, these cooperatives are socialist in their form and private in their substance. The Soviet leadership has finally managed to invent an organizational phenomenon that seemingly maintains the socialist system (owing to the socialist form of the new cooperatives) and at the same time eliminates from this system its intrinsic shortcomings (owing to the private substance of the new cooperatives). Then why not develop this organizational phenomenon as broadly as possible ultimately to encompass the entire Soviet economy and to open the way for sound economic development?

Employment of the new cooperatives has actually exceeded the limits outlined for them. They were allowed for purposes connected with the populace's demands for supplies and services. Creation of insurance cooperatives or those consulting Soviet entities with respect to organizational or technological problems was not intended when the Law on Cooperation was promulgated. Nevertheless, these and various other unpredictable cooperatives have appeared and continue to be developed. This development does not affect the fundamental tenet maintained by the Soviet leadership that holds that cooperatives must play a subsidiary and not principal or all-embracing role in the Soviet economy.[42] Such a view relies on different premises of varying importance.

As a modified form of individual property, the new cooperatives must be organized as small-scale enterprises. Gigantic cooperatives have arisen in a few cases, however only as amalgamations of numerous small cooperatives, not as unified cooperative entities. Meanwhile, the modern industry, transport, and other branches of the producing economy except for agriculture can reach their highest possible level if they are personified by large enterprises incompatible with cooperative forms. The issue of small cooperatives in the area of Soviet agriculture will be discussed below.[43] What has been considered here leaves no doubt that, in terms of the overwhelming majority of its components, the Soviet economy precludes the creation of cooperatives on a wide scale and the idea of cooperative comprehensiveness must be abandoned as completely futile.

There also exist certain branches of the economy whose decentralization is impossible either politically or economically. Collectively transformed individual property does not suffice for the purposes connected with these branches. For instance, Western countries can combine, even in the military area, the centralized customer in the person of the state or the government and decentralized producers in the person of numerous private companies. In the USSR, this activity as a whole must be in the grasp of the state, and since military production is carried out not only by military enterprises, the employment of cooperatives in this area encounters a broader barrier than seems at first glance. Consider also, for the purpose of illustration, Soviet railroad transport, which continues to play the role of principal carrier of goods. Although this transport functions with permanent irregularities, adherents of economic reforms in the USSR do not even contemplate modification of its organizational forms. Railroads are organized in the USSR as one line administered at different sections by various management units but handled as a whole from a unified center. This ensures a relative dependability of railroad transportation encompassing numerous sections, despite all of the defects characteristic of activities of Soviet railroads. Try to replace the government management by new cooperative entities, and collapse will be unavoidable, even if centralized administration is retained.

A number of other specific obstacles to recognition of the new cooperatives as the principal form of organization for the Soviet economy can be identified. These obstacles are of a specific character, and as such they cannot ensure a comprehensive explanation of the issue under discussion. The explanation becomes available only to those who consider the Soviet system as a whole with the absence of any intention of the new leaders to abolish this system and replace it with another that is more adjusted to reasonable demands of human life. Even if some Soviet ruler secretly cherishes this idea, there are more reasons to assume his defeat than the system's destruction. In assessing the creation of the new cooperatives only as one of the measures of within-the-system reform, the system itself must be recognized as the strongest obstacle for the "excessive" development of the new cooperatives.

The Soviet system represents unlimited political power of the ruling elite based on the economic monopoly of this elite. This system is characterized by cyclical development from strong centralism to a certain decentralization in the economic sphere insofar as the decentralization does not eliminate the centralization. Decentralization is necessary to prevent economic collapse and it is adjusted to restoration of the previous centralism as soon as the danger of collapse is over. In contrast, an all-embracing development of the new cooperatives as the principal form of the Soviet economy would be not a temporary but a permanent measure, signifying not a certain decentralization within the limits of the centralized economy but an actual replacement of the economic centralism by economic decentralization. As a result, the Soviet system would rely not on its own basis —state ownership undisguised or disguised by the collective farm/cooperative form—but on a basis alien to this system—individual property transformed by creation of the new type of cooperatives.

This change, revolutionary indeed, could occur if the Soviet leadership decided to abandon its unlimited political power in favor of a genuine democracy and therefore would not need to keep in its grasp the economic monopoly as the principal and the most dependable source of its power and the populace's obedience. But there is no sign presaging such a drastic turn.

Through general slogans, the Soviet leaders express their adherence to democratization. Separation of the Soviets and their agencies from interference of the Party and its bodies, as proclaimed by the Nineteenth Conference of the CPSU, could be one of the decisive steps in this direction. But according to the position maintained by the same Conference and previously discussed, one person must combine two offices—those of secretary of the appropriate Party committee and chairman of the Soviet's executive committee of the same level. Except for the combination of the offices of General Secretary of the CPSU and Chairman of the Presidium of the USSR Supreme Soviet or the Chairman of the USSR Council of Ministers, this organizational approach has never been employed during the whole history of the USSR. Thus, not democratization but an unprecedented centralism is, in fact, instilled.

In abstract promises, a new electoral system is so colorfully depicted that the replacement of fictitious elections by genuine ones should be expected. Remember that in defiance of all expectations, Gorbachev implemented his coup in the ruling agencies of the Party and the government by the same methods that Brezhnev and his accomplices had previously employed to settle with Khrushchev. Two meetings—those of the CPSU Central Committee on September 30, 1988 and the USSR Supreme Soviet on October 1, 1988—were called so suddenly (certain members of the Central Committee were returned from Moscow's Vnukovo Airport shortly before take-off) and with such disregard of the established procedure (for example, a rule requiring one month's notice for a meeting of the USSR Supreme Soviet) that no traces of democracy could be found.[44] Each meeting lasted only forty-five minutes, and

136

exclusively by means of information presented by the highest officials and voting implemented unanimously without discussion, the Politburo, the Presidium of the USSR Supreme Soviet, and the USSR Council of Ministers were shaken up substantially. As a result of this shake-up, Gorbachev supplemented his office of General Secretary of the CPSU Central Committee with the office of Chairman of the Presidium of the USSR Supreme Soviet. Those who seriously think about democratization would hardly act in such a way.

Even *glasnost'*, restricted as it is but enthusiastically accepted by the Soviet intelligentsia, cracks now and again. An incident connected with the publication of Aleksandr Solzhenitsin's works is typical of Soviet totalitarianism. For months, rumor spread that the most popular Soviet magazine *Novii Mir* would publish the principal books of Solzhenitsin. This rumor was confirmed by S.P. Zaligin, the journal's editor-in-chief, at a meeting with journalists, and according to dissident sources, the appropriate announcement was to be published in the October 1988 issue of *Novii Mir*. The same sources inform, a telephone call from the chancellery of the Politburo eliminated this announcement, and Radio Moscow deleted from the English translation of Zaligin's interview all mention of Solzhenitsin.

Certain signs of democracy appeared in the process of electing deputies for a new Congress of the USSR in March 1989. For the first time in Soviet history, voters could choose between two or more candidates on the same ballot. But almost one-fourth of the elec-toral regions retained the system of "one deputy, one candidate." In addition, the 1988 version of the Soviet Constitution establishes that one-third of these deputies shall be elected not by popular vote but by the CPSU and various societal organizations.[45]

Moreover, the USSR Supreme Soviet must be elected not by general elections but by the Congress of people's deputies convened only once a year.[46] From this point of view, the new version of the Soviet Constitution is even less democratic than its predecessor, if the latter can be considered as democratic at all, bearing in mind especially the practice of its application. Distinguishing between the appearance and substance of the new Soviet democracy leads to a definite conclusion that there is the appearance of democratic elements (for example, the extensive debates during the meetings of the Congress of People's Deputies) yet dictatorship in substance (for example, the election of Gorbachev as the President of the USSR and Chairman of the Supreme Soviet).

Replacement of unlimited political power by genuine democracy is not a valid prediction for the USSR. Without such threatened transformation, why should the Soviet leadership abandon its economic monopoly? These plans simply do not exist, and the property of the new cooperatives, though alien to the Soviet economy as transformed individual property earmarked for production purposes, is permitted along with numerous other measures to save the country's economy from the complete crash after its protracted stagnation. No more far-reaching implications of the development of the new cooperatives can be expected.

C. The Functioning of the Cooperative Economy

The issue of the functioning of the cooperative economy must be considered from two points of view: as the internal activity of cooperative entities and as the interconnection of cooperative and other types of property in the process of achievement of cooperative production or other purposes. It is necessary to make one preliminary remark before directly addressing this issue.

Interconnection of state property and the property of collective farms and other cooperatives has always existed, first and foremost because any type of cooperative activity can be implemented only on land belonging to the objects of the exclusive property of the Soviet state. This was the case previously and remains the situation now. During different periods, other forms of analogous interconnection have been employed. For instance, in the early 1930s when the farm collectivization process was largely completed, Stalin organized in the rural areas specific state entities called MTS (Russian acronym for Machine and Tractor Stations), which fulfilled the appropriate kinds of agricultural work and thus obliged the collective farm to pay for this work through providing grain and other agricultural produce for the benefit of the Soviet state. It was not until the late 1950s that Khrushchev liquidated MTS, sold agricultural means of production to collective farms, and consequently liberated these farms from the heaviest burden imposed on them by Stalin, along with numerous other obligations.

In this respect, Gorbachev's reforms have one very important peculiarity. He has introduced a number of new forms of interconnections between different types of property, including state, cooperative, and individual properties in the various combinations. These interconnections have been assessed by the new leadership as one of the principal methods of breathing new life into the Soviet economy. But Gorbachev's methods of establishing interconnections between different types of properties do not supplant the independent existence of each type. State, cooperative, and individual economies function not only on the basis of interconnections but also separately from one another. Interconnections must play the role of catalyst, not destroyer, and are considered separately in Chapter Four. At present, the functionality of the cooperative economy as such, independent of its interconnections with other economies, is the issue of scrutiny.

During the entire time before Gorbachev came to power, cooperatives representing transformed individual property—housing cooperatives, *dacha* cooperatives, garden societies, and so forth,—were of such a character that they could neither specify nor affect the Soviet economy. Their purpose was to satisfy the demands of their members, and from the viewpoint of the Soviet state, these cooperatives were important because they transferred a substantial portion of expenses from the state to the citizenry for purposes connected with satisfaction of individual demands. Only those cooperatives based on disguised state property —that is, collective farms and consumer cooperatives— could be qualified as a substantial component of the Soviet economy, and therefore only they must be considered in this regard.

Collective farms were formally characterized as self-regulating entities independent of the Soviet state. Legal provisions addressed to collective farms were construed as recommendations, not as commands. The actual situation had nothing in common with established legal forms. All collective farm activities were predetermined by the governmental plan of so-called obligatory state deliveries. This plan communicated to each collective farm precisely enumerated types and amounts of agricultural produce that had to be sold to state procurement entities during each season at prices below cost. At the same time, binding *normativi* mandated yearly creation and replenishment of the various collective farm property funds. It is clear that the collective farms confirmed their production plans "independently" only so far as these plans corresponded to the above-mentioned binding assignments. Creation and replenishment of the property funds were implemented by collective farms in the form of their internal activity. In contrast, the planned sale of agricultural produce relied on contracts between collective farms and state procurement entities according to the principle "contract is subordinated to plan."

The same principle actually regulates the supply of equipment and other items necessary for collective farm agricultural activities. As a matter of course, no imposed supply can take place with respect to collective farms; only as a result of their orders can they be indicated as purchasers in the plan of distribution if they need to purchase items whose sale continues to be limited, despite Gorbachev's reforms. In all other cases, collective farms can execute as a customer a contract of delivery on the basis of a free agreement with any seller. The actual economic situation does not ensure this freedom on a large scale. Therefore, plans affect the supplies of collective farms no less than other Soviet entities.

The only area in which contracts of collective farms depend exclusively on their own decisions, accepted by other contractual partners, is the sale of surplus agricultural produce either through consumer cooperatives or at collective farm markets. Qualification of surplus is applicable to that portion of agricultural produce that remains after a collective farm fulfills its other duties (connected with state procurement, replenishment of property funds, etc.). To sell this produce, a collective farm can execute an agency contract with a consumer cooperative, and by their own agreements the parties define retail prices, the fee to be paid by the collective farm to the consumer cooperative, and so forth. There is another opportunity to reach the same goal. Each city or urban settlement has its collective farm markets where both collective farmers and collective farms can sell their produce to individuals on the basis of free contracts. These contracts also define the price levels. Several attempts by local governments to regulate prices failed because, as a result of these attempts, the collective farm markets became as empty as state or cooperative food stores. Freedom of prices continues to dominate in collective farm markets as the only remnant of a free economy in the USSR before the present economic reforms.

Because the lion's share of the agricultural produce of collective farms must be transferred to the state at prices below cost, collective farms could not function as self-sufficient economic entities without the sale of a portion of their produce at collective farm markets. Collective farmers are also capable of making ends meet from their produce grown on subsidy plots as a source of family consumption and individual sale at collective farm markets. After Stalin's death, state procurement prices grew. The economic status of collective farms improved as they became capable of compensating for deficits with smaller resources. Collective farmers also began to receive higher payments for their labor. But the level of procurement prices has never reached cost levels, and this is true even now, despite Gorbachev's economic reforms. It is clear that under these circumstances Soviet agriculture cannot operate normally even if climatic conditions were more favorable and crops were brought from fields to stores without huge losses. Nevertheless, Gorbachev has not abolished the Soviet agricultural system created by his predecessors. He tries to save the situation not by undermining collective farms but by establishing certain interconnections between collective farm and individual properties.[47]

In contrast to collective farms, consumer cooperatives are not based on the labor of their members. As an all-union system of retail trade, these cooperatives hire workers and officials to implement their function of supplying rural populations who constitute the members of consumer cooperatives and to some extent urban populations. Customers facing empty state food stores can buy certain foods at substantially higher prices in consumer cooperative stores. Except for chairmen of various links of the cooperative chain, who must be members of a cooperative to occupy this official position, all other members of consumer cooperatives need only pay their membership dues to enjoy certain privileges (e.g., priority in the purchase of deficit goods).

As nonproduction organizations, consumer cooperatives are obliged under trade plans.[48] The indicators of these plans primarily depend on the general task defined by Gosagroprom or its new substitute and distributed among cooperative entities by Tsentrosoiuz. The execution of delivery contracts with suppliers of goods necessary for cooperative trade must depend on free agreement between purchasers and sellers, according to Gorbachev's reforms and new legislation dedicated to supply of consumer goods. Because shortages of these goods have increased instead of diminished, retail trade of consumer cooperatives remains dependent on planned limits more than on the cooperatives' discretion. The volume of trade can be enlarged by cooperatives themselves, free from the need to generate the planned prerequisites, if agricultural produce received by the cooperative as an agent for collective farms as clients is purchased by customers. Usually, this trade is employed in urban areas; in rural areas consumer cooperatives deal more with the sale of industrial products than agricultural produce.

In contrast to the external activities of consumer cooperatives, modified by the new legislation, the internal activities remain substantially unchanged under Gorbachev's reforms. Now as previously they cannot serve the purpose of improving the country's overall economic situation, namely increasing the efficiency of supply of commodities to the rural and urban populace in the USSR. As an embodiment of transformed state property, consumer cooperatives ensure the economic expectations of the Soviet leadership to no greater an extent than the state economy as a whole. All of the hopes of the authors of the present reforms are connected with the new type of cooperatives — those which, employing a socialist (cooperative) form, represent a specific modification of individual property. They create economic incentives for their members whose property is growing according to the economic achievements of their cooperative entity, and as a result these cooperatives must have a positive impact on the economic realms where they appear. Again, the new type of cooperatives are, in principle, separate entities. They can establish a district union or enter into the consumer cooperative system. But even in the latter case, the new cooperatives, though establishing organizational ties with consumer cooperatives, do not change their economic substance as a transformed embodiment of individual property. They remain separate entities, regardless of whether they establish their membership in cooperative organizations of a higher level.

As separate entities in the proper meaning, not in the distorted significance that attaches with collective farms and consumer cooperatives, the new type of cooperatives establish their economic relations with other entities or individuals only on the basis of contracts.[49] No planned task can be imposed on these cooperatives by a higher agency or by a government body of any level. Hence, in this case, either formula—the plan defines the contract or the contract defines the plan—is inapplicable. In economic relations with other persons, the new cooperatives can function only as contractual partners. For instance, an industrial combine in Magadan decided to rely for transportation on the cooperative Cheibukha instead of maintaining its own motor-transport pool; but to fulfill this decision, it was necessary to execute a contract between both parties on the basis of terms reciprocally acceptable.[50]

Despite the new role of contracts in the economic activities of the new cooperatives, it is a mistake to assume that no connections can exist between these contracts and certain acts of government planning.[51] The cooperatives need to be provided with equipment, materials, and other items necessary for production or other activities. They can acquire these items by means of freely executed contracts with either economic entities or individual owners. Acquisition of the appropriate objects from the planned resources allocated for the purposes of cooperative activities also is not precluded.[52] Under these circumstances, the larger the amount of resources allocated by the plan for the supply of cooperatives, the broader the economic opportunities created for the efficiency of cooperative activities. Considered from this point of view, cooperative contracts depend on the distribution plans economically, although legally the validity of even these contracts is not directly determined by the existence of the appropriate legal prerequisites.

Conversely, the new cooperatives can agree to fulfill governmental orders,[53] which, as explained above, are only a new name for centralized planning in its previous meaning. If a state order is accepted by a cooperative, the requisite supply ensuring the actual performance of such a duty will be provided by centralized planning.[54] Thus, the appropriate contracts of delivery executed between the cooperative and its suppliers must be based on and correspond to the necessary planned prerequisites. Otherwise the contracts will be invalidated in whole or in part. This signifies the restoration of the formula "the plan defines the contract" even with respect to the new type of cooperatives. As to the consent of a cooperative requisite for imposing upon it the performance of a state order, only future practice can demonstrate the extent to which this formal requirement will have actual force.

There are certain other centralized indicators binding for the cooperatives. For instance, in developing their plans, cooperatives are to employ longstanding *normativi* such as income tax rates, interest for extension of bank credits, tariff payments for use of natural resources, and so forth.[55] These binding *normativi* affect cooperative contracts either as contractual terms (such as in cases where bank credit contracts are executed) or as circumstances taken into consideration in the process of formulating contractual terms (such as those cases where prices must be determined with respect to merchandise produced as a result of the use of natural resources). It would be erroneous to consider the new type of cooperatives as completely liberated from centralized economic administration, including the centralized planning of production and distribution. But these cooperatives are bound by the centralized indicators much less than other economic entities in the

USSR, presenting, as a result, new economic phenomena capable of operating more efficiently than traditional components of the Soviet economy.

In defining the principles of cooperative activities, the 1988 Law on Cooperation formulates them in the same way as principles established for state enterprises and associations: full *khozraschet* and self-financing.[56] It seems a little astonishing that these principles explained above with respect to state entities are connected with cooperative organizations. State entities are not owners of the property they employ: this property belongs to the state and is allocated to state entities on the basis of the right of operative administration. To oblige the state entities to rely in their activity on only the property under their operative administration, without expecting receipt of other state resources, the law warns them that they must operate on the bases of full *khozraschet* and self-financing. In contrast, cooperatives are qualified as owners of their property. It is not because of full *khozraschet* and self-financing that they must use only their own income to compensate all expenses and financing. Full *khozraschet* and self-financing are principles of economic activities of nonowners. It is because they are owners that they have this independent economic responsibility. Extension of bank credits does not change this regulation because credits are repayable and, consequently, cannot be considered as government subsidies.

However, the law under discussion addresses cooperatives as a whole, not the new type of cooperatives separately. As has been discussed, there are two kinds of cooperatives—those representing transformed individual property (the new type of cooperatives) and those embodying disguised state property (collective farms and consumer cooperatives). In the latter case, that which the law calls cooperative property is in fact an object of operative administration. Where operative administration exists, principles of full *khozraschet* and self-financing are quite reasonable. This is why the 1988 Law on Cooperation declares these principles with respect to cooperatives. Whether full *khozraschet* and self-financing are applicable to cooperatives of all types, erroneously addressed to the newly-invented cooperatives, these principles nevertheless emphasize their complete economic independence from the state and property separation from the state economy. To ensure self-sufficiency under these circumstances, the new cooperatives must be endowed with a number of economic freedoms; the most important of these is the freedom to establish prices for their commodities and services. In principle, this freedom is legally established.

As Article 19(2) of the 1988 Law on Cooperation states, "cooperatives sell products and commodities of their own production, fulfill work and provide services on prices and tariffs established through agreements with customers or by cooperatives themselves." However, a general declaration expressed by Article 19(1) puts the observer on guard. This declaration reads as follows:

> Prices and tariffs on products (work, services) of a cooperative must mirror socially necessary expenses of the production and sale of products, taking into account consumer properties and quality of commodities (work, services), and consumer demand. They must be construed in consideration of reciprocal interests of both — cooperatives and consumers — as well as of the national economy as a whole, and facilitate the development of *khozraschet* and self-financing.

148

The two latter indications, though strange with respect to the new cooperatives, are favorable for them, strengthening the freedom of prices at least to the level requisite to cover the cooperative's costs and ensure a reasonable profit. But in all other components, the same provision evokes certain apprehensions.

The provision under discussion is formulated as a declaration or a call to action, not as a legal norm whose violation must entail employment of the appropriate legal sanctions. This legal technique can be interpreted as depriving an expressed legal provision of any impact on the designation of prices by cooperatives. However, the previous Soviet practice demonstrates that so-called declarative norms create the broadest opportunities for arbitrariness. It should suffice to mention the notorious Article 1 of the 1922 Civil Code, transferred to Article 5 in the 1964 Civil Code, and then to Article 39 of the 1977 Constitution. All of these articles are declarative: they call on Soviet citizens to exercise their rights and fulfill their duties in accordance with certain general principles differently expressed by different provisions (observance of the social purpose of rights and duties in the USSR, taking into consideration the fundamental interests of Soviet society, etc.). Nevertheless, a great number of Soviet citizens lost their houses, *dacha*, and other objects of individual property as a result of judicial decisions on the basis of these legal provisions. Bearing in mind this experience, it is possible that cooperatives can lose profits extracted by prices that contradict the declaration of Article 19(1) of the 1988 Law on Cooperation? Perhaps a reference to an interview given by the Minister of Public Health Evgenii Chazov will facilitate an answer to this question. The interviewer asked:

149

When medical cooperatives appeared, they entailed various judgments—from most ecstatic to extremely negative. For example, everybody hectically discussed a fantastic price, established by one Moscow cooperative for research on a computer which, incidentally, belonged to the state. It would be interesting to know your point of view concerning the cooperative movement.

The minister answered:

We support the medical cooperatives. But we strive to avoid excesses such as in the case mentioned by you. Imported, very expensive equipment is standing idle. We began to rent it out to cooperatives, but they began to charge the people extraordinary fees. Then we ordered the management of medical establishments to organize the employment of complicated equipment in two to two-and-a-half shifts.[57]

The Minister reveals nothing about the fate of the cooperative profit extracted by exaggerated prices. He mentions only one result: withdrawal of the appropriate equipment and the consequent deprivation of the cooperative's opportunity to implement certain medical operations. In fact, this result is more detrimental for the cooperative than regulation of prices implemented under the circumstances within reasonable limits. As to patients, they actually remained in the same situation after the measures mentioned by the minister were carried out. It is true that all state medical treatment is provided free of charge in the USSR. It is also universally known that patients who need a medical treatment requiring a high professional level must pay an "under-the-table" fee, and who knows whether in this specific case the actual expenses of patients were diminished or increased in comparison with the cooperative price? One thing is certain: even if a state medical establishment introduced three shifts to make full use of complicated equipment, patients will waste more time than they would receiving treatment from medical cooperatives.

In the case discussed above, the cooperative used its right to establish free prices in order to extract a superprofit. But sometimes the opposite situation arises. For example, during the harvesting season, millions of urban inhabitants are sent to collective farms in order to ensure the timely completion of this agricultural chore. These extraordinary measures are, of course, very expensive but not as costly as crops lost as a result of protracted harvesting that must be replaced with agricultural produce bought abroad. A collective farm in Latvia found another way out. It created temporary cooperatives at harvest times. These cooperatives consist of collective farm workers who ordinarily do not deal with harvesting: bookkeepers, agronomists, etc. Participation in these cooperatives provides them additional pay for labor fulfilled during time free from their principal job. The cooperative's charge and expenses are lower than the expenses connected with maintenance of temporary workers from urban areas. This conclusion follows from information that, in creating temporary cooperatives, the collective farm was liberated from the duty to pay imported city laborers.[58] But the temporary cooperatives and the collective farm that organizes them execute contracts as the legal basis for implementation of the appropriate work. These contracts provide the price—that is, the payment for an ordered task, and the members of the cooperatives agree to receive a lower price than that which is otherwise reasonable because they are simultaneously members of both parties to the contract—the temporary cooperative and the collective farm.

At the same time, the 1988 Law on Cooperation contains special provisions earmarked to restrain the escalation of cooperative prices. Article 19(3) establishes:

> Products (work, services), produced in accordance with contracts executed to fulfill state orders or manufactured from raw materials which have been delivered to a cooperative from state resources, shall be sold to procurement and other enterprises (organizations) or citizens for prices centrally defined, and, in cases where this is permitted, for contractual prices (tariffs). The same procedure is applicable to retail prices for commodities allocated to cooperatives from the state market funds for the purpose of sale to the populace as well as to prices and markups on commodities which are sold by cooperatives but have been acquired in the system of state and [consumer] cooperative retail trade.

Violations of this command shall be severely punished in accordance with subpart 4 of the same article. It provides:

> If a cooperative overstates prices (tariffs) on products (work, services) in these cases, income unjustly received as a result of this [overstating] must be withdrawn for the benefit of the budget. A cooperative which has overstated prices (tariffs) must also pay for the benefit of the budget a fine in the amount of income unlawfully received. The customer is entitled to cancel a contract executed between him and a cooperative in

cases where the cooperative overstates prices (tariffs) on products (work, services).

In consideration of both legal provisions, food and other goods must be distinguished to outline the area where the new type of cooperatives can lawfully exercise their right to free establishment of prices on products, work, and services.

Raw materials necessary to produce food can be bought by cooperatives at collective farm markets. Only in this case do prices depend on the food produced by cooperatives and on agreements between sellers and purchases, representing the category of free prices. Under present circumstances, such a restriction is, in fact, fatal to cooperative activity. For instance, the author of the article "The Markets are Crammed, the Shops are Empty"[59] describes the situation dominant in Leningrad in the realm of food supply considered only with respect to agricultural produce. As he contends, the state shops do not have this produce, while it can be found at collective farm markets in abundance and great assortment. As follows from the same information, prices employed by individual sellers are very high, and the number of cooperative sellers is so small that there is no competition between the former and the latter that could entail a decrease in prices. These circumstances also affect the level of prices for food produced by cooperatives from raw materials available at collective farm markets. On October 7, 1988, *Izvestia* published a very illustrative article called "A Bill for Lunch in a Café," meaning a cooperative café. An average price of a lunch in Moscow cooperative cafés is 10 to 15 rubles. Given average salaries of 180 rubles per month (according to official and obviously exaggerated data), this price exceeds the economic opportunities of the overwhelming majority of the Soviet populace. The situation is not improved by collective farm markets. A kilogram of meat at these markets in Moscow costs seven rubles, 81 kopecks. This signifies that the market price of 100 grams of meat is 78 kopecks, but cooked in a cooperative café it will cost three-and-one-half rubles.

From the viewpoint of the Soviet leadership, the objective behind the new cooperatives is to improve consumer supply, first and foremost, food supply. But because of prevailing food shortages, these cooperatives either do not affect the actual situation or may even worsen it. As a result, the final conclusion is not encouraging. The new type of cooperatives must be developed to facilitate solution of the food problem; but the food problem must be solved to stimulate development of the new cooperatives. A more complicated conundrum can hardly be imagined.

In putting aside food and addressing other goods earmarked for the supply of the populace, it is easy to ascertain that freedom of cooperative prices is actually compatible, as a rule, only with production of the appropriate articles by a cooperative from raw materials provided by customers. There are no free markets in the USSR where raw materials requisite for such production can be acquired by a cooperative. To carry out an activity of the appropriate character for those customers deprived of their own raw materials, a cooperative must buy them in the state or consumer cooperative retail trade system. But this precludes application of free prices. Prices are regulated under the circumstances, and offenders must be punished according to law.

Also, under the deplorable status of official supply, the new cooperatives cannot plan their activities, relying on state resources allocated for these cooperatives or the system of state and consumer cooperative retail trade as the sellers of the requisite items. Their expectations in this respect can be connected with only two sources: individuals' sale of used materials and the underground economy unlawfully producing materials whose production belongs to the monopoly of state enterprises. In the former case, the cooperatives will have no opportunities to satisfy the demands of their customers on the proper qualitative level. In the latter case, the purchase prices paid by the cooperatives will be very high, and as a result, the sale prices inevitable for the cooperatives must be even higher. Like food, other goods sold by the new cooperatives or work and services provided by them cannot be economically available to the majority of the populace.

At the same time, creation of the new cooperatives producing not only food but also other goods or performing work and providing services will stimulate the development of the underground economy, since the state economy fails to produce the desired supply. Exercise of the underground economy belongs to the category of economic crimes, severely punished in the USSR. Purchase of materials by the new type of cooperatives from producers from the underground economy, production of commodities from these materials, and their sale to customers also must be qualified as a type of criminal activity. This activity entails not only the punishment of guilty individuals but, at the same time, forfeitures of property, including income, gained by a cooperative as a result of such crimes. Thus, freedom of prices established for the cooperatives to stimulate development of new cooperatives on the one hand, and restriction of this freedom earmarked to prevent extraction of unlawful income on the other, can be transformed into disaster or collapse of specific cooperatives, to say nothing about the danger connected with this freedom for specific officials who strive to develop the activities of their cooperatives as broadly as possible.

Further, unavoidable interconnections between the cooperative and underground economies that stimulate the development of the underground economy, simultaneously undermine the state economy. The underground economy cannot function without unlawful reliance on the state economy. The forms of this reliance vary from illegal receipt of equipment and materials centrally distributed to illegal creation of private workshops or their parts at state enterprises. Regardless of the specific forms employed by the underground economy, it can be developed only at the expense of the state economy. As a result, the Soviet punitive agencies are in an incessant struggle against the underground economy, applying severe measures of criminal punishment. In assessing the new type of cooperatives from this point of view, not only a positive but also a negative impact on the Soviet economic system can be predicted. This impact is positive as far as the new cooperatives facilitate satisfaction of individual demand even at high prices affordable by only a very restricted circle of customers. But the same impact is negative because it entails migration of state resources to the underground economy prohibited by Soviet law and enhances the unlawful activities of the new cooperatives increasing application of property sanctions and criminal punishment. Once more Gorbachev's reforms face a vicious circle: the new type of cooperatives must be developed because the state economy cannot satisfy individual demand, but to ensure development of the cooperative system, the state economy in the USSR must operate at a level sufficient for the regular supply of the cooperative system.

Considering that the new cooperatives can disguise unlawful activities, the 1988 Law on Cooperation provides for employment in this case of all forms of control established for cooperatives of other types. Among these forms, financial control plays the most important role. Thus, Article 23(2) obliges the cooperative to have its accounts in the nearest bank, to deposit its money in these accounts, and to implement all payments through the banks in which the cooperative monetary resources are deposited. This creates an opportunity for the bank, implementing specific payments, to monitor the character of economic operations entailing the transfer of money and to prevent such operations generally prohibited in the USSR or that exceed those functions available to cooperatives according to specific laws in force. The state control over income taxes, which cooperatives must pay to the local budget, is no less effective. Financial agencies entitled to implement this control have broad opportunities to encompass by special audit all types of a cooperative's activity. They also have the right to apply severe sanctions provided for in Article 21(5) of the 1988 Law that establishes:

The cooperative is obliged to strictly observe the tax discipline. In the case of concealment or understating of income subject to taxation, the entire amount of the concealed tax and fines established by law shall be withdrawn from the cooperative for the benefit of the local budget. The second case of concealment (understating) of income by the cooperative entitles the appropriate financial agency to submit a request to the executive committee of the local Soviet of the people's deputies concerning termination of the activities of such a cooperative.

Taken by themselves, these provisions cannot evoke any criticism. Each state has its system of taxes and protects this system through proper remedies. The Soviet Union presents no exception to this rule. But a specific purpose pursued by the referred Soviet law is to guarantee, along with the receipt of taxes from cooperative income, comprehensive control over cooperative activities and decrease in their number, if necessary, by means of liquidation as a sanction for unlawful acts.

Activities of the new cooperatives generally can be implemented only by their members; hired workers can be used in extraordinary circumstances. Hired workers receive salaries that must be fixed by labor contracts and covered by the appropriate portion of gross revenue. Members must divide among themselves a portion of the gross revenue remaining after fulfillment by the cooperative of its other property duties.[60] This form of payments earmarked for members of the new cooperatives is the most important economic incentive virtually unknown to other cooperatives. Activities of consumer cooperatives are implemented by hiring workers who receive salaries. Salaries are also paid to officials elected from the members of consumer cooperatives. Incentive payments in the form of bonuses are in this case as inefficient as they are in state economic entities. Payments received by collective farmers also depend on distributions of gross income, and in this regard collective farms resemble the new type of cooperatives. But as discussed above, the major portion of agricultural produce must be sold by collective farms to the state procurement entities at prices below cost. Therefore, the intensive labor of collective farmers cannot greatly affect the size of payments they actually receive. In contrast, the new cooperatives function relying mainly on the labor of their members and bear no duties to sell their products to the state for less than cost. The higher the income of a specific cooperative, the larger the shares of distribution paid to each member according to the quality and quantity of his or her labor. In other words, because the property of these cooperatives is a modified form of individual property, this fact entails economic efficiency unachievable for other economic entities in the USSR. By introducing the new type of cooperatives, Gorbachev strives to eliminate stagnation in the Soviet economy by a phenomenon alien to that economy. This signifies that if his aspirations can be characterized as *within-the-system* modifications, the new type of cooperatives have no chance to exceed the framework of second-hand economic entities. The dominant role will still be played by the economy that remains directly in the grasp of the ruling elite as the economic monopolist and, consequently, as the holder of unlimited political power.

CHAPTER

3

The Individual Economy

In referring to the individual economy, Marxist-Leninist doctrine distinguishes between private enterprise and labor economies. Private enterprise relies upon the hiring of labor. In the early 1930s, Soviet citizens were prohibited from hiring labor. This prohibition coincided with the expropriation of all private enterprises in urban areas and the creation of collective farms in rural areas. At that time, private enterprise ceased to exist as a lawful activity in the USSR, and it could appear only as a result of violations of law in the form of the underground economy. In contrast, labor economies rely on individuals' own labor and that of their family members. Before the 1936 Constitution, not only the property of those who had their separate economies as individual peasants and artisans but also the estates of workers and officials of state and cooperative entities resulting from their salaries and wages were considered as individual labor property. The 1936 Constitution introduced Stalin's distinctions between individual labor and personal properties, distinctions that, although evolved to a

161

certain extent, were inherited by the present Soviet leadership.

A. Individual Personal and Labor Properties

When the concept of personal property first appeared in 1936, it was defined as "the right of citizens to their labor income and savings, dwelling house, and subsidiary household economy, and to domestic articles, and in articles of personal consumption and convenience."[1] This definition did not expressly indicate that it meant the property of persons who earned their livelihoods in the form of salaries and wages as officials and workers of so-called socialist organizations. But the appropriate conclusion followed from comparison with the interpretation of individual labor property as the basis of "the small-scale private economy of individual peasants and artisans relying on personal labor and precluding the use of another's labor."[2] In other words, property is individual labor property if it is connected with one's own economy based on one's own labor. This signifies that personal property can arise only from labor employed in socialist enterprises and other entities. In light of these distinctions, the second subpart of Article 6 of the 1936 Constitution seems especially interesting. It reads:

> Each collective farm household shall, in addition to the basic income from the social collective farm economy, have for personal use a small plot of land and in personal ownership a subsidiary husbandry on the household plot, a dwelling house, productive livestock, poultry, and minor agricultural implements, according to the charter of the agricultural cartel.

This property is also characterized as personal property. But it has certain peculiarities deviating from the general juxtaposition of individual personal and labor properties.

The following general distinctions exist between the two types of individual properties:

(a) personal property is derived from labor employed in the socialist economy, while individual labor property is derived from labor employed in the proprietor's own economy;

(b) the former is earmarked for consumer purposes, while the latter encompasses, along with consumer purposes, production goals; and

(c) citizens as personal owners can have only consumer goods, while as individual labor owners they can also possess certain means of production.

In analyzing the personal property of a collective farm household, one must come to a slightly different conclusion:

(a) this property is derived mainly from labor in collective farms and, in addition, from labor in collective farmers' own economies;[3]

(b) collective farmers' households are earmarked both to consumer and production purposes; and

(c) to the extent to which collective farmers' households are connected with production purposes, collective farmers are entitled to possess the appropriate means of production.

Along with the contrasting distinctions between individual personal and labor properties and peculiarities of collective farmers' households in comparison with other

forms of personal property, the 1936 Constitution and subsequent legislation developing it were designed to restrict
individuals' activities within the narrow limits established
for different groups of individuals. Officials and workers of
socialist entities could not exceed the limits of their labor
functions. If, nevertheless, they provided the populace with
certain services during their free time, these actions were
unlawful and could entail administrative sanctions, primarily financial, or even penal prosecution.

Individual peasant economies disappeared very soon
after promulgation of the 1936 Constitution, and their owners either entered collective farms or became workers and
officials of other socialist entities. As a result, this source of
necessary services was lost to the Soviet populace. Collective farmers' households alone, despite severe legal restrictions on their plots of land and available means of
agricultural production, managed to provide about one-
third of the agricultural produce supplied to urban areas by
rural areas. Yet because of the deplorable status of the food
supply resulting from the system of state and consumer
cooperative trade, even the significant contribution of collective farmers' households in this realm of the Soviet economy could not lead to any substantial overall improvement.
As long as Stalin was alive, employment of individual economic activities for the purpose of improvement of the
economic situation was out of the question. This tactic
could only be invoked by Stalin's successors.

This occurred in mid-1953 when for the first time in
Soviet history, Khrushchev, publicly describing the repre-
hensible state of Soviet agriculture, appealed to collective
farmers' individual economies as one of the sources for
improving a dangerous situation. As a result, the size of
plots of land allocated to collective farmers was increased,

the narrow limits of livestock available to them were extended, not only collective farmers but also other individuals were encouraged to develop their subsidiary household economies, and so forth. In this respect, personal property was liberated from certain previous restrictions, and individual economies became substantially more viable than previously. Several years later, Khrushchev himself stepped back from his innovations for fear that enriched peasants and others would be absorbed by their individual economies, disregarding their constitutional duty to work in collective farms and other Soviet entities. He restored the more restricted size of plots of lands allocated to collective farmers, narrowed the permissible range of livestock that could be possessed by individuals, completely prohibited the individual possession of livestock in almost all cities and urban settlements, and so forth. In addition, a concept that could be found only in certain judicial decisions in the time of Stalin was raised by Khrushchev to the level of a legal provision that prevented undesired growth of personal ownership. This was the concept of unearned income or, closer to the original Russian, "nonlabor income" (*netrudovoi dokhod*).

In 1961, this new legal provision established that "property in the personal ownership of citizens may not be used to derive unearned income."[4] It contained, however, no indications about the legal sanctions to be applied to violations. The appropriate legal sanctions were introduced in 1963-1964 by the union republic civil codes. For instance, the 1964 Civil Code of the RSFSR states in Article 111:

> If a citizen systematically uses any dwelling-house, dacha (part of a house or dacha) or any other property

owned by him to obtain unearned income, respectively this house, dacha (part of house or dacha) or other property must be withdrawn without reimbursement through judicial procedure according to the suit of the executive committee of the local Soviet of the peoples' deputies.

Even before these sanctions were established, and especially after they were promulgated, a number of Soviet citizens lost their houses and *dachi* because they received higher rents than that provided by law. Bearing in mind that the legal tariffs did not suffice to compensate the owner for expenses necessary to maintain these objects and that the overstating of legal limits could entail withdrawal of the property from its owner, citizens began to abstain from renting out their houses and *dachi*. The only victims of these consequences were, of course, those without their own homes because given the housing crisis in the USSR, their demands could not be satisfied. The blow directed against personal property also descended on the interests of those deprived of such property.

Brezhnev went even further than Khrushchev in the struggle against unearned income. Khrushchev included his prohibition only in the civil legislation. Brezhnev transformed it into a constitutional duty. The current Soviet Constitution, promulgated in 1977 during Brezhnev's era, states in Article 13 that "property in the personal ownership or use of citizens should not serve to derive unearned income or be used to the prejudice of the interests of society." Thus, the legal restrictions addressed to personal property became even stronger, encompassing not only individual owners but also individual users and prohibiting not only extraction of unearned income but also impingement of the interests of society. In fact, the struggle against unearned income broadly developed by Khrushchev was all but abandoned by Brezhnev. Brezhnev's rule was an era of corruption never matched during the entire history of the Soviet Union. Not long ago, Soviet media described the case of Nasriddinova, a former chairman of the Presidium of the Uzbek Supreme Soviet.[5] She managed to spend state monies and receive bribes from citizens and officials in amounts of hundreds of thousands of rubles. But each time a punitive agency began to prosecute her, higher officials in Moscow, including Brezhnev himself, ordered the immediate termination of those proceedings. As a matter of course, the leadership that maintains bribery cannot actively struggle against extraction of unearned income.

Along with the prohibition on the use of personal property for the purpose of extracting unearned income—a measure earmarked to prevent individual enrichment—Brezhnev included in the 1977 Constitution a norm pursuing the opposite goal—the increase of areas in which this property could be employed. Article 17 of the new Constitution, addressing the entire Soviet citizenry regardless of status as holder of personal property or individual labor property, declares:

In the USSR, individual labor activity shall be permitted in accordance with the law in the sphere of handicrafts, agriculture, domestic servicing of the populace, and also other forms of activity based exclusively on the personal labor of citizens and members of their families. The state shall regulate individual labor activity, ensuring its use in the interests of society.

The circumstances that induced Brezhnev's regime to introduce this innovation were clear from the outset. For decades, the official Soviet economy had proved its incapacity to satisfy the demands of the populace in all imaginable areas—from food supply to services. This can be demonstrated by numerous examples, for instance, automobile services. To hire a taxi legally is a difficult problem in Soviet cities. Yet individual owners of automobiles were prohibited from transporting passengers for a fee. Because economic demands are stronger than legal prohibitions, a number of individuals unlawfully employed their cars as taxis. Repairing the body of a private automobile in a state workshop requires months of waiting. Despite a legal prohibition, a number of professional mechanics and repairmen unlawfully provided numerous customers with the appropriate services. These facts of unlawful behavior were well-known to the government, but because no better solution could be suggested, the punitive agencies turned a blind eye to them. The way out of such a complicated situation was forced—the actual circumstances had to be legalized. This has been done by the Constitution in force. However, in Soviet practice, constitutional declarations do not function before their development is implemented by current legislation. Brezhnev managed to avoid such a legal development, and as a result, his constitutional declaration remained a dead letter for almost ten years, until Gorbachev began to announce his economic reforms.

Nonetheless, the constitutional innovation introduced by Brezhnev had its own legal consequences. Since individual labor activity became available to all Soviet citizens and could be combined with work in Soviet entities, this obliterated the former distinctions between individual personal and labor properties. The 1977 Constitution omits all terms other than personal property, defined in Article 13,[6] leaving the issue of types of individual property in the USSR as a subject of purely theoretical discussions.[7] At the same time, the Constitution in force has created the legal basis for further development of the current legislation on the indicated path. From this point of view, it must be assessed as a forerunner of the present economic reforms concerning the property of individuals and their labor activity.

B. A Flabbergasting Start

When in 1985, Gorbachev assumed the highest office in the country as General Secretary of the Communist Party of the Soviet Union and rumors about eventual economic reforms became widespread, the first expectations connected with individual property were based on the assumption that finally this property would be liberated from unbearable fetters. To the great astonishment of the whole population, Gorbachev has chosen another starting point —strengthening the struggle against unearned income extracted by individuals as a result of the unlawful use of either their own property or the property of the Soviet state, of cooperatives, or of societal organizations. On May 28, 1986, *Pravda* and *Izvestia* published under the same heading three enactments adopted by the three highest Soviet agencies: the Central Committee of the CPSU, the USSR Council of Ministers, and the Presidium of the Supreme Soviet of the USSR. The Central Committee and the Government decrees were adopted on May 15, 1986,[8] and the Presidium of the USSR Supreme Soviet dated its edict May 23, 1986[9] (the May enactments). This was unprecedented in Soviet legislative practice. The heading of each

169

enactment was "On Measures of Strengthening the Struggle against Unearned Income" (or "Against the Deriving of Unearned Income"). The first decree, from the Central Committee of the CPSU, is of a directive character. The second decree, from the USSR Council of Ministers, deals with the "struggle" activity by the appropriate governmental agencies. The edict from the Presidium of the Supreme Soviet of the USSR establishes administrative and criminal sanctions for individuals who violate the proclaimed prohibitions.

Those in the Soviet Union learned of these extraordinary innovations at once; those abroad had to wait a day or two for the specific details. The former were, of course, silent, whereas the latter reacted promptly. *The New York Times*, for instance, wrote on June 8, 1986:

> The Soviet Union, citing a need to use "the full force of the law" against corruption, has announced new penalties for embezzlement. . . . The targets of the new measures—"those living beyond their means"—apparently include not only the bribe-takers . . . , but also the large segment of the population involved in the underground economy. . . . Under Mr. Gorbachev, experimental rewards for incentive and initiative . . . have been introduced to divert enterprising workers away from the gray market. Having offered that carrot, the Government now appears to be brandishing a stick in the form of the new penalties for the sort of pilfering that makes the underground economy work.

While this statement represents the correspondent's attempt to characterize the true nature of the new legal rules, numerous questions were passed over in silence by *The New York Times* and other western media.

The declarative provisions of the three enactments emphasize the special importance of "intensifying the struggle" against the "stealing of socialist property, bribery, speculation and other mercenary crimes that are sources of unearned income." To be sure, stealing and bribery are also commonplace crimes in western countries where the concept of unearned income is not employed. But speculation, that is, the buying up and reselling of goods for the purpose of making a profit, is a peculiarly Soviet or even a peculiarly socialist crime. Soviet legislation has always deemed these crimes—stealing, bribery, and speculation—as dangerous, not because they result in unearned income but because of their incompatibility with the normal functioning of the Soviet economy or of the Soviet ruling mechanism. Now these crimes are combined with "other crimes" which share in common the deriving of unearned income. Why?

If stealing as a source of unearned income must be punished more efficaciously than previously, all types of stealing should involve an identical approach. But the May enactments pertain only to the stealing of property from the state, collective farms, and other Soviet entities (*socialist property*), completely disregarding the stealing of personal property. Why?

In contrast to stealing or bribery, other crimes leading to unlawful enrichment are mentioned generally, without specific characterization or even enumeration. Yet, in turning from general declarations to concrete provisions, it is evident that the most substantial innovations relate to "other" crimes or offenses: engaging in a prohibited trade, using state or individual living space for profit-making purposes, and so forth. Why?

All of these "whys" can be answered together: the Soviet legislator does not always directly say what he actually thinks. However, such an answer does not liberate researchers within the Soviet system, including Soviet law, to find the accurate solution of the problems arising from the study of the May enactments.

As demonstrated above,[10] the unlimited political power of the Soviet ruling elite is based on its economic monopoly that relies upon so-called socialist property. This is why a notorious Soviet law of 1932 known to young and old as "the decree of the 7th of August"[11] proclaimed that "socialist property shall be sacred and inviolable, and persons infringing against shall be enemies of the people." Accordingly, this law provided capital punishment as a rule and deprivation of freedom for ten years as an exception to the rule applicable to those infringing against socialist property. The law of August 7, 1932 was abolished long ago, but even the Soviet criminal law in force before 1989 established capital punishment for certain crimes directed against socialist property. Formally, this law introduced capital punishment for economic crimes, which contradicted certain international treaties ratified by the USSR. In fact, however, an infringement on socialist property undermines the economic source of unlimited political power and thus is a political crime. From this point of view, the Soviet leadership was quite consistent, strongly protecting the official economy. The May enactments observed this consistency, accentuating the struggle against violations of socialist property as the principal goal of the struggle against the derivation of unearned income. In contrast, stealing or other mercenary crimes that damage personal property do not undermine the official economy as the basis of unlimited political power in the grasp of the Soviet ruling elite. Although the May enactments are dedicated to the struggle against unearned income, they pay direct attention only to those sources of unearned income that belong to components of the official economy. Other sources are not mentioned because their use for the same unlawful purposes is not as dangerous as in cases where these purposes are achieved to the detriment of the economy dominant in the USSR.

Economic monopoly is necessary for the ruling elite to establish comprehensive dependence of individuals on the Soviet state and their unconditional obedience to governmental commands. But individuals can achieve their economic independence without harming the dominant economy, and this independence is dangerous *per se* as an undermining of political obedience. To protect not only the monopoly of the state economy but also the resultant economic dependence of Soviet individuals, the concept of unearned income has been devised to supplement the means of economic and political suppression by punitive prosecution. For instance, a professional chess player loaned money to a large number of persons on condition that the loans were interest-free, but in the event of a delay in repayment the lender reserved the right to require from the borrower fines that greatly exceeded the interest rate established for such violations of the law. The profit from the fines would have been sufficient for the lender to live as if there were no economic monopoly or unlimited power in the hands of the Soviet dictatorship. The court confiscated his profit as unearned income, and consequently, the "socialist" public order was restored in this specific case. Cases of the same character are countless in the USSR. The institution of the struggle against unearned income, which had become virtually dormant in Brezhnev's time, had to be revived by Gorbachev.

The new Soviet leader resolved this problem with the May enactments. He imparted a new vitality to a forgotten institution, transforming it into a phenomenon whose only rival in Soviet history would be the appellation *kulak* applied by Stalin to rich peasants in order to exile them to Siberia during the farm collectivization process in the late 1920s and early 1930s. Beginning with Stalin, continuing under Khrushchev, and ending with Brezhnev (Andropov and Chernenko had no time to resort to the same concept), the interpretation of unearned income corresponded to the literal meaning of the words employed. First, to be unearned, income must not have resulted from the labor of its beneficiary. For example, if an individual is engaged in a forbidden trade, he would be fined or subjected to another punishment, but the income derived was from his own labor and therefore could not be confiscated under the rules concerning unearned income. Second, unearned income as an object of confiscation must be unlawful by nature. Certain kinds of income are lawful, despite the fact that they are unearned, for example, inheritance, gifts, and so forth. Confiscation of such income should be completely precluded. In Soviet practice, there were attempts to introduce a broad interpretation of the concept under discussion. These attempts failed either immediately or shortly after their implementation. In several cases, Soviet courts tried to classify the high profit gained through cultivating and selling vegetables or flowers as unearned income. In the final analysis, the judicial decisions directed against such income were reversed because the produce sold was created through the labor of the defendants, and retail prices, subject to no official limits, were based exclusively on agreements between sellers and purchasers. After this practice was eliminated, unearned income again acquired its previous certainty: income was qualified as unearned if it were both unlawful in character and unearned in origin. Absent one of these features, income was either just or unjust, but it was evaluated under provisions other than those determining the fate of unearned income.

In comparison with these regulations, those established by Gorbachev resemble a mountain replacing a molehill. The volume of his innovations alone is staggering: instead of the several lines of the previous legislation, three lengthy enactments have been issued. Suppressive in content, these decrees are sinister in their declarations. The Central Committee of the CPSU, in its decree, considers "eradication of unearned income, alien to the nature of socialism, to be an important political, social, economic and educational task." As previous experience proves, this signifies in the Soviet jargon a command to stamp out with a crushing blow the multitude of cases of earning money beyond the limits of officially established levels, regardless of whether such behavior is criminal or simply undesirable to the guardians of the Soviet regime and whether it leads to limitless enrichment or only an insignificant increase in the beggarly payment for arduous labor.

The Soviet elite and habitual embezzlers aside, the average salary in the USSR itself compels tens of millions to look for extra money by means that are not legalized and that, nevertheless, hardly deserve to be "eradicated" by "the full force of the Soviet laws." A cleaning woman whose salary was seventy to eighty rubles per month would have violated Soviet law when Gorbachev's innovations were declared if she knitted women's jackets with her own wool based on orders from customers (a jacket could only be knitted legally with the customer's own materials). To tell this woman by means of a Communist Party decree that her actions were "incompatible with the socialist form of life," contrary to the "interests of laborers," and "entailing the just indignation of Soviet citizens," meant losing one's sense of humor (let alone a feeling for humanity). The gravity of the relationship between the tasks of "developing and carrying out concrete measures intensifying the struggle against deriving unearned income" and the call "to encourage the Party and the people to act against this evil" can hardly be appreciated.[12] Moreover, this task and this call were formulated only a month after the Chernobyl disaster, in complete disregard for the food and housing crises, the unavailability of domestic services, and so forth.

The May enactments are distinctive for more than just the timing of their adoption. First, the concept of unearned income acquires another, incomparably broader, content. Under the sources for deriving unearned income, the enactments link unconnectable phenomena: criminal and non-criminal behavior (for instance, the stealing of socialist property and the receipt of a higher rent than that provided for by law from a lessee of living space); actions that entail the deriving of income and those ensuring no income at all (for instance, mercenary use of Soviet entities' means of transport and the buying up in state or cooperative stores of baked bread, meal, groats, or other food products for feeding cattle or poultry); deriving income without labor and by means of unauthorized labor (for instance, the taking of a bribe and engaging in prohibited trade). The intentional linkage of different phenomena is not without practical design.

The criminalization of unearned income creates an opportunity to treat with "common disdain" any individual who strives to enrich himself by deriving that which is officially deemed unearned gain. This chastisement is very important for Soviet rulers, bearing in mind that, in contrast to infringements against personal property, successful enrichment at the expense of "socialist" property evokes envy or admiration rather than reproaches or condemnation. This is why the Central Committee of the CPSU "recommends" (read: "commands") that the Ministry of Culture, the State Committee of Cinema, and Creative Unions (unions of writers, artists, etc.) actively promote through their creative works "implacability against spongers, against a psychology stemming from private ownership, and against other antipodes of communist morality."[13]

Prosecution of those deriving unearned income in cases where actually no such income has been obtained, but merely certain other undesirable actions have been committed, must compromise an accused more than if his actions were not so characterized. In the USSR, a large number of individuals keep cattle or poultry within the limits established by law not for the purpose of enrichment but as a source of subsistence. A shortage of fodder threatens these individuals with irretrievable loss of that subsistence; to prevent such a disaster, they feed their cattle or poultry with food products such as breads purchased in state or cooperative stores. Who can blame them for a solution to which they have resorted only out of extreme necessity? But label them as parasites or egoists, and the psychological evaluation of their behavior can be materially modified.

Evaluating income created by individuals' own labor as unearned income is especially important from the viewpoint of the May enactments. This renders the concept of unearned income extremely uncertain, and as a result, broadly opens the gate for economic arbitrariness. The edict of the Presidium of the USSR Supreme Soviet establishes administrative or criminal responsibility only for "engaging in trade or other individual labor activity with respect to which there exists a special prohibition." But unearned income can be taken from an offender without resorting to penal or administrative measures, simply in the form of a property dispute initiated against an individual by a local agency of the Soviet government. Previously, a defendant could protect himself with reference to the labor source of his earning. At present this might not protect him, since despite its labor origin, the gain received can be deemed unearned income owing to its not irreproachable character. And moreover, in addressing unearned income, the same innovations replace in this respect a presumption of honesty on the part of Soviet citizens by the opposite presumption. In cases where the amount of an individual's transaction reaches an established level and in other cases where the local executive committee considers this reasonable, the acquirer of property must prove that he has used lawful sources to make this acquisition.[14]

The decrees are quite visibly flavored with demagogy typical of Stalin's rule and employed to some extent by Stalin's successors. When in the postwar period, Stalin at first unexpectedly abolished the death penalty but later repented his magnanimity, he rectified his blunder by referring to insistent requests purportedly submitted by vast masses of working people. This was Stalin's favorite approach in all cases where he considered it useful to announce publicly a new cruel measure. Khrushchev sometimes resorted to the same method, although in connection with relatively milder measures and with reference to fewer numbers of suppliants. In 1957, he postponed the repayment of state loans for twenty years and attributed his decision to satisfying the requests of workers in the industrial city Sormovo.

But this approach is too transparent to be left as an undiscoverable mystery, and it is no wonder that after Khrushchev's trick a widespread joke surfaced: We do not fear the Soviet government; we fear only the workers of Sormovo. Despite, however, the obvious primitiveness of self-justification with reference to popular support, Gorbachev appeals to it in the new enactments for reasons that are closer to Stalin's relying on the broad masses, as opposed to a separate collective body, to justify suppressive, not simply economic, measures. Referring to the working people in general, a decree of the Central Committee of the CPSU provides:

> In their application addressed to central and local agencies, they insist on the adoption of drastic measures for the purpose of eradicating unearned income. The Central Committee of the CPSU completely supports these demands, and it is of the opinion that activities of the Party, trade union, and Komsomol organizations, and of Soviets, economic and law enforcement agencies are in need of radical improvement.

To be sure, the question is of improvement of those agencies enumerated not as a whole but to the extent that their activities must aid in the elimination of any opportunity for deriving unearned income. The people mandate actions by the government, the government supports the people, and everybody is stirred to take part in the struggle against the principal evil. Only the fact that the struggle led by the government is directed against the people has not been expressed by this passionate rhetoric. However, a direction of the Party decree "to block all paths leading to deriving unearned income" signifies, after translation from political to colloquial language, that the income of the Soviet populace must not exceed earning predetermined by the Soviet rulers in a centralized manner. With this condition, the dependence of individuals on the monopolized economy will be comprehensive, and consequently, the obedience of citizens to the leadership's commands will be all-embracing.

Taking into consideration the measures discussed and the peculiarities of comparing epochs, as well as the individual differences between the two Soviet leaders that personify their respective historical periods, it becomes evident that in this case Gorbachev is actually following the path previously taken by Stalin.

Stalin's task, emanating from the nature of the Soviet system, was to eradicate any competing economy and to establish the economic monopoly of the Bolshevik political regime. This took about nine years (1924-1933), a relatively short time, bearing in mind that Lenin's heritage included a partly restored private economy in urban areas without much change in rural areas. Gorbachev has encountered a similar, though not identical, problem. He has not needed to reestablish the economic monopoly of the Soviet regime: this monopoly was inherited from his predecessors. There is, however, a new rival for the official economy—the underground economy—that has attained such strength that its elimination or, at any rate, its supplantation has become the principal requirement for the government to protect its economic monopoly. Compared to Stalin's economic task, the burden imposed on Gorbachev is in certain ways both lighter and heavier. It is lighter because the size of the underground economy does not compare with the size of the previously legalized private economy. The Soviet newspaper *Izvestia* contends in its May 29, 1986, issue that seventeen to twenty million people provide services privately, generating five to six billion rubles (seven to nine billion dollars). These figures are neither clear nor reliable because the article fails to explain whether the underground economy is taken into account, and if so, how the appropriate data were obtained.

Even such tentative data leave no doubt that the early private economy abolished by Stalin was tremendous in comparison to the underground economy functioning now. Viewed from another perspective, however, Gorbachev's burden is heavier than the task resolved by Stalin. Stalin saw the enemy whom he had to defeat. Gorbachev must discover the enemy before ensuring its annihilation. Stalin could inflict drastic blows with immediate effect, such as the collectivization of agriculture, the liquidation of *kulaki*, and so forth. Prohibiting unearned income was unnecessary, while these blows were objectively possible. In contrast, Gorbachev must resort to the long-term struggle against unearned income, meaning the underground economy, regardless of whether it originates from labor. This is why the May enactments are formulated so broadly, mobilizing the entire country and calling it to incessant struggle.

Stalin's methods of legally protecting the economic monopoly were always cruel and merciless. The decree of August 7, 1932, was replaced by new legislation in 1946 retaining the death penalty. Although the decree abolished the ten years' deprivation of freedom as a minimum punishment, it established twenty-five years' deprivation of freedom as a maximum punishment and alternative to the death penalty. The general mitigation of legal suppression resulting from the denunciation of Stalin also affected suppression with respect to the stealing of socialist property. Confirming the death penalty once more, Gorbachev's predecessors lowered the maximum sentence from twenty-five to fifteen years and differentiated more carefully among measures of punishment. A legal reform previously implemented has been mitigated by the new leadership, which abolished application of capital punishment to property crimes, probably for the same reasons that preclude an imitation of Stalin's methods of rule by means of mass execution in the years 1937-1938—a new time, different personalities, and modified approaches. Gorbachev has introduced one important novelty: the May enactments have rendered the prosecution of the stealing of socialist property, regardless of its value, all-encompassing to the extent that nobody convicted of such sins, heavy or light, could expect an official pardon. Such comprehensiveness must more than compensate for the failure to resort to the earlier atrocity.

C. A Comprehensible Continuation

The previous discussion has been based on the circumstances that existed when the May enactments were promulgated. At that time, no other explanation for the introduction of severe regulations concerning unearned income could be found. The conclusions deduced from this discussion are correct and they do not need to be modified as a result of certain subsequent events. These events necessitate the supplementation of the first formulated conclusions. On November 19, 1986, the Supreme Soviet of the USSR adopted a Law on Individual Labor Activity[15] (the November law). Considering this law against the above analysis of the May enactments, it seems quite reasonable that there may be certain doubts and that these doubts must be dispelled as much as possible.

At first glance, the November law is similar to Lenin's New Economic Politics (NEP) introduced in the early 1920s and quite different from any policy of Stalin or his successors. Lenin's NEP contained three components. First, it restored private enterprises and the private hiring of individual labor inside the economic branches where individuals could carry on such activities. The November law prohibits the private hiring of individual labor and limits private activities to the labor of individuals themselves and their family members, which may be utilized exclusively in the realm of consumer services.[16] Second, NEP replaced with goods and money exchange the uncompensated appropriation of agricultural produce in rural areas. The November law does not address this issue, and all other policies of the new Soviet leadership leave, in principle, the previous situation intact: collective farms are obliged to sell a certain amount of agricultural produce to the state at prices below cost as defined by the procurement plan, and any surplus of produce as well as the produce of collective farmers and other individuals may be freely sold at collective farm markets. Third, NEP introduced commercial (equivalent) relationships between state economic entities under the title "commercial accountability" (*kommercheskii raschet*). The November law does not concern itself with this issue either, and the new Soviet leadership,

though it strives toward substantial improvements, continues for good reasons to call its method of economic management not "commercial" (close to market) but "economic"
(remote from market) accountability (*khozraschet*). This
terminology from Stalin's time replaced the earlier "commercial accountability" because equivalent goods-money
exchange was transformed into a nonequivalent one, based
on artificially planned prices irrespective of reasonable cost
and just profit. The fact that Stalin's terminology remains
unmodified demonstrates that there is no sign of a return to
NEP in this case either.

Stalin never resorted to measures comparable to
Gorbachev's approach in regard to individual labor activity. Brezhnev, who made a long step back to Stalin after
Khrushchev's ouster, also implemented the first measures
that cleared the path for Gorbachev's reform in this respect.
As mentioned above, in contrast to Article 9 of Stalin's
1936 Constitution that recognized only small-scale private
economies of individual peasants and artisans as compatible with individual labor activity, Article 17 of Brezhnev's
1977 Constitution generally encourages such activities in
the sphere of handicrafts, agriculture, domestic services of
the populace, and so forth. Of course, the November law
must affect this development immeasurably more than the
appropriate constitutional provision. Effective regulation
of individual labor is an achievement of Gorbachev, not of
Brezhnev. This occurred, however, not because Gorbachev
rejected Stalin's approach but because he developed an
approach initiated by a stalinist Brezhnev. As the principal
speaker at the meeting of the Supreme Soviet dedicated to
the November law, Ivan Gladkii, Chairman of the USSR
State Committee on Labor and Social Problems, emphasized in his interview with representatives of *Pravda* that

"[t]he measures adopted do not signal a return to private enterprise activity in any shape or form. . . . The Law has been worked out in accordance with citizens constitutional rights"[17]—that is, the rights provided for by Brezhnev's Constitution and underscored by Gorbachev's law.

The second doubt must be connected with the assertion that, in essence, the Soviet system is one in which each individual is economically dependent on the Soviet state as the economic monopolist. If individuals are allowed to affect their economic activities privately, will they not acquire economic independence immediately after embarking on activities of any legalized types?

In expressing such a doubt, the specific circumstances that induced the Soviet leadership to issue the November law must not be disregarded. The Soviet literature, trying to elucidate these circumstances, distorts the genuine situation to paint it a rosier color. For instance, there is the following explanation:

> The real per capita income in the USSR has grown by more than 150 percent over the past 25 years. This rise in living standards has naturally led to an increased demand for various goods, especially high quality and fashionable consumer goods, and to new or greater needs for services. . . . The sphere of public services has been expanding rapidly; the number of personnel involved in it has increased by 24 percent over the decade beginning in 1975. . . . It has turned out, however, that this growth has not been fast enough. . . . Today, most of the problems have been resolved. . . . Citizens are free to engage in individual labor, while the state is encouraging them to do so. . . . [18]

In other words, individual labor activities are allowed and enlarged in the USSR because growth in citizens' income leaves behind expansion of the sphere of public services. Were this discrepancy not to arise, there would be no need for enlargement of individual labor activities. Is this explanation genuine or merely propagandistic? For instance, there are several hundred thousand individual automobiles in Leningrad and only two automobile body shops handling only forty cars daily. Will growth in the number of these body shops matched by growth in individual incomes resolve the problem? Individual income has grown more than 150 percent during the past twenty-five years. The same growth in the capacity to repair privately-owned cars ensures the demands of 120 customers out of the hundreds of thousands. Will this lead to substantial change? The author of the same book contends that, beginning in 1975, services in motor vehicle repairs increased by 422 percent. For Leningrad, this signifies that only 170 privately-owned cars can be repaired daily. Can one seriously take this growth into account?

The point is that services to the Soviet populace are in an even more deplorable situation than that of food supply. The Soviet leadership has been compelled to expand the employment of individual labor activities to prevent disaster in consumer services, disregarded for decades as a result of shortages of monetary and other resources. At the same time, they understand that it would be a flagrant political mistake to open such a dangerous gate without strong guarantees of the indestructibility of the Soviet system. These guarantees are provided for in the November law as follows:

Guarantee number one: Under Article 3, "housewives, disabled persons, pensioners, and students of legal age shall be permitted to engage in individual labor activity." The purpose is to draw on an additional labor force and not to permit the shift of labor from the "socialized" to the private sector. The Article continues, "Citizens of legal age who participate in social production shall be permitted to engage in individual labor activity during their hours off work in their principal occupation." This provision formally legalizes the limits of the allowed combination of labor in the official economy and individual labor activities, the combination existing before 1977 in fact, and then recognized by the Constitution in force. It seems quite possible that because unemployment has appeared in the USSR, the Soviet leadership will strive to cope with it, appealing not only to the officially dominant economy. As Soviet sources inform, unemployment developed in the USSR exists either as temporary,[19] as regional,[20] as that which arises in small settlements,[21] as concealed,[22] or as indirect.[23] If temporary unemployment must disappear *per se*, its other forms require special measures for their elimination. Judging from Soviet media, it is not individual labor activities but the new types of cooperatives that are preferred by the Soviet regime as the area where those losing their jobs must apply their labor. What about citizens who participate in social production but decide to quit first to run a household and then to engage in private activity under their new legal status?

Guarantee number two: Article 6 stipulates that "citizens who wish to engage in individual labor activity shall be required to obtain a permit from the executive committee." By refusing an application submitted by a person who previously participated in social production, the executive committee will oblige him to restore his previous status. Such a refusal cannot be appealed to the court because Soviet legislation does not provide for judicial review with respect to decisions of administrative agencies, except for a few insignificant cases directly indicated by specific legal provisions. It is true that a negative decision of the local executive committee can be appealed to a higher administrative agency. But neither those who reject a request nor those who decide the appeal are required to explain the reasons for their decision or to give any reason at all. Soviet media publish a number of articles emphasizing the significance of obstacles to the development of individual labor activities which stem from actions of the Soviet bureaucracy. Creation of those obstacles is not difficult in the ambiguous psychological atmosphere surrounding this area. According to the author referred to above:

> There has probably never been an enactment in the annals of the Soviet judicial system to have caused so much controversy as the Law on Individual Labor. . . . The Law took effect on May 1, 1987, but verbal swords continue to be crossed. Not everyone is "in favor" of it nor is everyone "against it." Those who raise both hands for individual enterprise would like better public service in the USSR. . . . Others . . . are scared by the word "private," as in private café, private taxi, private repair shops. . . . [24]

Such a psychological atmosphere strengthens the efficiency of the system of permits introduced for development of individual labor activities. This system proves to be capable of ensuring not only that labor will not shift from the socialized to the private sphere but also that private activities will not develop beyond that considered necessary by local agencies. What, however, if certain circumstances in different locations dictate that the number of individuals engaged in private activities in general or in a given realm must be reduced?

Guarantee number three: Article 6 provides that "the term of validity of the permit . . . shall not exceed five years." Does this mean that the permit cannot be invalidated before it expires? The law contains no express answer to this question. In enumerating the legal grounds for the revocation of a permit, Article 6 mentions individual labor activities that are contrary to "other social interests." The law does not explain whether it means intentional prejudicial behavior of an individual (a subjective criterion) or the type of activity that is itself prejudicial under the circumstances (an objective criterion). Either interpretation is possible. One thing is, however, completely clear. In Soviet legislative practice, two methods are employed to define the legal consequences of expiration of the established period of validity of legal documents: expiration of such a period either requires repetition of the same procedure (if the legislator has no intention of perpetuating the relations established) or automatically revives the same relations since they were not violated by any partner (if the legislator strives to perpetuate the appropriate relations). It is not the latter but the former approach that has been employed by Soviet law with respect to individual labor activities. The Soviet leadership considers its permission temporary, not permanent, and as soon as the decentralizing stage of the cyclical development of the Soviet economy is replaced by the stage of centralism, it seems quite possible that individual labor activities will be returned to the previous restricted limits or even reduced further. What, however, if a certain interpretation is inapplicable because of its obvious unlawfulness?

Guarantee number four: Under Article 5, executive committees and other organizations "shall render assistance to citizens who engage in individual labor activities with regard to purchasing raw materials, supplies, tools, and other equipment necessary for engaging in this activity, and for selling the goods that they produce." According to the text of the law, this assistance is discretionary. Bearing in mind the pervasive shortages in the USSR, refusal of such assistance may be equivalent to failure of the individual private activities. Of course, citizens deprived of official assistance can appeal to the underground economy. They will appeal to this economy usually because of the incapacity of the official supply to satisfy their demand even with the best intentions of the management of the appropriate agencies. But connections with the underground economy are unlawful and can *per se* entail the termination of activity of an individual enterprise as contradicting the requirements of law in force. At the same time, there are certain kinds of supplies that can be furnished only by state entities, not by those dealing with the underground economy. Non-residential premises adjusted to individual enterprises represent one of the most striking examples. These premises belong to the state and are objects of leases between local executive committees and their customers. As the same Article 5 establishes, on the one hand, executive committees "can make non-residential premises . . . available for leasing by citizens who engage in individual labor activity," but on the other hand, this type and all other forms of assistance "shall be rendered first to citizens who conclude contracts with enterprises, institutions, and organizations" and who carry on their labor activity in accordance with these contracts. All possible measures are provided to subordinate individual enterprise as an inevitable evil to

190

the official economy as the basis of the Soviet system, according to the principle "the less the appropriate activity is private, the more it must be encouraged." But what if an individual overcomes all these obstacles, and his or her income reaches a level ensuring a standard of living incomparably higher than that of the average Soviet standard?

Guarantee number five: In accordance with Articles 7 and 9 of the November law, citizens engaged in individual labor activity must pay income taxes or purchase licenses from state financial agencies. In regulating both issues, Soviet law strives to prevent the growth of individual income derived from individual activity substantially beyond the average income of other Soviet citizens. The distinctions between these issues are that taxes must be paid at the end of the year, while a license must be bought before one begins to implement individual labor activity. If individual income is at the level of average salaries, the size of taxes are the same as those paid by workers and officials: approximately 9.8 percent. This rate is applied to income up to three thousand rubles a year. The rates range between twenty and fifty percent for income of up to six thousand rubles with a rate of sixty-five percent for income exceeding this amount.[25] Payment for licenses, as Article 10 of the November law provides, "shall be determined on the basis of the average annual income of persons engaged in similar activity in state, cooperative and other enterprises, institutions or organizations, or persons who perform similar work as individual labor activity without a license according to the appropriate income tax rate." In accordance with Soviet policy, income remaining after periodic payments to the budget in the form of either taxes or license fees must not exceed or, at least, must not substantially exceed the average individual income in the USSR. This does not mean that even in a single case the Soviet regime cannot fail to achieve its goal. To say nothing about concealment of genuine income, Soviet media describe now and again individuals whose income is higher than average. These cases, simply because they are publicly described, are clearly not typical. Ascertaining this indisputable fact leaves no room for the purely logical deduction that the November law simultaneously undermines the economic monopoly of the Soviet state and the economic dependence of Soviet individuals on this monopoly. In fact, the November law strongly reinforces both the monopoly and the dependence.

There is no doubt that Gorbachev's innovation increases the opportunities for individual labor by Soviet citizens. In contrast to the situation under previous legislation, now individual laborers can use their own cars as taxis, open a café run by a family or group of individuals, create a workshop for automobile repair, manufacture household goods, footwear, and so forth. Even social and cultural activities are available as individual labor. The November law goes so far as to include in its enumeration of approved types of individual labor activities boarding services for tourists, sightseers, and other citizens.[26] Expansion of the limits established for individual labor activities entails enlargement of objects of individual ownership. For instance, a special governmental decree provides that individuals (possibly those involved in agricultural activities) are entitled to be owners of tractors, trailers attached to tractors, and self-propelled agricultural machines. Actually, such individual ownership has never been formally prohibited, and the appropriate prohibition has implicitly followed from the legal definition of personal ownership. A new governmental decree speaks not for personal ownership with respect to these items but to registration of their acquisition.[27] In fact, however, the Soviet government allows by virtue of this decree ownership with respect to tractors, and so forth. Such economic liberalism astonished Western observers who were sure that in this case the creation of private enterprises could not be denied by the most incorrigible skeptics. They did not notice, however, that boarding services were to be based on contracts with enterprises or other entities. If not for this oversight, it would be clear that the rule was intended to restrict private activity. It must be emphasized also that the prohibition against manufacturing certain articles from producers', and not customers', materials has been abolished. Thus, a cleaning woman who knits jackets with her own wool from customers' orders for the purpose of deriving a modest income to supplement her meager salary is no longer considered to be one of the criminal elements that must be "eradicated." What is more, individual production not for certain customers but for sale generally is allowed with respect not only to agricultural produce but also in the realm of various handicrafts.

At the same time, the November law prohibits certain types of individual labor activities. It is prohibited to manufacture chemicals, perfumeries, and toiletries; to maintain gambling houses, amusement parks, and baths; to organize games of chance, and sport-related and other similar business. One prohibition attracts special attention: it is forbidden to teach privately subjects that are not part of the public school curriculum. Abstractly, this provision can be explained as the desire of the Soviet leadership to be free of such ideological phenomena that either contradict the official ideology or are incompatible with specific political tasks under certain circumstances. For instance, the private teaching of Hebrew has been considered a crime for a long time because of the attitude of the USSR toward Israel and the problem of Jewish emigration from the Soviet Union. Judging from information from Israeli sources, now Hebrew can be a subject of private teaching, although it is not included in the curriculum of Soviet public schools, and certain Soviet universities, where such teaching takes place in connection with the study of the Middle East, do not entail any formal change because the law speaks about public schools, not universities. It is useful to remember in this connection that if it is necessary politically, the Soviet regime can disregard both prohibitions and permissions.

To understand the Soviet policy on individual labor activities, it is important to address once more the present formulation of the problem of cooperatives, especially those that could be called the new type of cooperatives. Consider, for instance, the 1987 decree of the Council of Ministers of the USSR "On the Creation of Cooperatives for Servicing the Populace."[28] According to this decree, these cooperatives are to perform labor activities that may be undertaken by individuals under the November law, and only the principle addressees of that law—housewives, disabled persons, pensioners, and students—are entitled to join these cooperatives. However, the cooperatives will enjoy governmental assistance unavailable to private individuals. It is needless to explain the genuine purpose of the decree under discussion: without impinging on the November law, it strives to attract additional labor from individual labor activity to the socialized economy.

Gorbachev's tactics with respect to individual labor activities are not as simple as they may seem superficially. The new legislation shows that individual labor activity is viewed negatively by the Soviet leadership, but since the circumstances compel that it be expanded, special measures must be employed as a restrictive counterbalance. Nobody in the USSR denies this fact. At the end of his report submitted to the Supreme Soviet of the USSR, Gladkii assures the deputies that "the state will, as always, regulate individual labor activity and ensure that it is used in the interests of society. The law introduced for your consideration is also proof of this."[29] Replace "the interests of society" with the true meaning of these words in Soviet parlance, and an official interpretation emerges of that which could be otherwise essentially misinterpreted.

A third doubt arises from the purposes of the May enactments directed against extraction of unearned income. As emphasized above, the May enactments augmented the interpretation of this concept to the extent that even the labor activities of individuals could not prevent the appropriate characterization of income if these activities exceeded a very restricted number of trades allowed to Soviet citizens at that time. Could these decrees pursue the goal of struggle against private activities if six months later a new law was adopted to achieve the opposite result? And even if such a goal was pursued at the outset, did the Soviet leadership not reject or modify it by promulgating the November law?

An alternative analysis demonstrates that the issuance of the November law rendered the May enactments neither ambiguous nor incomprehensible. On the contrary, the promulgation of the November law clarified what had been unclear in the May decrees—the broad definition of unearned income, the criminalization of the concept thereof, and the unprecedented comprehensiveness of punishment for violations. Broadening the limits within which individual labor activities may be pursued can have a negative impact on the Soviet system in two respects—by stimulating an upsurge of the underground economy and by injuring the Soviet system itself.

The underground economy acquires opportunities for expansion as a result of new approaches toward individual labor activities. Some might officially register for a permitted type of handicraft or service only to disguise other activities unavailable to individuals under the November law. For instance, an individual can register his enterprise as a jewelry repair shop to manufacture jewelry under this disguise. Because individuals are entitled to produce various articles for sale, they will in all likelihood sometimes resort to private middlemen to avoid either a complicated combination of production and sale or a disadvantageous relationship with state economic entities on the basis of contracts ensuring the sale of individual products. Despite the legal prohibition, hired labor can be used in the realm of lawfully performed individual activities with less risk and greater success than where such activity itself violates the law. Soviet law allows individuals to hire only housemaids, drivers, or personal secretaries. All other types of private hiring of workers are prohibited, and as a matter of fact, there will hardly ever be undisguised acts of this character. In contrast, the same acts properly disguised were previously employed, and they will be more broadly used under the present circumstances. At any rate, underground economic activity may be substantially facilitated by the new legal regulations.

A worker hired by another individual can purchase a license at the expense of his actual employer and thus provide their unlawful relationship with a legal appearance. The concept of family members in Soviet practice must be helpful to those wishing to engage in prohibited use of hired labor. Persons not connected by marriage or kinship are nevertheless considered family members if one is a dependent of another or if both are in other specific relations. It is not difficult to contend that an actual worker is a dependent of his actual master, whereas the burden of disproving such a relationship can be very cumbersome, especially if the hired workers are disabled persons or students. Achievement of these goals is further simplified by a provision that allows a group of persons to jointly implement private labor activities. According to the meaning of the law, all participants in this group must be partners; but it is easy to employ hired workers under the disguise of partners. Thus, the creation of new areas where individual labor activities can be implemented and the procedure established for the exercise of these activities facilitate employment of privately-hired workers by representatives of the underground economy, despite the fact that both are forbidden by Soviet law.

The unavoidable linkage between legalized and underground private economies will also develop because of the problem of supplies for individual labor activities. For instance, the November law provides that automobile repair may be an authorized individual handicraft. But automobile repair usually requires the appropriate spare parts. It is well known that purchasing an automobile in the USSR can take several years of periodic registration and necessitates overcoming numerous obstacles. Acquiring spare parts is sometimes more difficult than buying a new car. Similar situations exist in almost all other spheres in which individual handicrafts are encouraged. Although the November law calls for governmental assistance in assuring the requisite supply, economic resources that can be allocated for this purpose are less than minimal compared to the new demand. When the additional demand is unsatisfied, it increases the overall shortage rather than leads to an abundance. The underground economy keeps pace with any shortage, and the greater the shortage, the broader the underground economy. The demand for individual handicrafts unsatisfied by official supplies will be unofficially satisfied by the underground economy.

These violations entail deriving unearned income only in part, for instance, as a result of using hired labor. In other respects, for example in cases of unofficial supply, the individual handicraft nevertheless leads to the derivation of labor income as this concept was interpreted before the adoption of the May enactments. Even if an individual owner of an enterprise has given a bribe to receive the required supply, not he but the appropriate planner has extracted unearned income in its proper meaning. However, the purpose of the May enactments is to interpret bribes as unearned income considered from both points of view—those of the giver and the receiver. To speak more generally, to prevent the undesirable development of individual handicrafts and simultaneously intensify the struggle against the underground economy, new legal provisions have so defined unearned income that its definition could apply under certain conditions to any income, regardless of whether it has an individual's own labor as its sole or principal source.

The Soviet system must be protected at the outset and throughout the entire process of performing individual labor activities. When an individual submits an application to the local executive committee, a dangerous situation arises. Since the acceptance or rejection of this application is within the discretion of the local bureaucracy, unrestrained by a normative enumeration of the respective legal grounds for whatever decision is taken, a more favorable inducement for bribery is inconceivable. Next, the problems of workplaces and supplies arise. Work premises can be leased through relationships with the local executive committee as a rule. But in this case, too, a positive decision depends on the official entitled to adopt it, and there is no reason to assume that each decision will be lawful and disinterested. Obtaining supplies at the expense of government resources, if the materials cannot be procured through retail-trade enterprises, requires the perpetration of two interdependent crimes: stealing of the requisite objects by workers from entities having these objects at their strictly-earmarked disposal and purchasing what has been stolen by the private enterprises.

Stealing can be combined with other crimes, should individual producers establish a direct relationship with official planners. The planners may unlawfully allocate the appropriate materials to an enterprise whose manager or other high official will be able then to transfer these materials to the interested individuals. It is unlikely that either activity will be engaged in without a bribe.

These unlawful methods are not matters of fantasy. They rest on the Soviet judicial practice of punishing crimes connected with the underground economy, modifying this practice in accordance with the peculiarities of the legally-approved private economic activities. These activities will also create their own offenses. For instance, Article 9 of the November law provides for taxing citizens' income derived from individual labor, requiring entrepreneurs to keep accounts of all revenues and expenditures connected with their businesses and to present to the local financial department a statement declaring the amount of new profit.[30] It does not require much imagination to predict how many violations will be perpetrated by working individuals and how profitable the prospects are for officials of governmental financial agencies.

Given these prospects, it is easy to understand the Soviet legislature's disposition to criminalize the concept of unearned income in contrast to its previous inclination to consider the perpetration of crimes and derivation of unearned income as separate types of unlawful conduct. Such farsightedness can be explained, however, only on the assumption that the May enactments, chronologically preceding the November law, logically resulted from the decision adopted in favor of the development of individual economies. And this chronological sequence, though logically contradictory, is psychologically irreproachable. Had the chronology been reversed, one could not interpret this other than as a substantial restriction of individual labor activities by means of intensifying the struggle against the derivation of unearned income. Owing to the actual sequence, another interpretation, less damaging from the viewpoint of propaganda, has been suggested: the struggle against unearned income is mitigated by the expansion of individual labor activities. To prevent any optimistic delusion in this respect, however, Article 1 of the November law warns its addressees: "Individual labor activity which . . . pursues the goal of deriving unearned income . . . shall not be permitted." What does "shall not be permitted" signify? To answer this question, the May enactments must be reviewed with great care.

CHAPTER

4

Interconnections between Different Economies

As demonstrated above, the state economy as such — in its undisguised (for example, state industrial enterprises) or disguised forms (such as collective farms or consumer cooperatives) — cannot, at least currently, guarantee the requisite economic efficiency, despite all the efforts of the Soviet leadership through new economic reforms. The same is not true for the economies that, in principle, are beyond the limits of the Soviet economic system. Individual labor activities and activities of the new cooperatives representing transformed individual property have yet to produce a substantial upsurge in the economic development of the USSR. However, these forms of economic activities alone have proved capable of creating certain new economic phenomena which, being developed to the level of actual demand (the volume of the appropriate activities, the level of prices available to the mass customer, etc.), can indeed encourage an economic upswing unknown in Soviet history. How can the Soviet rulers utilize this undisputable conclusion? Which organizational measures must they consider as the most reasonable in assessing the first results of their economic reforms?

Since these new economic phenomena, strange by definition to the Soviet official economy, have proved to be the only successful ones, they must be, of course, retained and developed. But their development cannot occur at the expense of the official economy because this would finally destroy the Soviet system itself—a consequence exceeding the actual goals of the new Soviet reformists. Thus, in their proper substance, these phenomena must not exceed certain restricted limits outlined by those who are entitled to decide how to save the Soviet economy from collapse and at the same time to prevent its transformation into another economic system. Despite their positive impact, the new economic phenomena cannot be developed without limits. Heavy reliance on them would compromise the Soviet leadership politically because it would be perceived as revision of the existing system under the guise of its perfection through reconstruction. Since the official economy does not work, despite all the applicable measures, and those economic phenomena that do work are foreign to the official economy, only one solution is possible—to invent organizational methods that could entail development of the official economy as a result of the appropriate employment of alien economic forms.

These organizational methods have been found. Generally, they can be called the methods of interconnections among different economies—state and cooperative, cooperative and individual, individual and state, and so forth. The types of interconnections differ. The only condition requiring a strict observance under all circumstances is that the interconnected economies are indeed and not merely terminologically different. Interconnections between state enterprises and collective farms, for instance, lead to nothing because both represent the state economy, though under different titles. Replace collective farms with the new type of cooperatives or interconnect collective farms and individual labor activities, and the desirable result will become achievable.

Resorting to interconnections between different economies as the only efficient method of rescuing the entire economic system, the Soviet leadership uses different approaches for industry and agriculture. Present day industry is based mainly on large enterprises. Small enterprises play an appropriate role; however, they are not the reason that the USSR is an industrial power. The leading role for state industrial property has never been doubted by Soviet rulers, despite the use of combinations of state, cooperative, and individual properties in this area as a stimulating factor for economic development.

In contrast, agriculture personified by small economies develops better than in cases where this activity is implemented on a larger scale. In order to stimulate development of small agricultural economies, avoiding at the same time disparagement of state and collective farms, Gorbachev declared at a plenary meeting of the CPSU Central Committee in March 1989:

> Today, it is a question of recognizing equality of different forms of socialist ownership of means of production and methods of economic activities based on them. We must open the path to many different forms of economic activities—to collective farms, state farms, peasant economies, subsidiary households, agricultural workshops of industrial, construction and

other nonagricultural enterprises, subsidiary trades, etc.[1]

This tenet seems very strange and obviously incorrect. For instance, in the USSR land is an exclusive object of state property, representing at the same time one of the principal means of production in the realm of agriculture. How can nonstate socialist ownership be equal to state ownership in this regard? In addition, socialist ownership must be represented by a collective body. Then how can peasant economies and subsidiary households rank on a par with state and collective farms? But in this case, theoretical problems do not trouble Gorbachev. He is interested in pushing the development of Soviet agriculture by combining different economic phenomena. He disregards their differences and declares their equality.

The teaching of combining different economic phenomena is at a very low level in the USSR for the time being. Soviet law, dealing with the same issue, is not very developed to date. There are numerous hints in Soviet media that the appropriate legislative development is in the process of preparation. In contrast to the law, Soviet economic practice has managed to create numerous patterns of the requisite character. The most important and the most typical of these patterns deserves to be analyzed specifically. The suggested analysis will encompass both peculiarities of each specific method and the types of economies interconnected in this way.

A. Contracting and Leases in the State Economy

Before Gorbachev's reforms, relations between employers and employees were based on labor contracts, while relations between state entities and outsiders performing ordered jobs required execution of contracts of independent work. The distinctions between these two legal forms are obvious. In the former case, employees are obliged to work within an established period in accordance with the task and under the supervision of employers who, in turn, must pay a guaranteed salary based on the time spent, even if the entire job is not completed. In the latter case, contractors are obliged to perform ordered projects independently from the customers who, in turn, must pay for these projects if they are completed and transferred to them. In contrast to labor contracts dealing with relationships inside an entity between its administration and its workers, independent work contracts regulate relationships outside an entity between the entity and its contractors.

Innovations stemming from the present reforms in this respect consist of attempts to supplement labor contracts with independent work contracts, using both for the purpose of regulating relationships within economic entities. Labor contracts are by definition adjusted to this purpose. Independent work contracts, on the contrary, represent an usual vehicle for such a goal. In combining these different institutions, the Soviet reformists strive to spur the development of the official economy from the outside, since it does not work to rely only upon internal factors.

The labor contract is an individual contract; it must be executed between the employer and each employee. The independent work contract introduced by the new economic reforms into the internal activities of state economic entities has a different character as outlined by the 1987 Law on the State Enterprise (Association).[2] It must be employed in relationships between an economic entity and its teams (*brigadi*) "as the basic collective form of labor organization and stimulation."[3] *Brigadi* are constituent parts of workshops, sections, or other principal units of enterprises. They are headed by foremen and consist of workers, but if necessary for application of independent work contracts, *brigadi* "may include engineers, technicians and other specialists."[4] Along with the *brigadi*, workshops, sections, and other similar units also may function as partners of their economic entities in the realm of independent work contracts.[5] Common practice has gone even further. For instance, there are state enterprises completely distributed among various groups of their workers by means of independent work contracts.[6] The same worker, acting as a partner of an individual labor contract, may simultaneously participate in two independent work contracts—as a member of a *brigada* and as a worker of a workshop, section, other unit, or the enterprise as a whole.

To take part in an independent work contract, a *brigada* or a workshop must be organized on the principle of economic accountability, *khozraschet*. But the *khozraschet* of these constituent parts of an economic entity must not be confused with the *khozraschet* of the economic entity itself. Earlier, the distinction was made between full *khozraschet* and internal *khozraschet*. Full *khozraschet*, applicable to economic entities, signifies that they may establish relationships of goods-money exchange with other entities, acquiring rights and bearing duties in these relationships, including the duty to be responsible for their acts separately both from a higher organization and the Soviet state. In comparison, internal *khozraschet* means that a constituent

206

part of an economic entity, provided with the necessary equipment and materials, receives a planned task from its entity defining the quality and quantity of output, their cost, etc. No contracts outside the economic entity are permissible for a constituent part. But at the end of a planned period, its actual results must be compared with planned indicators, and the receipt of bonuses or their deprivation or reduction will depend on the character of a deduced proportion as favorable or detrimental to the appropriate constituent part of an economic entity.

This internal *khozraschet* can be supplemented by independent work contracts. The impact of internal *khozraschet* on the income of workers is well-known: a planned task must be fulfilled or overfulfilled in order to receive ordinary or increased bonuses. Yet the permanent portion of an established salary cannot be affected by the success or failure of internal *khozraschet*. What about independent work contracts executed between the administration of an economic entity and a workshop or *brigada*? Until now, no model contract of this type nor specific contracts actually applicable have been published. At any rate, this contract employed to regulate the labor activities of an economic entity's own workers must differ immensely from an independent work contract executed between the same entity and another individual or collective partner.

First, both partners of the independent work contract in its proper meaning must be subjects of law—physical or juridical persons (legal entities). *Brigadi* or workshops as constituent parts of an economic entity cannot be juridical persons. They are also precluded from qualification as groups of physical persons because each is organized as a single whole, and an independent work contract is executed with this single whole, not with all of its workers. Hence, there is a new independent work contract executed between an economic entity and its constituent part.

Second, a new type of independent work contract cannot eliminate legal guarantees allocated to workers by the labor legislation. In this respect, two guarantees are especially important:

(1) a worker must receive a minimum of salary even if he has not completely fulfilled his labor task by the established time; and

(2) the risk of the accidental loss of performance is borne by the employer, not by the worker.

These are the legal consequences of all labor contracts. The independent work contract entails the opposite consequences:

(1) nonperformance of an ordered task precludes payment to the contractor; and

(2) the contractor bears the risk of loss from an accident.

It is not the individual workers but the appropriate constituent parts of an economic entity that function as contractors in the new type of independent work contract. If a contractor receives no payment for as long as the work is uncompleted, it will have no resources for payment of salaries to its workers. At the same time, it is the workers who must compensate for accidental damage, since the contractor bears the risk of loss. Under these regulations, the independent work contracts could indeed stimulate an increase in the productivity of the official economy. But on the one hand, this new stimulation has only a punitive character and contains no positive incentives. On the other hand, it contradicts the certain privileges mandated by labor legislation and left intact by the present reforms.

The most realistic predictions of the specific forms of the independent work contracts employed under new circumstances for the achievement of specific purposes follow:

(a) Nonperformance of ordered tasks must entail fines imposed on the contractor and compensated by the fund of bonuses allocated to it in larger amounts than in the absence of an independent work contract. It is also possible that the guaranteed minimum salary will be decreased for workers participating in the activity of a constituent part that is a partner of an independent work contract executed with its economic entity;

(b) A great number of other incentives may be withdrawn more from workers of a contractor than from other workers who do not perform their labor tasks (for example, incentives connected with the distribution of living space, places in nursing homes, sanatoriums, etc.); and

(c) All of the positive incentives provided by laws in force for certain labor achievements will be increased in the realm of relationships based on independent contracts. This must affect the size of bonuses for timely or accelerated performance of the ordered jobs, the preferable allocation of living space, and other goods whose distribution depends on labor achievements.

The efficiency of certain moral factors must also be considered. If the effort of each worker affects the results of the entire collective body of a contractor, there will be peer pressure to push the activity to the highest possible level.

However, all these stimuli arising from the employment of independent work contracts in the official Soviet economy do not appear to be as highly efficient from the hindsight of the eventual result. The point is that to call the execution of these contracts within an economic entity an interconnection of different economies is a great inaccuracy. Of course, a state economic entity and its workers included in a team (brigade) or workshop (section) represent different interests in an executed contract. But these interests exist within the same enterprise or association, and the impact of outside factors on official economic activities cannot be too successful under the circumstances.

A different nature is intrinsic to family contracts entailing performance of independent works. This system is also covered by the same legal provisions.[7] It is clear, however, that in contrast to teams (brigades) and workshops (sections), separate families as partners in the contract under discussion can perform only very restricted types of tasks. The 1987 law itself considers this indisputable fact in emphasizing that independent work contracts shall be "basic collective forms of labor organization and stimulation" with respect to teams or brigades, while with respect to families, these contracts can be applied only "if necessary."[8]

From the viewpoint of its legal character and economic efficiency, family independent work contracts substantially differ from those executed between an economic entity and any of its constituent parts. A family as a contractual partner does not consist of workers connected by a labor contract with the other partner—an economic entity. In this

210

case an interconnection between different economies actually exists: an economic entity represents state property, while the family personifies individual property. As a result, the economic efficiency of contracts executed with families must be higher for an economic entity than in relationships with its own constituent parts.

According to Soviet law, a family is not a subject of law as a single whole. It consists of two or more physical persons connected either by marriage or kinship. To consider a whole family as a partner of a contract, this contract must be signed by all family members or by the head of the family legally acting as its representative. It does not matter whether certain members of this family are or are not workers of an economic entity under contract. Under all circumstances, family members take part in independent work contracts as strangers with respect to the economic entity, the other contractual partner. This signifies that even if a member of a family is a regular worker at the economic entity, a labor contract between them has no connection with an independent work contract involving the same family. As a matter of course, such a family member must fulfill his duties arising from a family contract only during his free time from his duties based on his labor contract.

If a family executes an independent work contract only as a group of physical persons, this institution cannot be considered as a family contract. Each family member would be obliged to fulfill his or her duty, remaining unaffected by the nonperformance or improper performance of other family members. This would, of course, diminish the stimulating role of family contracts. To oblige a family as a whole by an executed contract, it is necessary to establish its joint liability for contractual performance. Liability is joint *per se* if an ordered work is indivisible, as for instance, construction of a barn. Divisibility of a contractual endeavor, entailing the production of a certain number of homogeneous items, requires inclusion into the contract of a special term providing joint liability. Only because of such a term does an executed contract acquire the features of a family contract.

A family contract of independent work is not connected with the labor contracts of family members, and as a consequence, privileges arising from labor contracts cannot affect the appropriate family contracts. Family contracts can be qualified as independent work contracts in their proper meaning. This signifies that an economic entity as a customer must define the work whose performance is imposed upon a family and provide this family with materials and other items necessary for performance. Accidental damage to materials or other items is the risk of the economic entity. The family's duties are to use proper care with respect to materials and other items received from the customer, to employ them economically in the process of production, and to perform the work according to the customer's order and in the time agreed between partners. The family as a contractor bears the risk of an accidental loss of performance. The contract can provide two forms of payment for ordered tasks—either by installment after completion of each work stage or at once after completion of the entire job. Regardless of the specific form chosen, the contractor acquires the right to receive payment only after performance of the appropriate work. Payment of an advance can be provided, but a guaranteed minimum payment is not applicable in this case.

From the standpoint of economic stimulation, family contracts for independent work are more advantageous

than independent work contracts executed between an economic entity and its constituent parts. But such independent work contracts are preferable to family contracts from
another point of view: constituent parts of economic entities can fulfill on the basis of an independent work contract
the same tasks that they have to fulfill in general, while
families as partners in independent work contracts are
capable of dealing only with certain types of work requisite
for an economic entity. Assessing various legal constructions employed by economic entities to establish interconnections between different economies, it must be concluded
that the contract for the lease of a state enterprise or one of
its constituent parts encompasses various works necessary
for the appropriate entities. The idea for such leases has
been expressed by Soviet officials in numerous cases. Its
most eloquent expression can be found in a report submitted by the USSR Minister of Finance, B.I. Gosteev, to the
Eleventh Session of the Supreme Soviet of the USSR on
October 27, 1988.[9]

At first, the Minister characterized the deplorable
financial situation of numerous state enterprises:

> It is necessary to decisively refuse the existing practice
> of automatically covering losses [by the state budget].
> Unprofitable enterprises exist at another's expense,
> they bear great losses, but they do not feel those losses
> in the realm of payment for labor. The sharpness of the
> situation is evidenced by the fact that as a result of this
> cause 10-11 billion rubles of the people's money are
> yearly lost. About 24 thousand enterprises of different
> branches work unprofitably.[10]

Trying to find a way out from these difficulties, the Minister formulates his suggestion:

> Large reserves are embodied in the development of lease relations with respect to means of production not only in the realm of agriculture but also in other branches. The lease has as its economic basis the increase of responsibility of interests of labor collectives to improve employment of socialist property.[11]

The problem, however, is the legal significance of the lease of an enterprise or its constituent part if rented by the labor collective of either. Neither collective body is a subject of law—a juridical person. How then will they be able to rent an enterprise or a constituent part of this enterprise, as according to *Izvestia*, a department store's labor collective in Gorky has already done?[12] The Minister answers this question as well:

> In accordance with a governmental order, ministries and departments of the USSR, and Councils of Ministers of Union Republics have developed a plan for the liquidation of unprofitable enterprises, in principle, during the next year. . . . It is necessary to broaden the transfer of unprofitable enterprises and separate production sections through leases to labor collectives, by transforming them into cooperatives.[13]

Legal problems cannot, of course, be explained in such a way, but the economic necessity employing this unusual legal form entails no doubts. The ministerial call was preceded or answered in various forms. For the purpose of illustration, the following example can be used, despite the fact that it preceded the Minister's report. Three days

214

before this report was issued, *Izvestia* published an article entitled "Arguments in Favor of the Lease—Why a State Enterprise Longs to Become a Cooperative?"[14] The author states:

> A workshop manufacturing consumer goods within the Tomsk oil-chemical combine . . . was a burden on the enterprise. Its plan called for the production of 14 million rubles worth of products per year, but it managed to produce only 3 million in half a year. . . . The general manager of the combine [decided] to disband this unprofitable workshop and to transfer it on the basis of a lease to a cooperative called Avangard. . . . The first thing that the cooperative did was to retain only 85 of the 140 previous workers. And a local miracle occurred: in two months production increased 2.5 times. Output per cooperative member increased to tens of thousands of units—triple the previous rate. Avangard began not only to perform its contracts of delivery but also to pay the debts of the previous workshop. It is clear that the workers' salaries were also increased.[15]

What does this anthem in favor of cooperatives mean in comparison with the very low economic results achieved by its predecessor, a state enterprise's workshop? Is this a call to replace the state economy with a cooperative one in its proper significance, or must Gorbachev's reforms be interpreted differently?

As a matter of course, the Soviet leadership does not intend to completely transform the state economy into a cooperative one. Leasing state economic entities or their constituent parts is employed with respect to small enterprises or their workshops and only in cases where the latter proved to be unprofitable. Bearing in mind the increased freedom of cooperatives, especially in the realm of prices, cooperatives are capable of extracting a profit especially where state enterprises suffer unprofitability. What is more important, through leases, the state enterprises or their constituent parts are not transformed into components of the purely cooperative economy. The Soviet state represented by its entity as a lessor retains the right of ownership with respect to rented objects; accordingly, cooperative organizations acting as lessees are only users, not owners, of the same objects. In these cases the executed contracts contemplate not the transformation of the state economy into a cooperative one but the combination of both economies interconnected in a form that ensures employment of state property by cooperative organizations. Because this combination is based on contracts of lease, the state acquires new dominant advantages over the cooperative sectors.

A contract of lease can contain various terms, including those that restrict the cooperative's discretion guaranteed by law. For instance, the 1988 Law on Cooperation includes two important provisions:

(1) Cooperatives sell products and goods of their own production, fulfill orders and provide services in accordance with prices and tariffs established by agreements between cooperatives and consumers or independently by cooperatives;[16] and

(2) A cooperative is entitled to voluntarily accept fulfillment of state orders.[17]

The first provision concerning prices can be modified in various directions by a contract of lease, for instance, requiring that a cooperative abstain from exceeding certain price levels, that it pay rent by in-kind tendering of a certain amount of produced products free of charge, that it sell at a discount a defined quantify of manufactured items either to the lessor or a third party, and so forth. The second provision concerning state orders can also be modified by a contract providing that the lessee must not only pay rent in the appropriate form but also accept state orders encompassing a certain portion of produced products. Such a contractual term will result in other restrictions on the cooperative activity implemented by the lessee. Under these circumstances, the lessee will be obliged by the 1988 Law on Cooperation to take into account the accepted state orders in the process of developing its economic activities,[18] and apply centralized prices to products furnished in accordance with state orders. It is true that if in executing a contract a state partner burdens a cooperative partner with duties reducing almost to zero the cooperative's economic freedom, the interconnections between the state and cooperative economies will hardly be efficient. Within reasonable limits, leases of enterprises or their constituent parts executed between state entities as lessors and cooperative organizations as lessees can play an important role as a state regulator of cooperative activities.

One special consequence of the interconnections between state and cooperative economies results from provisions concerning cooperative membership. As emphasized above, Soviet leaders strive to prevent a shift of labor from state entities to cooperative organizations. In principle, they accept such a shift only in cases where a worker of a state entity functions as a member of a cooperative during time off from his or her official job or where cooperatives are created as outgrowths of state entities. The transformation of a labor collective into a cooperative as an eventual lessee with respect to a state enterprise or its constituent parts has a different character. As the lessee, the cooperative will be connected with the lessor personified by a state entity. In this regard, the new cooperative can be considered as another form of a state entity. In such cases another point seems more important. As a rule, unprofitable enterprises or their constituent parts must be used, if possible, as objects of leases between state entities and cooperative organizations. According to Soviet policy with respect to unprofitability discussed above, these entities or their departments must be liquidated. Practice will demonstrate the extent to which the proclaimed policy is realistic and implementable. But one thing is clear from the outset: each case of liquidation will result in numerous cases of unemployment. The creation of cooperatives will detract labor from the state economy only to the extent that this labor is surplus. Such a shift in labor seems quite reasonable, and employing this form of interconnections among different economies, the Soviet leadership actually strives to simultaneously achieve two goals—preventing unemployment and avoiding unprofitability.

B. State Trade and Cooperative or Individual Economies

Cooperative and individual economies can be connected with state trade on both sides—supply and sale. The forms of these connections differ. The only thing that must be taken into account is that state trade in the USSR means not only state stores but also consumer cooperative stores. As demonstrated above, consumer cooperatives are in fact disguised state entities, and there are advantages to the Soviet system owing to this disguise. A particular advantage stems from the employment of consumer cooperatives as a means of selling products and providing services resulting from cooperative or individual labor activities. State shops are bound by centrally established prices. Even second-hand state consignment shops selling used consumer items define prices on the basis of agreements between these shops and their customers and must observe certain limits introduced by law in force. In contrast, consumer cooperatives are bound only by agreements between them and cooperative or individual producers in the process of defining prices for the goods or services to be provided. This is why a foreigner visiting Soviet food stores is so astonished by the striking difference between state and cooperative trade entities—low prices and empty shelves in the former in contrast to expensive yet sufficient supplies in the latter.

There are certain cooperatives that completely depend on the appropriate state entities in the process of their activity and its material maintenance. For instance, an enterprise in Yerevan created a cooperative labeled S.I.M.[19] The purpose of this cooperative is to eliminate emotional stress through a twenty-minute session in a psychologist's office. It is clear that, providing workers and officials within a given enterprise's premises with its service, S.I.M. could neither exist nor function without permanent relationships with this enterprise. The same is also sometimes true for individuals implementing private labor activities. Individuals are prohibited from owning photocopying machines in the USSR. This ban retains its force even in the epoch of Gorbachev's *glasnost'*. If an individual worker specializes in the repair of these machines, he can apply his labor only on the basis of orders received from Soviet entities. It is obvious that owing to such peculiar connections between state and cooperative or individual economies, the state entities acquire extraordinary opportunities to regulate the activities of their partners, either cooperatives or individuals. These same connections strengthen the economic efficiency that is vital to the Soviet system. The Soviet state can provide useful services without spending its own time and money, as the existence of the S.I.M. cooperative persuasively illustrates. It can also satisfy certain specific demands of state entities and avoid the creation of some state enterprises, as exemplified by the individual repair of photocopy machines.

Putting aside certain extraordinary circumstances, one must clearly understand the general character of the interconnections under discussion in the area of supplies received by the cooperatives or individuals from the state and the sale of products and provision of services through the state by cooperatives or individuals.

Beginning with the problem of supply, materials and other products necessary for cooperative or individual labor activities can be bought at collective farm markets where free prices prevail. Specifically, cooperatives and individuals establish prices for their products and services exclusively by agreements executed between them and their customers. This form of supply, though the most broadly available, has substantial shortcomings. Prices at collective farms are incomparably higher than in the state system of trade. As a result, the prices charged for cooperative or individual products or services must be that much higher. Nevertheless, cooperatives and individuals can compete with the state system of trade, where prices are lower but supply is far behind demand. At the same time, the new type of cooperatives and individual labor activities have not yet reached the demand posed by even the rich layers of the Soviet populace. Competition between cooperatives and individual workers cannot result in any decrease in prices. Such an impact does seem unavoidable in the future, when cooperative and individual economies will be more broadly developed. If, at that time, the food supply produced by the state does not change its present inadequate status, prices at collective farm markets will retain their very high levels, while cooperatives and individual workers will be compelled by reciprocal competition to diminish their prices, and consequently, their economic crash will be inevitable. By attracting certain customers of the state system of trade now, the new cooperatives and individual workers mitigate the economic difficulties at the present time. But this effect is only temporary, and if the state supply is not substantially improved during a restricted period, its own collapse will cause the collapse of the system of cooperative and individual labor activities.

Another critical fact is that collective farm markets can provide only food, while the new cooperatives and individual workers more frequently require technical and technological inputs. Unlawful supply aside, there is a restricted number of ways to resolve this problem.

The new type of cooperatives can generate the requisite supply through purchase in the state system of retail trade. This source of supply is unreliable because of the deficits permanently prevailing in the state retail shops. In resorting to this form of supply, cooperatives immediately lose one of their most important privileges—freedom of prices. They must apply centrally established prices or tariffs. Certain mark-ups are possible only if cooperatives add their own labor to items bought in a state retail shop.[20] For instance, the repair of an automobile by using a spare part from a state store can and will be more expensive than the centrally established price for the spare part. If a cooperative only resells items bought in a state retail shop, this procedure is economically senseless both for the state, which does not even slightly mitigate the economic difficulties of the populace, and for the cooperative which must resell at prices equal to purchase prices. In contrast, the same procedure acquires significance for the entire economy if cooperatives add their labor and provide the populace with services that, as in the case of private automobile repairs, exceed the capacities of the state economic system. In this regard, interconnections between state and cooperative economies function as a positive factor. But the new type of cooperatives have no privileges as purchasers in the state system of retail trade compared to citizens as the principal customers in this area. Therefore, retail trade can hardly play a significant role in the supply of cooperative activities.

The second source of supply available to cooperatives can be created by contracts of delivery executed either directly with a state producer or at so-called wholesale fairs.[21] The contracts of direct delivery are available to cooperatives only with respect to portions of a producer's product that exceed the indicators of state orders. As previous experience proves, these excess portions either do not exist or they are reduced to insignificant amounts. Wholesale fairs are periodically sponsored by Gossnab and are usually held in Moscow. Each economic entity is entitled to sell products in amounts defined by planned limits. A seller can be chosen by any purchaser allowed to take part in these fairs. The necessary permission to buy and sell is given only to Soviet entities, not to Soviet citizens. Since cooperatives also have such a right, they can acquire the requisite goods by means of contracts of delivery executed at these wholesale fairs. However, acquisition of goods either by direct contracts of delivery or by those executed at wholesale fairs brings the same consequences that arise from acquisition through the state system of retail trade. The above-mentioned restrictions legally and economically resulting in the state system are also applicable to the wholesale fairs.

The third source of supply opened by law to cooperatives is connected with state orders. As the 1988 Law on Cooperation emphasizes, all economic relations between cooperatives and other entities are to be based only on contractual principles: "The contract is the only legal and economic document regulating all economic relations of cooperatives."[22] The same principles must be applied to state orders: it is not governmental commands but executed contracts that impose on a cooperative a duty to fulfill a state order.[23] Execution of these contracts significantly affects supply; a state entity functioning as a customer must provide a cooperative as a contractor with objects necessary to fulfill a state order. In these cases, prices of products furnished by the cooperative or services provided by it are defined either centrally or, if the laws allow, by contracts based on state orders. As a result, economic opportunities retained by cooperatives are substantially diminished. Nevertheless, acceptance of state orders can be reasonable for cooperatives if, deprived of other supplies, they must use this specific source. In addition, fulfillment of state orders ensures a certain profit to cooperatives, taking into account the application of their own labor and the possibility of defining prices by free contract. For the appropriate state entities, imposition of state orders on cooperatives is reasonable without exception. Otherwise they would not execute a contract with a cooperative obliging it to fulfill a state order. In this case, too, interconnection between state and cooperative economies is economically efficient.

In contrast to the new type of cooperatives, individual labor activities have even fewer sources of supply. They can employ neither state orders nor contracts of delivery, both direct contracts and those executed at wholesale fairs. Along with materials submitted by customers, individual workers functioning lawfully strive to provide themselves with raw materials, tools, and other equipment either at collective farm markets or in state retail shops. But like the new cooperatives, they realize the well-known fact that collective farm markets supply only food, and state retail shops have never had the entire assortment of objects necessary for individual labor activities. In addition, the mere resale of purchased objects by individuals (not by cooperatives) constitutes the Soviet crime of speculation. To avoid committing criminal acts, individuals must add their labor to acquired objects before selling them to their customers. Has the Soviet law dedicated to individual labor activities ignored the problem of supply of these activities? The November law contains only an abstract provision declaring that local executive committees and other organizations must assist citizens who engage in individual labor activities with regard to purchasing raw materials, supplies, tools, and other necessary objects.[24] These words present only an abstract declaration, not a legal provision. An individual has no right, referring to such a declaration, to demand from an executive committee the requisite supply, and the executive committee bears no correlative duties toward an individual. Of course, a higher governmental agency, auditing activities of a subordinate executive committee, can note shortcomings in the organized supply of individual labor. Even if this occurred, criticism addressed to the local executive committee could be significant only for relationships between this committee and a superior governmental agency, not for individual rights in relation to the Soviet government. Gorbachev's reforms, enlarging the legal opportunities for individual labor, waste no efforts in assisting this labor economically. How can the authors of the present reforms assume that they will achieve the appropriate results by means of expansion of individual labor? What facts have been taken into consideration?

The Soviet leaders know that the underground economy exists in the USSR. As a matter of fact, they also imagine the approximate volume of this economy. Maintaining a strong struggle against the underground economy, they understand that its complete elimination is impossible because economic demands have always been stronger than legal prohibitions. Through the liberalization of individual labor activities and the concurrent protection of supply, the Soviet rulers silently proceed from the supposition that sources of this supply will be found by individuals themselves where the punitive hand of Soviet law has proved to be powerless. It is clear, however, that serious governmental policy cannot be based solely or even primarily on such an assumption. Other steps have been taken, and economically they deserve more attention, namely because in this case, too, interconnections between various economies play a decisive role. To understand these other steps, it is necessary to leave the issue of supply and concentrate on sales transactions represented either by individual workers or by the new cooperatives.

It is interesting that the same legal declaration that calls on local executive committees to assist individual workers with their supply needs contains a special reservation establishing that this assistance must be rendered first to those who conclude contracts with enterprises, institutions, and other organizations and who carry on their labor activity in accordance with these contracts.[25] The purpose of this command is clear. Individual workers, although entitled to deal directly with their customers, must prefer to function through Soviet entities as intermediaries in the process of selling goods produced or providing services by individual labor. To establish this intermediary step, it is necessary to execute a contract that can embody numerous important terms, including the transfer of products to a Soviet entity or provision of services according to the indications of this entity and the corollary receipt from the entity of all supplies necessary to fulfill its orders. As a result, the official Soviet economy receives additional products or services, while the individual Soviet economy is assured with the requisite supply. Once more, interconnections between different economies, not a separate functioning of that which is allowed as something accessory or subsidiary, serves as a method to achieve positive results in the process of implementation of new economic reforms. This is why the most important forms of legalized individual labor activities such as boarding services for tourists, sightseers, and others can be implemented only on the basis of contracts with state enterprises or other Soviet entities.

The appropriate Soviet entities can function as intermediaries with respect to products and services connected not only with individual labor but also with the activities of the new cooperatives. First of all, the 1988 Law on Cooperation, dealing with contracts available to cooperatives, generally establishes that cooperatives can execute contracts with various customers for their products, works, and services. Among these customers, individual citizens occupy the lowest place. The enumeration begins with a reference to state, other cooperative, and societal enterprises and organizations.[26] Sometimes these customers acquire cooperative products as direct consumers, for instance, if a cooperative produces constituent parts of products assembled at a state enterprise. There are no obstacles, however, to purchase for the purpose of resale, such as a consumer cooperative acquiring products from a cooperative of the new type. Products, works, and services originating with the new type of cooperatives can be connected with production or sale implemented by other Soviet entities. This interconnection must be based on reciprocal advantages. Cooperatives, losing price freedom, can impose on their partners the duty of supply, while their partners, burdened with this duty, can liberate themselves from certain types of activities better suited for the functions of cooperatives.

A general provision discussed above is implemented in the 1988 Law on Cooperation by two special rules concerning state orders:

(1) a cooperative is entitled to accept performance of a state order; and
(2) in this case the requisite supply must be ensured by the customer — that is, by the appropriate agency of the state.[27]

The guaranteed supply attracts the new type of cooperatives to accept state orders despite the loss of price freedom, while the Soviet state thus acquires opportunities to include the cooperative activities into the all-embracing development of the planned Soviet economy. Relying on interconnections between different economies in this case, the Soviet reformists strive to use a private economy in a cooperative form as a stimulus for development of the dominant economy in the grasp of the ruling elite.

C. Collective Farms and Combinations of Leases and Independent Work Contracts

The forms of interconnections between different economies under discussion here and especially below pertain exclusively to agricultural activities. Because a general CPSU program concerning these activities was set forth by the March 1989 plenary meeting of the CPSU Central Committee, first and foremost, by Gorbachev's report entitled "On Agrarian Politics of the CPSU under Contemporary Conditions,"[28] it seems reasonable to describe this program briefly and then address different forms of its implementation actually employed before promulgation of the appropriate Party decisions.

The declared program gives the general impression that the Soviet leadership, understanding the inefficiency of agriculture based on the collective (state) farm system, intends neither to liquidate this system nor leave it unmodified. The March plenary meeting, developing its program, relied on the following premises:

(a) Collective and state farms must remain now as previously as the principal link of agricultural production. However, the structure of collective farms

228

must be radically renovated to transform them into "cooperatives of cooperatives." The same approach is actually applicable to state farms;

(b) This transformation requires creation of cooperatives of lessees of the appropriate constituent parts of collective (state) farms' economies that will perform agricultural activities in accordance with contracts executed with collective (state) farms as lessors. Under certain specific circumstances, collective (state) farms can function either as before or they can rely on independent work contracts with brigades, links, and other internal departments in exceptional situations;

(c) Agricultural activities of peasant families and individual peasants must be restored on the basis of the lease of land whose development will play one of the decisive roles in the process of reconstruction of economic relationships in rural areas. The rights of subsidiary households of laborers (not only collective farmers) also must be completely restored; and

(d) In the future, individual and collective producers will be independent in the resolution of all problems connected with their agricultural activities and price freedom will stimulate them to produce what is necessary for the state and society. However, free prices cannot be introduced immediately. During the transitional period (its duration is not even approximately outlined), the mandatory discipline of the state procurement of agricultural produce must retain its binding force.[29]

To begin the analysis of the various forms of agricultural activities developed in practice and approved by the CPSU Central Committee, it is necessary to consider leases and independent work contracts combined by collective farms.

As discussed above, collective farms, considered formally as cooperative organizations in the realm of agriculture, are actually state entities disguised in a cooperative form. Bearing in mind their actual substance, many of the causes of the inefficiency of Soviet agriculture can be understood. Previously one of the greatest suppliers of agricultural produce in the world market, the USSR began to lose this position in 1928, precisely when the policy of replacement of individual farming by collective farms began to be implemented. At the present time, more than sixty years after the beginning of the mass creation of collective farms, the USSR is one of the largest importers of agricultural produce because domestic production cannot completely satisfy the populace's demand. This reveals the low productivity of collective farm labor.

To raise this productivity, Stalin's successors, particularly Khrushchev, have tried to approach the problem from two different sides—state procurement of agricultural produce and organization of labor in collective farms. During Stalin's time, state procurement was so organized that almost all agricultural produce had to be transferred to the state on the basis of purely symbolic prices completely unrelated to cost. As a result, collective farmers received almost nothing for their labor and earned their living by cultivating small plots of land allocated to them by collective farms. After Stalin's death, the system of state procurement of agricultural produce was gradually modified. The amounts extracted became relatively stable for five-year periods;

these amounts did not encompass what was necessary for the current activity of collective farms, and procurement prices reached higher levels, but still lower than cost. Even increased payment for individual labor in collective farms, resulting from all of these substantial changes, did not suffice to stimulate the labor activities of collective farmers. Their own small economies continued to be the principal source of their livelihood. Therefore, numerous attempts were made to reorganize the labor process in collective farms and appropriately renovate the system of compensation for collective farmers' labor. These attempts failed, as would be expected, considering the low priority given to economic incentives. It became obvious that to push agricultural development a different approach had to be employed. This approach consists of interconnections between collective farm and other economies in different forms.

At first, independent work contracts were applied to relationships between the board and brigades or other sections of collective farms. These contracts relied on principles identical to those discussed above with respect to state economic entities. Each brigade or other section began to work on the basis of internal economic accountability, *vnutrennii khozraschet*, and actual economic results were compared with the task outline established by the collective farm's board. This comparison determined the payment received by a brigade or other section and, in the final analysis, the remuneration due to each collective farmer.[30] The previous analysis of this method in connection with state economic entities referred to its shortcomings and resultant economic futility. The same conclusions are true for independent work contracts whose partners are brigades or other sections of collective farms. The point is that these contracts combine collective farms and outsiders only in appearance. In reality, brigades or other sections are constituent parts of a collective farm, and therefore they cannot spur the development of a collective farm's economy as a stimulus generated from outside. As a result, managers of state and collective farms often replace contracts by orders in these cases, as has been reported on a state farm in the Saratov region.[31] As a matter of course, instead of a combined lease and independent work contracts, which define the rights and duties of both parties, the orders of the managers enumerate only the state farm's rights and the lessees' and contractors' duties.

Taking into account the negative results of internal leases and independent contracts, the 1988 Law on Cooperation proclaims collective or independent family contracts as the principal form of economic/production relations within collective farms.[32] Previously such a combined contract was unknown to Soviet law. There existed two different contracts:

(1) the lease, entitling one person, the lessee, to the temporary use of the property of another, the lessor, who, in turn, acquired the right to receive payment for the use of the property; and

(2) the independent work contract, according to which a contractor is obliged to fulfill a specific task at his or her own risk under an order of a customer either from the contractor's or the customer's materials, and the customer is obliged to accept and pay for the work fulfilled.

Combination of both contracts under the title collective or family lease and independent contracts has resulted from reforms addressed to Soviet agriculture, being first formulated by the 1988 Law on Cooperation. This law considers the appropriate collectives and families as labor sections of collective farms; however, they must function on the basis not of internal *khozraschet*, as in the cases of brigade independent contracts, but of full *khozraschet*, like collective farms themselves. Moreover, a combined contract can entitle these *khozraschet* collective bodies to sell independently their products, use extracted profit, including payments for labor and other expenses, and to open their own accounts in banking establishments.[33] As a result, collective bodies organized in this way function more as economically separate outsiders than as relatively independent sections of collective farms. In these cases different economies—those of collective farms and of groups of individuals—are interconnected not only formally but also in fact.

Consider the example of a married couple who were the first to execute a combined contract in the region of Orel.[34] A local collective farm had a piggery that would be cheaper to burn than maintain (the cost to produce a metric centner of pork was 800 rubles). The couple, the Mutsanovs, entered into a combined lease and independent work contracts in connection with this piggery. The contract obliged the couple to supply the collective farm with pork at the price of 130 rubles per ton. Nine months passed, and the couple recorded the first results: expenses—67,000 rubles, receipts—86,000 rubles, cost—seven times lower than the collective farm's.

In assessing this example, bear in mind a peculiarity of Soviet media: they have always exaggerated the successes of new measures adopted by the Soviet leadership, and this peculiarity has not disappeared despite *glasnost'*. Of course, the contract under discussion can end up with not only successes but also failures. The article referred to actually recognizes such a possibility, finishing the story with the words, "Such masters . . . as the Matsunovs can feed the entire country, others cannot."[35] Despite the exaggeration, one fact seems doubtless: because this combined contract pushes the private initiative to the foreground, it can revive the agricultural economy of collective farms whose present status is more pitiable than ever before. The limits of this initiative differ. For instance, the Novonikolaev district of the region Volgograd is one in which all collective farms but one have been completely transferred to this organizational method. As a result small groups of collective farmers of the entire district can enjoy economic freedom previously unavailable to them. However, the contracts executed between collective farms and numerous groups of collective farmers predetermine the amounts of produce and land that must be used to achieve this goal. Thus, the actual economic freedom of partners of collective farms has proved to be more restricted than expected.[36]

What sort of psychological atmosphere surrounds this new economic construction? The policy of the Soviet leadership seems sufficiently clear: the new arrangement must be maintained and developed. This can be demonstrated by numerous examples such as that of a meeting in the CPSU Central Committee on May 13, 1988 dedicated exclusively to this issue. The report on this meeting is entitled "The Combined Lease and Independent Work Contracts Are the Closest Way to Food Sufficiency."[37] In his introductory speech at the meeting Gorbachev emphasized:

> We formulate the issue as follows: nobody can refuse or preclude a person from employing an independent work contract, including combination of this contract

with a lease. Nobody is entitled to refuse them. Moreover, one cannot be trusted with the administration of a collective farm or state farm[38] if one takes the path of refusal and precludes the transformation to these new forms of work.[39]

In contrast, lower level officials often behave differently. Consider, for instance, the article "Is It Easy to Become a Lessee?"[40] The following excerpt from this article illustrates how certain bureaucrats meet the suggestions on the availability of free labor by means of combining leases and independent work contracts:

A dry intellect of a staff official could not assimilate imagination on and about swing of free labor. While a story was told [by an eventual lessee] the manager [of a state farm] only calculated how much the lessees would earn if they would be able indeed to supplement cows with gooses and karps. . . . [Then a discussion between two eventual partners arose.] Klimov [a lessee] asked a farm for a five-year lease, but the manager gave it only for one year. . . . The lessee desired independence, but he was compelled to accept the supervision of specialists. He desired to ensure his own supply of fodder, but the manager insisted that all produce be sold to the state farm and that fodder be bought from it, prohibiting the establishment of any relations with outsiders besides the state farms.[41]

In other words, the manager of the state farm did everything possible to preclude execution of a contract that represented a group of contracts supported by the Soviet leadership.

Lessees also receive hostile treatment from those peasants who are reluctant to follow the same pattern. One journalist published an article under the title, "Envy and Laziness Hinder the Family Lease and Independent Work Contracts."[42] According to this article, a family that executed a contract of lease of a stock breeding farm was characterized in its own village as a *kulak*, meaning a representative of private enterprise liquidated in the USSR long ago. Condemning this family, one inhabitant of the village said, "Many were offered the chance to employ the family lease and independent work contracts in the realm of stock breeding, but only this family agreed."[43] It is evident that the new forms of agricultural activities do not yet evoke the trust of the Soviet peasantry.

Another problem, that of relations between collective or state farms and their contractual partners, is also important. Must the partners be equal or is rigid subordination of lessees to lessors more preferable? The question is not as easy to answer as it looks at first glance. Compare two examples.

One group of agricultural managers thinks that lessees must be independent, and "if we [collective farms or state farms] need produce from a peasant, we must interest him economically."[44] The same author continues: "For instance, we tell vegetable growers: 'Sell vegetables to our state farms, and we will pay 20 rubles per metric centner under the state procurement price of 15 rubles.' Tell me, will they then bring their vegetables themselves?"[45] Is this not genuine economic freedom completely acceptable for lessees? It would seem so if the author did not explain how this state farm could avoid losses under such a purchasing scheme. But he did: "The state farm has no surplus money. In order to avoid losses, we will sell you [the lessees] sowing seeds more expensively but of better quality. We will also sell water more expensively but deliver more quickly. . . . In one word, the difference in money which we have lost must be compensated in accordance with the requisite profitability."[46]

Another group of agricultural managers maintains the opposite view: lessees must be strictly subordinated to lessors—collective and state farms. For instance, to feed cattle a lessee needs grassland. The chairman of a collective farm was ready to rent out 150 hectares but on the condition that the lessee would fulfill a portion of state orders accepted by the collective farm and all other duties proportionally connected with this land.[47] The lessees dealing with collective or state farms cannot require economic freedom. Their detailed dependence on these farms must be retained despite the execution of leases and independent work contracts.

Which method is preferable—economic freedom or binding subordination? No one can answer this question better than the lessees themselves, especially if their opinions coincide with the lessors' views. In this respect, an article "What Is the Risk of the Lessee"[48] is illustrative. It deserves to be quoted in depth, demonstrating not only the attitude of lessors and lessees toward the issue under discussion but also the actual impact of the new phenomenon on the old collective farm system.

A journalist asks the chairman of a collective farm in the Saratov region:

Did your lessor become a genuine independent master enjoying full rights? He is strongly bound to the collective farm: you dictate to him what and how much he must cultivate, and to whom and at what price he must

sell that which has been cultivated. He cannot dispose
of at his discretion even that portion of produce beyond
the task defined by the contract. He is obliged to sell
exclusively to the collective farm also those products
produced over and above the plan, and the price is the
same as with respect to planned products. . . . It is
needless to say that the lessee must go to the collective
farm for any trifle, for instance, a spare part: otherwise
it can be bought nowhere. The lessee has no bank
account and no legal guarantees. Then, how can one
speak about his independence?[49]

The question formulated by the journalist itself proves that
the previous system of detailed surveillance, typical for
collective farms, remains intact despite the declared independence of lessees in the agricultural area. But the answer
of the chairman demonstrates that the same surveillance
dominates over collective farms, too. He says:

It is true that the lessor sells products produced over
and above the plan to the collective farm, as provided
for by a contract. . . . And what can you advise us to do?
The collective farm has a state order, and there also is
the desire to eliminate the backing of the former years.
Where can the collective farm take, let us say, the same
grain? That ideal lease discussed by you looks as if it has
been dropped by the existing system of planning and
production/economic relations in agriculture. Our collective farm fulfilled a state order for grain in August
and sold over and above the state order 800 tons of
wheat. It seems that after that we could act at our own
discretion, let us say, with respect to corn. . . . However,
nothing like that has occurred. We were told that we

238

could not use for any other purpose even a single hectare planned for corn. All this is issued not at the district level nor by the region. Thus our lease is adjusted to the actual circumstances.[50]

The chairman's last sentences hint that the same "center" that initiates the independent activities of collective farms and their lessees simultaneously maintains rigid supervision over the former and thus compels similar rigidity in the administration of the latter. But what about the lessees? Do they favor their actual dependence on their collective farms? Read the opinion expressed by a lessee in the same article:

> The lease in all its forms is a risk, first of all a risk for the lessee. It is nice that this year has been lucky. . . . The rainfall was timely, and we received 53 metric centners per hectare, instead of the planned harvest of 33 metric centners. But what if the situation were the same as in 1983, when the harvest of 15 metric centners was considered a great one? I would be a debtor with such a debt that I could not foresee paying. Under complete independence, I would be finished as a lessee. . . . But under our form of lease, I am for the collective farm its provider, regardless of any circumstances. It will not abandon me, and after an unlucky year it will help me by extending credits and other necessities.[51]

Is it not astonishing that a lessee prefers to be dependent on his collective farm despite the fact that his economic independence is a central purpose of the new economic arrangement introduced by the Soviet reformists? No, it is not, considering that the new reforms are based on a combination of the dominant economic system and alien economic phenomena. The lessee has a certain independence; otherwise the innovation in the form of combined lease and independent work contracts could not function at all. But he is afraid of complete independence because it leads to loss of economic assistance from the dominant economy under extraordinary circumstances, and as a result, the risk of independence seems to him less acceptable than the advantages of economic dependence.

Because the independence of lessees has not always reached the requisite degree, governmental agencies sometimes apply to lessees those approaches usual for relationships between these agencies and collective farms. Here is an impressive example described by the article "Why Does the Lessee Need an Inspector?"[52] according to which, lessees are asked to submit periodic reports containing about fifty indicators. A lessee asks:

> Tell me, please, why do I, a lessee, need all this paperwork? I must daily account for the number of cows, yield of milk, matings, calvings, calves, texture and quality of milk. . . . [The lessee goes on to enumerate the account indicators he must submit weekly and monthly.] . . . In fact, however, I shall deal only with two pieces of paper: the contract and checkbook. What is the legal ground for checking my every step?[53]

Mere bureaucratic obstacles hamper the normal implementation of lessees' activities. Sometimes, however, serious barriers result for political reasons. For instance, according to data of the Estonian Academy of Sciences, only two to four percent of farmers are ready to become lessees.[54] In this connection, one writes in *Izvestia*:

But why do even those who desire to not hurry to do so? The negative social memory restrains them. Yes, there is such a somewhat concealed influence. This is the memory of the liquidation of *kulaki* and coercive collectivization. The memory of coercion is, of course, alive. . . . [The author then refers to the heavy labor demanded of agricultural lessees.] . . . They work at least 14 hours a day, without days off and holidays. To bring oneself to such a thing by one's own will . . . !?[55]

This new phenomenon, though advocated by the highest officials, cannot yet be developed to the extent necessary for any palpable upsurge of Soviet agriculture. In an effort to eliminate or at least mitigate impediments to the development of combined lease and independent work contracts, Soviet media criticize the amount of red tape, strive to attract collective farmers to these contracts by reference to higher incomes that compensate the intensive labor, and so forth. Special attention is also paid to the political interpretation of these economic reforms, foreign to socialism in its Marxist-Leninist interpretation and therefore frightening to a number of those otherwise inclined to take part. Of course, agricultural production based on individual lease and independent work contracts cannot be characterized as a component of the socialist economy in its traditional meaning. However, without such a characterization, it is hardly possible to eliminate the fear restraining numerous collective farmers from acceptance of these contracts. In response, the Soviet press has begun to develop new approaches to the economic restructuring based on the present reforms.

In this respect the article "Socialism without Dogma"[56] is especially significant. Presenting a review of letters received by *Izvestia*, the article accentuates the following ideas:

(a) The Soviet reforms under way deal with fundamental grounds of the existing economic and political systems. Therefore, they often engender alert among those accustomed to the dogmatic tenets of previous times. Letters received state, "Socialism as a social formation needs no innovations" or "Is there [in these innovations] no deviation from socialism in force achieved through our suffering and acquired authority all over the world?";

(b) In contrast, those who maintain the positive role of the new reforms develop the opposite opinion. They contend: "One must not approve by the holy flag of socialism our progressing lag behind developed countries, the slavery of various lines, production of defective merchandise, and barbarian mismanagement, and to consider the purification of society from these events as violations of principles"; and

(c) Leases and other concepts new to the Soviet system must not be assessed as contradicting this system or as alien to it. This assertion is explained by the appropriate arguments, "We try not simply to adjust an economic mechanism which does not work as necessary or to reconstruct administrative structures. The substance of economic reform, implemented in this country, consists of modification of property relations." Therefore, results of this modification, including combined lease and independent work contracts, cannot be considered as deviations from Marxism-Leninism. "Transform the laborer into the master of his labor, and . . . we will push *perestroika*." This approach must be assessed as a restoration of Lenin's view and not as a revision of Marxist-Leninist doctrine,[57] considers the same group.

The discussion itself proves that the combination of official and private economies employed by the Soviet reformists has not gone unnoticed. As a matter of fact, it is impossible to conceal this obviousness by means of propagandistic theories. One needs more drastic measures to achieve a desirable goal. These measures were found in the combination of collective farms as a disguised section of the state economy and the new type of cooperatives as a private economy embodied in a "socialist" form.

D. Collective Farms and New Cooperatives

Families and other collective bodies as partners of combined leases and independent contracts executed between them and collective farms function on the basis of full *khozraschet* in their capacity as internal sections of collective farms. In addition, the 1988 Law on Cooperation establishes that, "relying on the consent of a collective farm, these collectives [including family collectives] can be created as primary cooperatives."[58] The words *primary cooperatives* have a double significance. As *primary* cooperatives, these collectives are subordinated to collective farms. The dependence of the former on the latter, so appreciated by the lessees themselves, is retained, though a cooperative as an entity cannot belong to the internal sections of a collective farm. As primary *cooperatives*, the same entities preclude their qualification as private enterprises. They represent the socialist economy and those desiring to create these cooperatives must not be frightened away by political reasons. This trick has proved to be quite successful.

Both types of cooperatives have been and continue to be created. For instance, the cooperative *Koster* in the Orel region is in fact a family cooperative. It consists of a father, mother, two sons, and a daughter-in-law. They lease 530 hectares from their collective farm. They have built or bought a number of other items by themselves and with the use of bank credits. This cooperative specializes in cultivating seeds and perennial grass.[59] Cooperatives created by other collectives vary greatly. Usually they are separated from their collective farms in the process of production activities, fulfilling orders issued by collective farms and receiving from the latter any necessary economic assistance. One collective farm introduced full *khozraschet* in thirty-eight sections, but in order to establish permanent links among them, these sections were included in a cooperative as a primary entity of the collective farm.[60] Sometimes temporary agricultural cooperatives are organized, such as those made up of students during their summer vacations. They execute leases of land from collective farms and designate income for the achievement of certain common goals: repair of hostels, acquisition of sports equipment, textbooks, and so forth.[61]

It is not the variety of the forms but the volume and pace of the spread of agricultural cooperatives that is most significant. To have a clearer view, certain specific data must be considered. For instance, as Soviet media report, all collective farms in the Maikop district have introduced combined lease and independent work contracts and the economic relations arising from these contracts are organized as agricultural cooperatives.[62] According to another report, something extraordinary has happened in the collective farm *Rodina* in the Pskov region. Instead of five farms, they created fifteen cooperatives of lessees, five leasing cattle and land, and ten leasing cattle, buildings, technology, and a little land. They acquire fodder from other agricultural cooperatives.[63] Certain managers within the Soviet agricultural system complain that the process of creating agricultural cooperatives is unnecessarily dragged out. A chairman of a collective farm in the Astrakhan region says, for instance:

> The combined lease and independent work contracts are so new for us that we do not know from which point we must begin. . . . In my opinion, the most important mistake in this regard is elongation of the transition to the new form of economy. Now the collective farm has only five separate collectives. . . . This does not seem to be too much. But even such results have eliminated the problem of cadres, for example, in the realm of milk production. Today the cost of milk is one-half the previous level. . . . It is necessary to go further. . . . But this is impeded by the elongation of a transition [period]. . . . We plan to revise all of our livestock breeding and farming operations in accordance with leasing principles.[64]

Almost daily the situation changes in favor of accelerating the process of creating primary cooperatives on the basis of combined lease and independent work contracts.

Izvestia in late 1988 reported about collective farms completely encompassed by these contracts.[65] Because one of
these collective farms transformed into cooperatives only
its four principal departments and all other types of agricultural activities are implemented by families or other groups
of collective farmers as lessees that do not form cooperatives, the chairman of the collective farm is at the same time
the chairman of the association of four cooperatives.[66] This
process affects the structure of the collective farms and the
methods of administration. Collective farms in the Maikop
district were mentioned above as completely transformed
into groups of lessees — merely collectives of primary cooperatives. A chairman of one of these collective farms tells a
journalist that now the offices of the board of the collective
farm are almost empty. The administrative "top" consists
only of the chairman, the principal economist, and several
other officials. Beyond these limits, the previous adminis-
trators work not in the board of the collective farm but in
the cooperatives subordinated to the farm.[67]

The problem that arises as a result of such a development was precisely formulated in an interview given by the
president of the Soviet Academy of Agricultural Finances,
A. Nikonov:

> Question: Suppose that all obstacles for combined lease
> and independent work contracts are eliminated. Then
> what will remain of the system of collective and state
> farms?
>
> Answer: Do not worry about that happening. Collective
> farms and state farms are only forms of socialist enter-
> prises. Production relations are determined in both by
> relations dominant in the whole society. The collective

farm can be a barrack with performers deprived of rights and even internal passports, as was the case in Stalin's time. But it also can be a cooperative of independent collectives or families of lessees entitled to adopt decisions and bear the entire economic and legal responsibility. . . . A lease is neither an obstacle nor an alternative to collective and state farms. Speaking generally, small units (a family or a group collective) is only a structural cell of large production based on *khozraschet*.

In other words, the system of collective and state farms must be reconstructed to facilitate the higher productivity of agriculture and strengthen the rights of agricultural producers. This reconstruction does not mean liquidation of the appropriate system.[68] The speaker above further emphasizes that collective and state farms do not exhaust all of the forms of organization of agricultural production. This production requires more pluralism than uniformity.[69]

The idea of pluralism was initially maintained and developed by Gorbachev at a special meeting sponsored by the CPSU Central Committee on October 12, 1988.[70] First of all, he called for the employment of new methods of agricultural management without which, in his view, the agricultural problem could not be resolved. These methods signified, in his interpretation, reconstruction of economic relahotions. Therefore Gorbachev thought that agricultural cooperatives would implement production activities, while collective and state farms would organize these activities, consult with the new cooperatives, provide them with agricultural specialists, and so forth. This thought differs from the assertion that the system of collective and state farms remains as such despite a number of new forms of agricultural production in the USSR resulting from application of combined lease and independent work contracts. In summing up the same meeting, Gorbachev argued somewhat differently. Two of his tenets seem the most important:

(1) I do not deny any of the forms which have been discussed here. Collective and state farms, cooperatives, lease relationships . . . must be on the basis [of other forms]. And even here different approaches are acceptable because collective and state farms can also be different;

(2) It is necessary to integrate collective and state farms with the individual sector through contract, to include the individual sector in production relationships and thus to provide them with an even more socialist character. Not a private trader (*chastnik*) as sometimes one says with indignation, but the genuine and zealous master has to be integrated with a collective farm on the basis of socialist property.[71]

These two tenets must entail a substantial conclusion. As is obvious, though informed about the economic weakness of collective and state farms—weakness as a system, not as a mere result of organizational shortcomings—Gorbachev is not inclined to dissolve them. He only thinks that other forms, such as cooperatives and leases, must be introduced in addition to develop the productivity of Soviet agriculture, avoiding the suggestion of a unique model of correlation between the old and new methods. "I treat very cautiously and with a certain fear the suggestion to create a model economy."[72] He does not preclude any option: collective and state farms with cooperatives and without them, cooperatives connected with collective or state farms and separated from them, group and individual lease and independent work contracts executed between collective or state farms and these members (workers) or outsiders. Although expressly preferring small cooperatives surrounding collective and state farms, Gorbachev frankly recognizes that it is impossible to formulate a uniformed solution to the problem. From this point of view, it is interesting to compare Gorbachev's position and the ideas expressed in discussion by a local party leader, V.V. Ushakov. Ushakov contends:

> Collective and state farms must be retained as fundamental cells of the socialist state. The matter is about further development of collective and state farms as cooperative associations and reconstruction of their activities on cooperative principles. They [these farms] become associations of primary cooperatives functioning on the basis of independent work and *khozraschet* principles.[73]

The speaker exaggerates, of course, in announcing that collective and state farms have been already transformed into cooperative associations. The number of "reconstructed" farms continues to be smaller than the number of those constructed on the previous model. It also sounds a little strange that state farms are simultaneously cooperative associations, recalling that, according to the official Soviet view, state and cooperative properties are different forms of socialist property. However, the general opinion presented by the speaker is clear: collective and state farms are at the top of the structure as the fundamental cells, while cooperatives are at the bottom as subordinate units.

Gorbachev does not dismiss this hierarchy. In principle, he considers all acceptable organizational methods—collective and state farms, agricultural cooperatives, and groups or individuals acting as partners of combined lease and independent work contracts. Moreover, primary cooperatives can arise only on the basis of combined lease and independent work contracts. Remembering the notorious "complete collectivization" of the late 1920s and early 1930s, Gorbachev says, "I would be very reluctant to see the process of complete leasing [combined lease and independent work contracts] encompassing all collective and state farms."[74] Different tenets of the Soviet leader seem neither entirely clear nor consistent. But certain things are doubtless. He strives both to retain and to renovate the system of collective and state farms. *To retain* signifies that these farms must exist, depending on the circumstances, either in their traditional form or as organizers of primary cooperatives, collectives, or individual lease and independent work contracts. *To renovate* means to combine collective and state farms with new methods of agricultural management reviving private initiatives that have almost completely languished during previous regimes.

Specific methods approved by Gorbachev leave no doubt that he considers his goals achievable by establishing interconnections between state and private economies in the agricultural area. But what about his call to integrate the official agricultural system with the private sector and consequently strengthen the socialist character of the entire Soviet agricultural economy? This call evidently demonstrates that the Soviet leader strives to avoid the existence of an independent private sector in the agricultural area and to prevent such a situation by contractual connection of this sector with collective or state farms. If the private sector fulfills the tasks imposed by official farms, receives from the latter the necessary supplies, and sells agricultural produce either to them or in accordance with their orders, the dominant agricultural system established in the USSR will not undergo substantial modification. Not so much in light of practice but from the viewpoint of Marxist-Leninist dogma, Gorbachev's assertion that the contractual connection of the private sector with collective and state farms will transform the private sector into a socialist element is astonishing.

According to classical Marxism, the socialist property that arises after establishing the proletarian dictatorship exists as the property either of the entire society (the state) or of numerous collective bodies (collective farms, other cooperatives, societal organizations). Under all other circumstances, there is private property which can belong either to individuals or to their groups, for example, to co-owners or to a family. The official doctrine and Soviet law have employed not the words *private owners* but rather, *personal owners* with respect to the majority of individuals who possess no economies of their own and earn their living by labor in enterprises, institutions, or other Soviet entities. Even the property of these individuals represents not a socialist but an individual estate.

The individual sector, as Gorbachev calls it, cannot be qualified by Marxism-Leninism as a bearer of socialist property, regardless of whether various individuals use in their economies their own or leased means of production. No critics of Stalin's regime would disagree with the assertion that only after "collectivization" of individual farming was private property replaced by socialist property in rural areas, although individual farmers based their economies on the land that belonged to the Soviet state. It would seem that also at the present time individual economies of collective farmers, though employing the combination of lease and independent work contracts, do not personify socialist property. But Gorbachev maintains another view, speaking about the socialist character of the individual sector insofar as it has contractual connections with collective and state farms. This view, expressed by the Soviet leader and thus acquiring official significance in contrast to other disputable issues, probably results from two circumstances.

First, Gorbachev imagines contracts earmarked to connect individual and socialist sectors not merely as those regulating leases and independent work. In his view, the suggested connection must establish reliable control over the individual sector and its strong dependence on the official economy. This, of course, undermines his strength in the struggle for improvement of Soviet agriculture by interconnections among different economies. In the final analysis, preservation of the official economic system is to him, as to other Soviet leaders, more important than upsurge of this system.

Second, in his report dedicated to changes of the Soviet Constitution, Gorbachev addressed the problem of renovation of the concept of socialist property. He stated:

> It is necessary to separately discuss suggestions in favor of broader and further modifications of the Constitution of the USSR. These [suggestions] deal with the fundamental revision of the preamble, a new concept of socialist property, cooperation, self-administration, the rights of citizens and other important issues. It is true that a number of things must be renovated in the 1977 Constitution. But this belongs to future activity.[75]

Judging from these words, the constitutional definition of socialist property whose development is temporarily postponed, must be formulated so that the individual sector will also acquire all the requisite socialist features. This will, of course, promote propagandistic advantages to the Soviet reformists striving to preserve the socialist system but who understand that it does not work in its "uncontaminated" appearance. Such a propagandistic advantage turns into a substantial disadvantage in practice. A dogmatic word restrains the actual activity. The new Soviet leaders have invented methods of interconnecting different economies to save the dominant economic system from stagnation. But their devotion to Marxist-Leninist dogma precludes making this invention a reality in the Soviet economy to the extent necessary to avoid an economic collapse. This is why successes of agricultural reforms in the USSR seem more impressive in literary descriptions than in daily life.

Soviet media do not miss a day in recounting encouraging stories about how new methods of agricultural administration are spreading throughout the country, the unimaginable results achieved soon after introduction of these methods, and how these results will improve the food supply of the populace. Between the lines of these stories, the reader can ascertain that the number of collective and state farms introducing new methods is small, that along with some efficiency, the new methods entail their own difficulties, and that even the achieved efficiency does not yet extend beyond the gates of collective and state farms. In food stores, the situation is either the same or worse than before. Perhaps real changes will occur in the remote future. Assessed in light of the present time, however, agricultural reforms implemented in the USSR are either futile or doomed to failure; they are by no means a genuine success.

253

E. State Land and Individual Leases

For the more than fifty years of its existence, the system of collective (state) farms has negatively affected the productivity of agriculture. It has also entailed a process called by the Soviet reformists *raskrestianivanie*. The precise connotations of the word, stemming from "peasantry" but acquiring the opposite meaning, render it unworthy of direct translation and therefore its significance can best be explained by describing the consequences of the above-mentioned process. *Raskrestianivanie* results in two principal consequences.

The first consequence is that numerous villages have been abandoned by their inhabitants, remaining empty for decades. In the official Soviet jargon, these villages have been called "villages without prospects." According to the official data, in the Orel region the number of such villages is more than 700. But the Orel region belongs to the so-called "non-*chernozem*" areas where natural conditions are not very favorable for agriculture.[76] In contrast, the Ukraine, situated in the *chernozem* area, has always been considered as the breadbasket of the country. Nevertheless, the same process is also under way in the Ukraine, as a journalist reports, citing the example of the Kirovgorod region.[77] To revive agriculture, Soviet leaders must attract new inhabitants to rural areas. How can this problem be resolved? It is clear that not a single urban inhabitant, even if a peasant in origin, will return to a village to become a collective farmer or a worker in a state farm. Other methods must be employed.

According to a recent article entitled "A Village Invites You to Live,"[78] a collective farm in the Kaluga region received 6,000 positive letters in response to an invitation to work in the farm on the basis of collective or family lease and independent work contracts. The author colorfully describes the successes of those who left their homes caused in part by the strong assistance given by the collective farm to newcomers. This description suggests more of a propagandistic approach rather than an accurate description. A journalist who studied the situation in the Pskov region paints a more gloomy picture. As he reports, even if only the lease of land without membership in a collective farm is offered, these offers are usually refused, often because of the move from a city to a village. Sometimes they are refused as a result of the fear that the new policy may very soon be abolished and the inability to predict what will happen to these new lessees.[79] To achieve substantial change in this regard, the Komsomol (Communist Youth Organization) Central Committee sponsored a special meeting to stop the shift of youth to urban areas and to attract young people to villages as lessees of land—its genuine masters, a newly created generation of Soviet peasantry.[80] Despite this meeting, there are more "rent myths" (using *Izvestia*'s expression)[81] than actual lessees coming from cities to rural areas. Where there is no peasant, there is no agriculture, regardless of the character of reforms proclaimed by the Soviet government.

The second consequence is the disastrous decrease in the number of those who possess peasant skills, those able to nurture and respect the land. As one author writes, "the poet was worried about the person to whom the lyre had to be transferred, [while] the peasant [thinks] to whom to transfer his land."[82] He continues: "In a little more time, there will be nobody [to take on the land]. But so far there are [such people]."[83] Whom does he mean? He means children who study in schools and ride the tractors after school.

"An old and low-powered tractor stands by a house until the young master has his dinner after school. . . . Each morning the chairman of a collective farm's car is driven 15 kilometers to school and back to pick up a single schoolboy. What a privilege, a personal car, allocated to a schoolboy of the first grade!"[84] It is difficult to describe more eloquently the second consequence of the lengthy process of *raskrestianivanie* resulting from the creation of the collective farm system in the USSR.

This issue attracted the special attention of Gorbachev at the meeting referred to above. He declared:

> Man has been torn away from the land, from the means of production in collective and state farms more than in other branches of production. . . . The worker ceased to be a peasant dealing with land and farming, as he must be. Ours is a living world—land, nature and its processes. One must know how the land lives, how it breathes, how it must be treated. . . . Tearing a man away from land, from means of production, we transformed the master of land into a worker by the hour.[85]

To overcome *raskrestianivanie*, it is necessary not only to attract labor to villages but also to return to the land its master.

Sooner or later the Soviet rulers had to come to this conclusion. Because of the shortage of labor in villages millions of urban inhabitants—workers, officials, students—were sent annually since the end of World War II to collective farms during harvest season. To say nothing about the poor capacity of these people to farm and large losses resulting from such a harvesting organization, their work was expensive because they retained their right to salary and acquired the right to be maintained by collective farms. When urban inhabitants were forced to work in the collective farm fields, the collective farmers themselves strove to remain at home, dealing with their own economies and disregarding their collective farm duties. As a result, the harvest process dragged on and large amounts of grain rotted on the stalk, remaining in the fields through the rain and even snow seasons. In addition, there are a number of other types of agricultural work which collective farmers must themselves fulfill. If the principal labor force consists of elderly people and children, these tasks become back-breaking burdens. All these circumstances prove that the settling of villages and inculcating of peasant skills in new-comers is an urgent goal for the Soviet agricultural system. This goal cannot be achieved through drastic measures. Even those who decide to move from a city to a village to set up permanent residence must spend numerous years before becoming peasants by profession. The entire life of a whole generation is necessary to eliminate *raskrestianivanie*, and to allow true restoration of the peasant skills necessary for efficient agricultural activities. But how can urban inhabitants be attracted to the country?

Collective farms have compromised themselves to a degree that repulses outsiders instead of attracting them. Even if the offers referred not merely to eventual member-ship in a collective farm but also to execution of combined lease and independent work contracts, almost no results would be likely. Another approach had to be employed—lease of land for its cultivation individually, without collec-tive farm membership. Nor is this membership necessary if one would like to combine the lease of land and independent work. Does this signify the return to individual farming, at least within certain limits, or a new development of so-called socialist forms of Soviet agriculture?

As mentioned above, Gorbachev contends that contractual connections with collective farms must provide the individual sector with the socialist character. Expressing this idea, he probably means a special contract establishing not merely connections but ties that could transform the individual sector into a special section of the collective farm system, in fact if not in formality. Soviet scholars analyzing the same topic maintain an abstract but quite clear point of view. For instance, R. Praust, the head of a laboratory of the Soviet Academy of Agricultural Sciences, argues:

> Recently our theoretical views were based on the premise that leases and/or independent work are incompatible with the principles of socialism and with the concept of socialist property. . . . Our social production of all branches, all spheres and all regions is based on the system of hired labor, or, if one would like to be more precise, on the system of hired labor with its well known estrangement of the worker from means of production and from the results of his labor. In the framework of this system, socialist property began to be transformed into something which belonged to nobody, i.e., into alien property. This is the source of many of our failures, especially in the realm of agriculture where violation of eternal connections of the peasant with land proved to be very painful.
>
> Leases and independent work are special forms of hiring of property, i.e., qualitatively another system of

organization of social production and production relationships under socialism, returning opportunities for individual peasant economies. At the same time, this is also labor used to fulfill tasks which are imposed on the collective or state farms. . . . There is no place for estrangement. If a ruble is spent for nothing, it goes from one's own pocket, but at the same time each additional kilogram either of harvesting or of milk yield is a pure profit of the lessee.[86]

The mere fact that the lease is based on a contract with a collective farm and transfers the fulfillment of certain tasks from the collective farm to the lessee transforms the individual sector into a component of the socialist economy.[87] Without a lease, land is an object of state property but it has no master (a proprietor without master), while, because of the lease, the proprietor is supplemented along with the master (the master is not the proprietor, and, vice versa, the proprietor is not the master). A very peculiar theory!

It is impossible to understand how it can occur that an object has a proprietor but no master, and on the other hand, it is necessary to explain by what miracle a master of an object cannot be its proprietor? What are the legal differences between the proprietor and the master, as a result of which a subject of law can become a master of an item without the property right, or the bearer of the property right cannot be the master of the same object? These questions are theoretically very important, bearing in mind that legislation dealing not only with agriculture but also with industry distinguishes between the proprietor and the master. This terminology is employed by new statutory acts without any comments explaining the meaning of the word *proprietor* and *master* in their comparison and their peculiarities.

Perhaps the best way under the circumstances is to put aside all these theoretical controversies and assume that Soviet leaders themselves, although they employ the terms *proprietor* and *master*," do not realize the genuine distinctions between them. Such confusion has taken place more than once in Soviet history. For instance, during the 1965 reform, Kosygin and his adherents suggested orally and in legal provisions that a distinction can be made between administrative and economic management. Officially this distinction has never been explained, and Soviet economic and legal theories have had to resort to extraordinary efforts to express the necessary rationales. These efforts failed, especially when certain scholars of sound judgment began to ask: Do these concepts not belong to different logical realms, and why can an administrative decision not rely on economic calculations, or, vice versa, why must economic calculations preclude adoption of an administrative decision?

Referring to this historical precedent, one would be hard-pressed to outline the distinctions between the proprietor and the master as a purely theoretical problem. At the same time, in light of common sense, the problem is completely clear. If the entire state or a huge collective body called a collective farm is the owner, but state workers or members of a collective farm cannot consider the same object as their own, at least in restricted and conditional meaning, then the appropriate estate belongs to the entire whole and to no one personally. According to the Soviet reformists, to eliminate this perverted situation, peasants must be returned to the land, not as its owners (it belongs to the Soviet state) but as its actual masters in the capacity of lessees, performers of independent work contracts, or in any other capacity attaching the peasant to land as its nurturing parent and, in this regard, to something that is his own.

Awareness of these circumstances is a credit to the new Soviet leaders. They have introduced a number of ways of facilitating the accomplishment of that very significant task. These methods can be classified between two groups: those connected with collective farm memberships and those free of this connection. The former is employed, as a rule, with actual members of collective farms in the form of leases of land or other property and more often in the form of leases combined with independent work contracts. The latter is experienced mainly with respect to outsiders who, though not members of collective farms, are ready to establish lease relationships either with a collective farm or with a local executive committee. Not infrequently these relationships encompass the lease of land and/or other property and fulfillment of independent work contracts. But in this regard, the lease of land presents special interest and attracts direct attention.

The fact that such leases are not very widespread can be easily demonstrated. *Izvestia* on December 10, 1988, pictured someone named Valentin Burochkin with his daughter accompanied by a short article under the title "Lessees." Those familiar with Soviet media and their methods of operation understand that such attention on the part of *Izvestia* could be paid only to an event that is rare in practice but whose dissemination is officially welcome. Even this fact alone demonstrates that the Soviet leadership have a long way to go until the empty villages are completely settled, to say nothing about the time needed to teach new-comers the skills of peasants in the proper meaning — masters of land, not merely its users. However, the requisite first steps to instill leases of agricultural land have been made and they deserve to be analyzed.

Until recently, there was no law regulating the individual lease of agricultural land. At the meeting referred to above, Gorbachev promised only that the appropriate law would be adopted.[88] Before implementation of his promise it was not law but practice that served as a source of legal regulation of the lease under discussion.[89] This practice was multifarious. At first, the contracts for the lease of land were limited to two to three years. Such a short period did not stimulate execution of these contracts because the lessee could not predict what would happen with his investment after the contractual term. Therefore, at the meeting sponsored by the CPSU Central Committee on May 13, 1988, one of its participants said:

> We came to the conclusion that land must be rented out for longer time-periods: 10-15 years. This forms a quite different human psychology. When we created a system of lease and encompassed by it the entire state farm, another situation arose: workers themselves began to count, estimate, and plan; the previous style of command does not fit anymore. The individual began to consider himself a master, not a hired worker.[90]

Expressing this view, the speaker meant not only workers of his state farm but also newcomers who decided to become lessees.

At the next meeting invoked by the CPSU Central Committee on October 12, 1988, new trends became visible. For instance, taking into consideration peculiarities of the Baltic republics, a speaker representing this area contended:

> I think that under these conditions the method of lease of land is not convenient. Suppose that a person has executed a contract for 20 years, that he created on this land his own economy and began to handle his business. But these years passed, and he could be told that there would be no contract anymore. And nobody can give a guarantee that it would not be so.[91]

There were suggestions to establish fifty years as the limit for land leases. But the same speaker submitted to the meeting an extraordinary claim. He announced:

> I am a natural farmer in the direct meaning of the word. . . . I received land for eternal use by a decision of a district Soviet of the people's deputies, I work employing my own means of production, and I have my own cattle. Thus, I am not a lessee.[92]

Relying on these examples, which give an accurate illustration of practice in recent years, it can be ascertained that:

(1) the individual farming encouraged by Soviet reformists can be based on the lease and on the eternal (unlimited in time) use of land;

(2) leases can be established for a short time, for example, two to three years and for longer periods, for example, ten to fifteen or even fifty years; and

(3) independent work contracts can accompany leases, or leases can be established without independent work agreements.

This practice was legalized by the edict of the Presidium of the USSR Supreme Soviet of April 7, 1989 "On the Lease System and Lease Relations in the USSR."[93]

The edict deals not only with leases of land and not only with cases where individuals are lessees. It encompasses all types of leases discussed in this chapter—internal and external, for example, those established between an entity and its internal sections or those connecting a given entity with individual or collective outsiders; separate leases and leases combined with independent work contracts; leases of land and other objects (enterprises, their subdivisions, equipment, etc.). Almost all leases are regulated by this edict in accordance with patterns developed in practice and analyzed above. As to leases of land, they have numerous peculiarities that must be separately emphasized.

Citizens as lessees can function either individually or as an organized group. The other parties to these contracts, the lessors, can consist of either state entities entitled to rent out plots of state lands (such as local executive committees) or in cases covered by law, the land's primary users (such as collective farms). The latter situation is similar to a sub-lease, which is generally allowed to the lessee if he has the consent of the lessor. The question of leasing land within an economic unit is decided by this unit (a collective farm, a state farm, etc.). However, local executive committees are entitled to compel a unit to execute contracts or even to withdraw from the unit's unused or irrationally used lands for the purpose of creating a reserve of leasable land.

The size of plots of land that may be leased by each peasant holding must not exceed the possibility of these plots being worked by the personal labor of members of the peasant holding. Hence, the hiring of labor is prohibited to individual farmers. But at the same time all members of peasant holdings are liable for social insurance and social security on a par with workers and employees, and therefore peasant holdings must contribute to the state social insurance fund from their own income. They also must pay taxes to the state along with the lease payment due to the lessor.

The duration of the lease of land is ordinarily arranged on a long-term basis—from five to fifty years or even longer. As a rule, annulment of the lease contract may take place only on mutual agreement. The lessee is, in principle, attached to a plot of land until expiration of fifty years or longer. If the lessee dies, his rights are transferred to one of his heirs who lived and worked with him until his death. Needless to say that this provision is also designed to attach to the land the entire family of each lessee.

The edict establishes that the lessee independently determines the directions of his economic activity and disposes of the output he produces and the income he generates. As the edict states, these rights must be exercised in accordance with current legislation and the lease contract. This legislation and especially the contract can impose on the lessee various duties, including those called by Gorbachev "the discipline of state procurement" which according to him, must be retained during the whole transitional period whose duration is completely uncertain. From this point of view, the independence of lessees of land proclaimed by the edict seems illusory.

In assessing the decree as a whole, its preamble is important, especially the following words:

As a new, progressive form of socialist economic management, the lease system is becoming increasingly important in the system of measures to improve production relations and effect the far-reaching, qualitative renewal of production forces.

In other words, what was earlier an "anti-socialist" institution has been transformed into one of the most important means of Soviet economic and social development.[94] It could not be otherwise, since the new Soviet leadership considers interconnections of different economies as the only reliable method to prevent the irreparable crash of the Soviet economic system. In dealing with individual leases of land, three special circumstances must be taken into consideration.

First, as mentioned above, Gorbachev requires that contractual connections be established between collective (state) farms and the individual sector to provide the latter with the socialist character. It is evident that projected contracts will impose numerous duties on lessees compelling them to work for the benefit of the state personified by collective and state farms.

Second, the contracts for the lease of land must be indissoluble at least unilaterally, like almost all other Soviet contracts. If a contract is executed for fifty years, neither the lessor nor the lessee can cancel it before expiration of that period. As a result, not only lessees themselves but also their future generations as heirs interested to retain economies of their ancestors will be attached to the land, and consequently, by means of contracts any opportunity to leave the rural area will be precluded.

Third, to create the individual sector in Soviet agriculture as a substantial and dependable structure will require decades. But without the private sector, the agricultural economy of collective or state farms cannot improve as needed, regardless of whether the functions of lessees are imposed on newcomers or members (workers) of collective (state) farms. Although lease and independent work contracts are officially characterized as the best and closest route to food sufficiency,[95] this method will require a very long wait for the achievement of any palpable results.

Conclusion:
Understanding the Actual
Causes of the Soviet
Economic Failure

The foregoing analysis of the numerous economic measures adopted by Gorbachev and his adherents to date leaves no doubt that the Soviet leadership of the present time genuinely strives to achieve substantial improvement of the Soviet economy. The real-life situation is developing from bad to worse. Soviet official data do not contradict this assessment. The only purpose of the official information is to attempt to substitute statistical reports for the objective economic reality. To deduce the correct conclusions, the results of calculations made by Western sources on the basis of an experienced analytical approach to Soviet information must be utilized. A *New York Times* article entitled "The Soviet Economy: Worse Than We Thought" states:

Economic might. C.I.A. estimates suggest that Soviet national output is currently a little more than half as large as America's, with per capita output a little less than half the American level. Last year, however, an economist with the Soviet State Planning Committee (Gosplan) published a Western-style reckoning of the Soviet gross national product in rubles. Even at the ruble's artificially high official exchange rate, these numbers would make the Soviet economy barely a third the size of ours and would put Soviet per capita output at just over a quarter the American level.

269

Growth rates. The C.I.A. estimates that the Soviet economy has grown by an uninspiring 2 percent a year since the mid-1970s. But earlier calculations, Soviet commentators now say, did not make adequate adjustments for inflation (a phenomenon whose existence was previously denied). Last year, in a now famous article two Soviet economists suggested that per capita output was slightly lower in the mid-1980s than it had been a decade earlier. . . .

Defense burden. C.I.A. figures put military spending at 15 to 17 percent of Soviet output. This is harder to check, because, despite *glasnost'*, the Red Army's budget remains a closely guarded secret. However, if Soviet and American military expenditures are roughly comparable (as many Western experts believe) and the Soviet economy is smaller than was thought, its defense burden would have to be higher than present C.I.A. figures suggest. The Gosplan G.N.P. numbers, for example, suggest that Soviet defense spending could easily reach 25 percent of total output.[1]

As a matter of course, the military build-up detracts most of the Soviet Union's financial resources that could instigate more sound economic development if employed in other economic branches. Perhaps the principal cause of economic failures in the USSR is found here, and as a result, restriction of military expenses may be a more reliable way to strengthen the Soviet economy than all the economic reforms announced by Gorbachev. The necessity of this restriction is understood by the Soviet leadership; the program of unilateral reduction of Soviet military forces submitted to the United Nations in 1988 and proclaimed several times afterward mirrors this understanding. In comparison with Soviet economic demands, the restriction proclaimed is very modest, and from this point of view, nothing has been modified in the realm of distribution of financial resources. Is this a consequence of the shortsightedness of Soviet rulers or of circumstances independent of their volition?

In considering this specific issue—Soviet military build-up—it must be realized that for this economically weak country military strength is the only way to maintain its position as one of two superpowers. Abandoning this position exceeds the genuine capacity of any Soviet leader. Any attempt would meet with failure resulting from pressure on the part of the whole system represented by others in power. The USSR must maintain its significance as a superpower based on military strength, demanding huge expenses for maintenance of this position. Substantial reduction of military expenses cannot serve as a source of additional financing for the Soviet economy.

Even if the Soviet rulers managed to find financial replacement for resources spent for military purposes, this could only mitigate economic difficulties, not eliminate them. This assertion becomes clear as soon as it is understood that it is not the huge military budget or any other economic irrationality that principally causes incessant economic failures. The cause is embodied in the Soviet system itself, and as long as that system exists, the economic failures will recur. Those western Sovietologists who recognize this genuine situation precisely are brave in their recommendations. As Igor Birman writes, "the only way out: a capitalist economy."[2] In his opinion, the same view is maintained by a Soviet scholar Tat'iana Zaslavskaia in her famous report reviewed by principal American newspapers and published in Russian abroad,[3] although Zaslavskaia herself has never expressly formulated this conclusion.

The economy is a component of the entire system of a given country. It is obvious that substantial changes in the economy cannot leave intact this system as a whole. This close interdependence between the former and the latter seems quite clear to the Soviet leadership. In his report submitted to the Supreme Soviet of the USSR at a meeting dedicated to changes in the Soviet Constitution, Gorbachev emphasized that "tasks formulated both for the short-term and prospectively can be resolved only by combination of economic reforms and political transformations, democratization and *glasnost'*."[4] If the economy is modified but not replaced by another economic structure, the system as a whole remains identical, despite its changes resulting from economic reforms. In contrast, if the economy is not merely modified but replaced by another economic structure, the entire system dominating in the country must also be replaced. The Soviet system does not disappear as a result of fostering economic decentralization by diminution of economic centralism (increase of rights of enterprises and restrictions in the power of central planning agencies), supplementation of state property by the property of the new type of cooperatives (creation of a new form of transformation of individual property), or expansion of individual labor activities in the realms exceeding the capacities of the state economy (employment of individual labor in the spheres of production of consumer goods and supply of the populace with daily services). Economic innovations of this character are called by western Sovietologists *within-the-system* modifications. A specific suggestion discussed separately can be acceptable or unacceptable, but in principle, *within-the-system* modifications cannot be rejected by the

Soviet leadership because they are by definition compatible with the Soviet system. Compare these modifications with the suggestion of replacing the Soviet economic structure with a capitalist economy: transformation of state enterprises into private ones (functioning either as corporations or objects of individual property), rejection of the cooperative disguise of certain portions of state property (as in collective farms) or of individual property (as in the new cooperatives), free exercise of private individual activities (including hired labor), and so forth. In implementing such a suggestion, the Soviet leadership would eliminate the Soviet economy, replacing it with another type of economy. Accordingly, all other components of the Soviet system would also be replaced. In the final analysis, the matter is about the liquidation of the Soviet system and the creation of a system on the pattern of contemporary democratic countries. Perhaps this development is justified historically. But it has nothing in common with attempts to improve the Soviet system, and as ruling representatives of this system the Soviet leadership can deal only with the latter task. Any suggestions that would not leave the Soviet system intact cannot be an issue of discussion by Soviet official agencies, regardless of whether these suggestions emanate from western Sovietologists or from Soviet scholars.

As emphasized from the outset,[5] the Soviet system is a system of unlimited political power of the ruling elite based on this elite's economic monopoly. In assessing the Soviet economy, its political and economic efficiency must be distinguished.

The political efficiency of the Soviet economy is a specifically Soviet phenomenon. It signifies the capacity of this economy to protect the unlimited political power of the

273

ruling elite by establishing economic dependence of the populace on the state. To implement this function successfully, the economy must possess at least two features:

(1) it must be completely and exclusively the object of state property; and

(2) it must be administered as centrally as possible.

Unfortunately for the Soviet leadership, it is impossible for both features to be all-embracing. Because consumption for production does not preclude individual consumption, individual property must be allowed to a certain extent, despite the overwhelming domination of state property. At the same time, since the centralized plan cannot foresee everything, a certain initiative must be guaranteed to those who directly exercise state economic activity (state associations, enterprises, and other lowest economic entities headed by their managers). Despite this inevitable necessity, Soviet rulers have always managed to take it into account to the extent compatible with the economic maintenance of their own unlimited political power.

The specific correlation between the economic monopoly and its antipode or between economic centralism and decentralization has not always been the same. For instance, during the War Communism years, economic monopoly and centralism reached their apogee, in contrast to the period of Lenin's NEP which weakened to some degree both these elements. However, centralism has accompanied the Soviet regime during all of its history. Thus, from the political perspective, the Soviet economy has always been efficient and not a single failure can be found in its development.

In contrast to political efficiency as a specific feature of the Soviet economy, economic efficiency is a generally accepted indicator of economic development. This efficiency is usually measured by national output and output per capita. Taken separately, the appropriate figures do not give a complete picture: national output can be large because of the large population but inefficient per capita, and vice versa, though efficient per capita the economy of a small country can be insignificant from the viewpoint of national output. In addition, an economy's efficiency is expressed by the living standard it affords. Output per capita can be high, but if it is represented mainly by products of heavy industry with little regard for consumer goods, the given country has a poor living standard. Under the circumstances, when the populace can acquire a sufficient amount of consumer goods, the living standard is also sufficient, even if national output and output per capita are not as high as in certain other countries.

Does the Soviet system provide any economic efficiency, or can it rely only on the political efficiency of its economy? Political efficiency is embodied in the guarantee of the economic monopoly of the ruling elite. If this monopoly has been established, then the higher the economic development, the stronger the economic might of the political rulers. Therefore, they cannot be indifferent toward economic efficiency. On the contrary, they strive to do their best to achieve economic indicators as high as possible. But economic efficiency is subordinated to political efficiency. This subordination affects both the structure and the methods of economic development.

The structure for economic development in the USSR is predetermined by the purpose of strengthening the country's economic might. Heavy industry has always had a priority in comparison with light industry, and as a result, shortages of consumer goods have become a permanent feature of the Soviet system. The first attempt to plan for relatively rapid growth of light industry was made in 1953 by Georgii Malenkov, Stalin's direct successor. But in the process of his ouster from the leading position in 1955, he was accused of apostasy from Marxism-Leninism because of this idea. Brezhnev's five-year plan of 1981-1985 was the first legislative act in Soviet history to provide for limited priority development of light industry over heavy industry. In fact, nothing changed because of underfulfillment of the plan precisely within the indicators concerning light industry. In 1988, Gorbachev began to maintain planning priority in favor of light industry in an amount insignificant *per se* but still slightly larger than in the last Brezhnev plan. No one knows whether this is a permanent policy or an extraordinary measure, to say nothing about the substantial differences between plans and their fulfillment. In addition, the shortage of consumer goods has reached such a level in the USSR that with just several percent higher growth in light industry in comparison with heavy industry *per annum* it would take decades to modify the structural development of the Soviet economy. Because such a modification of economic efficiency contradicts political efficiency, the emphasis on light industry development is doomed while heavy industry retains its primacy.

The methods of economic development in the USSR depend on the cyclical character of this development — from centralism to a relative decentralization when there is danger of economic collapse, and then back from a relative decentralization to a strong centralism when the danger of the loss of economic monopoly as the principal source of unlimited political power of the ruling elite appears. The previous development of the Soviet economy corroborates the incessant functioning of this regularity. Experience accumulated during seventy years cannot be disregarded. The further in time the Soviet Union has moved away from the very small and inefficient tsarist economy, the less significant the rate of its economic progress has proved to be. As mentioned above, beginning with the mid-1980s, the Soviet economy either ceased to progress or began to move backward. These results could be predicted as natural according to the cyclical regularity. After each new cycle, the distance between its stages has been shortened. Relative decentralization has yielded to centralism before substantial economic results were achieved, while centralism has displayed its negative consequences sooner than the Soviet leadership has been ready to appeal again to a relative decentralization. This signifies that the entire system has begun to completely exhaust its economic capacities, and the cyclical regularity that previously rescued the Soviet economy has transformed itself into an economic danger. Because this regularity is inseparable from the Soviet system, to abolish the former would destroy the latter. Since the same regularity has demonstrated itself as both the method of economic improvement and the cause of the economic failure, it has to be supplemented by a new method eliminating the negatively functioning cause. This was the dilemma whose solution fell to Gorbachev's lot.

On the one hand, Gorbachev employs an habitual method — restriction of centralism and expansion of decentralization. In words, he expands decentralization more broadly than any of his predecessors. To illustrate this trend, it suffices to refer to the complete abolition of centralized distribution with respect to consumer goods and beyond the limits of state orders with respect to production-technical products. The degree of implementability of unplanned distribution seems, in fact, dubious. Production-technical products were completely encompassed by state orders in 1988, and thus a substantial innovation in planning was hanging in the air. A promise to reduce state orders to forty-five percent of produced products in 1989 must be checked in practice before its economic seriousness can be assessed. Because of the huge shortage of consumer goods, they could not be reasonably distributed even by planned procedures. How the free sale of these goods can guarantee the supply to the entire country if goods production demonstrates no signs of increase is an enigma for the authors of the reforms just as it is for the addressees of the reformed legal provisions. Greater expansion of decentralization proclaimed by Gorbachev does not necessarily mean the possibility of achieving more significant results than those reached on the basis of previous economic reforms. At any rate, large-scale utopian promises are more dangerous, in the final analysis, than relatively realistic programs of a less promising character. Also it must not be forgotten that the economic reforms under way retain certain of the former centralizing measures (as in the transformation into production units of those enterprises included in associations) and introduce certain new forms of centralism (for example, creation of Gosagroprom and its successor as the ruling central agency for the entire agricultural system and adjacent economic branches).

On the other hand, Gorbachev resorts to a new method—combination of the socialist economy, as the latter is officially called, with outside economic elements. The forms of this combination have been discussed above. Now they must be generally qualified. The method of team or brigade independent work (for instance, the method employed in industry) is a form of fulfillment of work in favor of a socialist entity on the basis of common efforts of a group of workers connected by collective responsibility. Lease and independent work contracts (for instance, those employed by collective and state farms), assuming distribution of products (in this case, agricultural produce) between lessors-customers and lessees-contractors are a form of the feudal corvée,[6] regardless of whether the internal departments of collective (state) farms, families of collective farmers, or newcomers lease property and fulfill independent work for socialist entities. In principle, the same situation arises on the basis of leases of land, since individual farmers are obliged to settle up with their landlords (the state or its collective farms) by submitting the appropriate portion of agricultural produce.

Cooperatives of the new type are either organized by state entities or connected with them by contracts (including contracts of lease of state enterprises or their appropriate parts), and they represent a combination of transformed private property with socialist property under subordination of the former to the latter. Other new cooperatives represent less obviously the same combination because they cannot exist without state land or other objects of state property (like workplaces), state supply at least to a certain extent, and so forth. Individuals exercising their own labor activity possess private property. Functioning on the basis of contracts with cooperatives, they create directly or indirectly a combination of private and socialist properties. Without these contracts, they nevertheless depend on the state (for supply, workplaces, land), directing their activities where the populace's demands cannot be completely satisfied by the socialist economy.

A new method of development of the Soviet economy invented by the reformists of the present time consists of combination of the socialist and private economies that sometimes includes even feudal elements but more often is represented by individual property, either undisguised or transformed by the creation of new types of cooperatives. Despite this combination, socialist property retains its dominant position, while private property plays a subsidiary role because of its amount and its direct or indirect subordination to the socialist economy. The questions remain as to why Gorbachev and his adherents resorted to this combination, and to what extent can this new method ensure the normal development of the Soviet economy in the future.

The first question, concerning the causes of the established interconnections between socialist and other economies, is easy to answer. The new Soviet leadership has understood two things:

(1) that the socialist economy does not work but must be retained; and

(2) that in order to compel it to work it must be combined with other, strange economic components that spur its activity. As the authors of the Soviet reforms believe, these alien economic components must be only catalysts for economic development, not a counterpart of the socialist economy. Therefore, they resort to numerous measures. Among these measures, the following must be considered:

(a) The socialist economy shall be quantitatively prevalent, and the other economic phenomena shall not exceed the limits of subsidiary economic factors.

(b) Protection of the socialist economy against pernicious impact of the alien economic phenomena shall be ensured as broadly as possible. For instance, state enterprises or their sections can be rented out to cooperatives, not to individuals, and the lessees must be subordinate to and dependent on their lessors. The same ideas entail the establishment of connections between the private sector and the socialist economy in the form of contracts, through the system of permission and registrations, through the supply of materials, equipment, and premises, by control over the results of nonstate economic activities, and so forth.

(c) The stability of official forms of agricultural activities shall be maintained. Collective and state farms are retained and their relationships with representatives of the outside economic concepts are based on the subordination of those concepts by means of contracts keeping all forms of private economic activities under control. The attachment of peasants to land, established by Stalin, is preserved. But Stalin accomplished this task by means of the passport system and rigid restriction of the freedom of movement of collective farmers at the discretion of collective farms. Now when collective farmers have their own internal passports, only their specific numbers indicate that their bearers cannot leave a rural area without permission from collective farms. This has changed the form but has not abolished the attachment of peasants to land. At the same time, a certain modification of the form of the attachment has been supplemented by new methods subjected to the same purpose. Contracts of lease of land combined or uncombined with independent work contracts are, as a rule, indissoluble for both parties, first and foremost for lessees. This means that until the expiration of the contractual term, which can reach fifty years or be eternal, neither a peasant nor his descendants can leave the rural areas and break their attachment to the land.

(d) The labor activities of individuals and cooperatives of the new type shall be connected with activities of the socialist entities by means of contracts, which are not necessary only if a new cooperative has been created by a socialist entity. These contracts formally confirm the dependence of nonsocialist economic phenomena on the appropriate socialist economic entities. Therefore, the combination of different economic substances does not impinge on the dominant position of the socialist economy. But even if these contracts are not executed, the same dependence is at hand. It is guarded by legal procedures established for the creation of new cooperatives or initiation of individual labor activities as well as by numerous other factors (supply of materials and equipment, providing of premises, and other items).

(e) Government control over the activities of nonsocialist economic phenomena shall be designed to eliminate any threat on the part of these phenomena to the dominant socialist economy. The basis of this control is created by introduction of declarations on income taxes and the governmental right to check the entire economic activity to verify the preciseness of these declarations. In addition, the appropriate governmental agencies have discretion to allow the economic activities exercised by individuals or by the new cooperatives as well as to prohibit these activities either generally (by a statutory act) or specifically (by a prohibition of economic activities of a certain person or a certain cooperative).

Due to all these circumstances, the socialist economy is strongly protected in the USSR, despite its combination with other economic phenomena.

The second question, concerning the degree of normal development of the socialist economy supplemented by the unusual economic phenomena, cannot be answered unequivocally. This extraordinary combination under the dominant position of the socialist economy and specific combinations introduced by the present reformists has been employed for the first time in Soviet economic history. No answers can be formulated on the basis of history or experience to date. Only abstract assessment is possible. From this point of view, it seems reasonable to distinguish between two different situations: components of the private economy are either accompanied or not by relatively adequate market relationships. Market relationships are restricted in all economic sectors of the USSR, and as a result, complete adequacy between these relationships and components of the market economy is impossible. But distinctions between approximate adequacy and its almost absolute absence can nevertheless be ascertained.

Activities of individual laborers and of the new cooperatives addressed to the populace's demands are based on a comparatively free market. They will, of course, come across supply difficulties necessitating a resort either to governmental assistance or the black market. But freedom of prices, free choice of contractual partners, free development of contractual terms, and so forth, are guaranteed in these cases. Normal economic functioning can be assured under the circumstances if governmental agencies do not interfere, disregarding the law in force and relying exclusively on their own discretion. The economic development of this character only replaces the socialist economy in the areas where the latter has insufficient or no capacity to satisfy the populace's demands. The situation for consumers will be improved if the services of individual laborers or of the new type of cooperatives are economically available to them. But the socialist economy as such will feel no impact from this economic development.

All other types of economic activities, regardless of whether they are implemented by socialist entities or by the private sector, individual or cooperative, are deprived of free market devices. The Soviet Union is not yet mature enough to introduce freedom of prices. Prices are regulated completely or substantially with respect to both the socialist economy and the private sector. Where there is no freedom of prices, there is no market freedom. Gorbachev and his adherents have decided to combine the socialist economy and private economic concepts to introduce genuine economic incentives. In comparison with the socialist economy, private economic phenomena are infinitesimal in the

USSR, and consequently, they cannot quantitatively affect the socialist economy to the extent necessary for comprehensively normal economic development. In addition, since even the private economic phenomena permitted in the USSR are deprived of adequate free market relationships, their own capacity to economically stimulate labor productivity is diminished so substantially that they cannot be relied upon in connection with the general purpose of improving the development of the Soviet economic system as a whole. As a result, there are no dependable reasons to think that the new economic reforms will be more successful than previous ones. This pessimistic conclusion follows from essential contradictions intrinsic to Gorbachev's economic policy.

He strives to save the socialist economy by employment of private economic constructions. At the same time, his purpose is to retain the socialist economy in its principal features and to prevent the penetration of ingredients typical for the private economy. It is obvious that the former goal is precluded by the latter purpose. Sooner or later, this contradiction will become clear to the Soviet leadership. Their eventual decision is unpredictable. One can speak only about the available alternatives: either rejection of the entire system or return to strong centralism.

Endnotes

Introduction

1. M.S. Gorbachev, *Speeches and Writings* (Oxford-New York: Pergamon Press, 1986), 131.

2. V.I. Lenin, *Collected Works*, 44: 99-100 (1958), cited in M.S. Gorbachev, *Speeches and Writings*, note 1, supra, at 154.

3. E.g., Marshall I. Goldman, *Gorbachev's Challenge* (New York-London: W.W. Norton and Company, 1987); E.A. Hewett, *Reforming the Soviet Economy* (Washington, D.C.: The Brookings Institution, 1988); Padma Desai, *Perestroika in Perspective*, (Princeton, N.J.: Princeton University Press, 1989). At the same time, certain works, especially those written by Russian emigres are sometimes sharply critical. E.g., Aleksandr Zinoviev, *Gorbachevism* (New York: Liberty, 1988). See also Judy Shelton, *The Coming Soviet Crash* (New York-London: The Free Press, 1989); George Feifer, "The New God Will Fail," *Harper's Magazine* (Oct. 1988): 43.

4. See a new governmental decree on the sale of liquor in *Izvestia*, 19 Sept. 1988.

5. For details, see Robert Conquest, *The Harvest of Sorrow* (New York-Oxford: Oxford University Press, 1986).

6. E.g., note 1, supra, at 25.

7. E.g., N.A. Ryzhkov, the Chairman of the USSR Council of Ministers in his speech at the CPSU's 27th Congress, *Izvestia*, 4 Mar. 1986.

8. 1977 Soviet Constitution, Article 108.

9. *Izvestia*, 3 Dec. 1988. Although the first Congress of People's Deputies in May and June of 1989 gave the appearance of democracy, in fact all of the decisions suggested by the summit of the CPSU for this meeting were adopted by the Congress. See, e.g. *Izvestia*, 26 May—15 June 1989.

10. 1988 Soviet Constitution, Articles 128-136.

11. Materials of the CPSU's Conference have been published in various editions. Publications in *Izvestia* of 29 June to 5 July 1988, will be used herein.

12. Id. See also the Law on Election of People's Deputies of the USSR, *Izvestia*, 4 Dec. 1988.

13. *Izvestia*, 29 July 1988.

14. There are numerous realms, not only those connected with military secrets, that are closed for *glasnost'*, according to the statements of Soviet media. As, for example, the magazine *Ogonek* states in issue no. 32 from 1988, "despite *glasnost'*, the labor-correctional establishment deprived of fresh air from freedom, stews in its own juice. . . . In separating a camp with a blank, impenetrable fence, completely removing 'the zone' [campgrounds] from the realm of our criticism and '*glasnost*'", the agency of ITU [Russian acronym of labor-correctional establishments] are not very interested with what happens there, beyond the fence."

15. *Moskovskie Novosti*, no. 32, 7 Aug. 1988.

16. Harold J. Berman, "The Possibilities and Limits of Soviet Economic Reform," *Soviet Law and Economy*, (O. Ioffe and M. Janis, eds.) (Dordrecht, Netherlands-Boston: Martinus Nijhoffe, 1986), 29-40.

17. *Izvestia*, 1 July 1987.

Chapter 1

1. *Sbornik Normativnikh Aktov po Khoziastvennomu Zakonodatel'stvu* (*Body of Statutory Acts on Economic Legislation*) (N.S. Malein ed.) (Moscow: 1979), 9.

2. Id. at 63, 86.

3. See the 1987 Law on the State Enterprise (Association), *Izvestia*, 1 July 1987.

4. M.S. Gorbachev, *Speeches and Writings* (Oxford-New York: Pergamon Press, 1986), 38-39.

5. See note 3, supra.

6. Abel Aganbeguian, *Perestroika — Le double défit Soviétique*, (Paris: Economica, 1987).

7. Id. at 10 et seq.

8. See note 4, supra, at 35-36.

9. See note 6, supra at 18.

10. Foreign Broadcast Information Service, 3 Nov. 1987, 51, 64.

11. *Ogonek*, Dec. 1988, no. 52: 12.

12. Moreover, as occurs with all officially proclaimed ideas in the USSR, *khozraschet*, designated only to one addressee, the Soviet economy, has been borrowed in certain other areas where it cannot be applied according to its actual substance. For instance, *khozraschet* for territories — several union republics and provinces — is introduced according to the Law on the 1989 Plan (*Izvestia*, 27 Jan. 1989). It is interesting that *Izvestia* itself emphasizes the inapplicability of this concept to territories in accordance with its meaning with respect to plants or factories. The newspaper prefers the term "economic mechanism of a territory" (Id.).

13. *Izvestia*, 27 Jan. 1989, 58.

14. *Overseas*, London, 1986, 112.

15. See note 11, supra.

16. *Izvestia*, 24 Jan. and 3 March 1989.

17. *Izvestia*, 3 Feb. 1989.

18. See note 10, supra at 51.

19. See note 4, supra at 25.

20. 1936 Constitution of the USSR, Article 6.

21. E.g., A.V. Venediktov, *Gosudarstvennaia Sotsialisticheskaia Sobstvennost'* (*State Socialist Ownership*) (Moscow-Leningrad: 1948), 328-29.

22. 1961 Fundamental Principles of Civil Legislation of the USSR and Union Republics, Article 21.

23. *Ved. SSSR*, 1981, no. 44, item 1184.

24. *Sovetskoe Gosudarstvo i Pravo*, 1988, no. 6: 19-34; 1981, no. 1: 132-38.

25. Iu. Kalmikov, "Obshchenarodnaia Sobstvennost' i Trudovoi Kollektiv," *Khoziaistvo i Pravo*, 1988, no. 12, p. 56.

26. *Izvestia*, 30 Nov. 1988.

27. It is interesting that the enterprise can rent out its functioning fundamental assets and sell those that become surplus. However, the 1987 Law does not mention the different conditions to be observed in the former and in the latter cases. These conditions are referred to only to indicate the funds to which sales receipts must be diverted (Article 4.4). Such a legal technique entails an erroneous impression as if the fundamental assets are also encompassed by the enterprise's right of disposition of the whole volume.

28. See the 1987 Law, Article 3.

29. Id., Articles 2 and 3.

30. Igor Birman, *Ekonomika Nedostach (The Economy of Shortcomings)* (New York: Chalidze Publications, 1983).

31. See note 6, supra, at 10.

32. 1987 Law, Article 6(2).

33. Id., Article 6(3).

34. Id., Article 6(5).

35. *Izvestia*, 22 Aug. 1988.

36. *SP SSSR (Collection of USSR Governmental Decrees)*, 1949, no. 9, item 68.

37. *SP SSSR*, 1962, no. 12, item 94.

38. *SP SSSR*, 1959, no. 11, item 68.

39. 1964 RSFSR Civil Code, Article 160.

40. *SP SSSR*, 1965, no. 19-20, item 153.

41. *SP SSSR*, 1981, Part I, nos. 9-10, item 62.

42. See note 10, supra, at 21, 42.

43. *Izvestia*, 22 July 1988.

44. Id.

45. Id.

46. Id.

47. See note 36, supra, at 42.

48. Id.

49. See note 37, supra.

50. Id.

51. *SP SSSR*, 1988, nos. 24-25, item 10.

52. *New York Times*, 26 Sept. 1988.

Chapter 2

1. Compare Articles 52 and 57 of the 1922 Civil Code of the RSFSR.

2. See the 1969 Model Collective Farm Charter, *Resheniia Partii i Pravitel'stva po Sel'skomu Khoziaistvu* (1965-1971) (Moscow, 1971), 419-39.

3. See the Model Charters of Local and Central Links of Consumer Cooperatives, *Sbornik Normativnikh Aktov po Grazhdanskomu Zakonodatel'stvu*, Part I, (Moscow, 1984), 130-59. All these charters are renovated by the Twelfth Congress of Consumer Cooperatives (*Izvestia*, 20 Mar. 1989).

4. A decree issued by the CPSU Central Committee and the USSR Council of Ministers and published by *Izvestia* on 23 Nov. 1985.

5. *Izvestia*, 8 June 1988.

6. The draft of this charter, published by *Izvestia* on 10 Jan. 1988, was confirmed by the All-Union Council on the Matter of Collective Farms.

7. See note 4, supra.

8. *Izvestia*, 16 Mar. 1989.

9. Id.

10. See note 3, supra.

11. *Izvestia*, 27 Feb. 1989.

12. *Izvestia*, 17 Sept. 1988.

13. 1988 Law on Cooperation, Article 12(2).

14. *Izvestia*, 31 Dec. 1988.

15. *Izvestia*, 2 Jan. 1989.

16. *Ogonek*, 1988, no. 29:4.

17. *Ogonek*, 1988, no. 39:2.

18. *Izvestia*, 10 Mar. 1989.

19. To prevent excessive enrichment of these cooperatives and their members, the USSR Council of Ministers established progressive taxes for these cases (*SP SSSR*, 1988, no. 15, item 41). However, taxes had been so high that an edict of the Presidium of the USSR Supreme Soviet of 23 Feb. 1989 (*Izvestia*, 23 Feb. 1989), diminished their amount.

20. 1988 Law on Cooperation, Article 18(1).

21. See note 13, supra.

22. See note 14, supra.

23. See note 8, supra.

24. *Izvestia*, 10 Jan. 1988; 1988 Charter of the Collective Farms, Article 15.

25. Id.

26. See note 17, supra; 1988 Charter of the Collective Farms, Article 12.

27. Id.

28. See note 3, supra.

29. Article 46.

30. Article 47.

31. Article 48.

32. Article 3(2).

33. Articles 7, 11.

34. Article 11.

35. Id.

36. Article 20.

37. Articles 40-44.

38. *Ogonek*, 1988, no. 23:4-5.

39. Id. at 5.

40. Id. at 4.

41. See note 19, supra.

42. As will be discussed in Chapter Four, this official view is modified by Soviet leaders themselves only with respect to agricultural activities.

43. See Chapter Four.

44. *Izvestia*, 1 and 2 Oct. 1988.

45. Article 95.

46. Articles 108-11.

47. See Chapter Four.

48. Consumer cooperatives possess a number of small plants for processing agricultural produce before its sale, but these plants do not play a serious role in the cooperative's activities.

49. 1988 Law on Cooperation, Article 17(3).

50. *Izvestia*, 12 Oct. 1988.

51. Plans developed by cooperatives themselves on the basis of executed contracts are not taken into account in this respect. 1988 Law on Cooperation, Article 18(1).

52. Id., Article 19(4).

53. Id., Article 18(2).

54. Id., Article 19(3).

55. Id., Article 18(3).

56. Article 17(2).

57. *Ogonek*, 1988, no. 42:2.

58. *Izvestia*, 13 Oct. 1988.

59. *Izvestia*, 1 Sept. 1988.

60. 1988 Law on Cooperation, Article 20.

Chapter 3

1. 1936 Constitution, Article 10.

2. Id., Article 9.

3. This correlation is declared by the 1936 Constitution. In fact, however, especially in Stalin's time, the collective farmers' private plots ensured the principal source of their earnings, and labor in collective farms, previously unpaid, does not suffice even now to satisfy the reasonable demands of collective farmers and their families.

4. 1961 Fundamental Principles of Civil Legislation of the USSR and Union Republics, Article 25.

5. *Izvestia*, 2 Nov. 1988.

6. However, the former terminology is employed by the civil codes and certain other statutory acts. As will be discussed below, Gorbachev has substantially enlarged the limits of individual labor activities, introducing even individual lease of plots of land. Therefore, certain scholars suggest eliminating the consumer character as a feature of personal property, frankly recognizing that the latter can be employed for production purposes also (*Sovetskoe Gosudarstvo i Pravo*, 1989, no. 1:132-38). However, Gorbachev and other Soviet officials use the name "individual labor property," dealing with property arising as a result of individual labor activities. Accordingly, certain scholars contend that in the USSR individual personal property and individual labor property must be distinguished. They also insist on broader

development of legislation dedicated to the latter than developed at the present time (Id.).

7. See, e.g., *Sovetskoe Grazhdanskoe Pravo, Part 1*, (Leningrad: 1982), 375-81.

8. *SP SSSR*, 1986, no. 21, items 119-21.

9. *Vedomosti SSSR*, 1986, no. 22, item 364.

10. See the Introduction herein.

11. *SZ SSSR*, 1932, no. 62, item 360.

12. *SP SSSR*, 1986, no. 21, item 119.

13. Id.

14. *SP SSSR*, 1986, no. 21, item 120.

15. *Izvestia*, 21 Nov. 1986.

16. Therefore, Soviet authors themselves have emphasized that the November law does not introduce a new NEP in the USSR. E.g., Miroslav Kondratev, *The "Pros" and "Cons" of Individual Labor*, (Moscow: 1987), 3.

17. *Pravda*, 21 Nov. 1986.

18. Kondratev, note 16, supra, at 5-6.

19. *Novii Mir*, 1987, no. 6:148.

20. *Voprosi Ekonomiki*, 1986, no. 9:99.

21. *Sotsialisticheskii Trud*, 1987, no. 6:71.

22. *Sel'skaia Zhizn*, 24 Mar. 1987.

23. *Voprosi Ekonomiki*, 1987, no. 8:61.

24. See note 17, supra, at 1.

25. Id. at 9.

26. Article 15.

27. *SP SSSR*, 1988, no. 31, item 88.

28. *Izvestia*, 13 Feb. 1987.

29. *Izvestia*, 20 Nov. 1986.

30. November law, Article 8.

Chapter 4

1. *Izvestia*, 16 Mar. 1989.
2. Article 14(3).
3. Id.
4. Id.
5. Id.
6. E.g., *Izvestia*, 8 Feb. 1989.
7. Id.
8. Id.
9. *Izvestia*, 28 Oct. 1988.
10. Id.
11. Id.
12. *Izvestia*, 7 Feb. 1989.
13. Id.
14. *Izvestia*, 24 Oct. 1988.
15. Id.
16. Article 19(2).
17. Article 18(2).
18. Article 18(1).
19. *Izvestia*, 19 Sept. 1988.
20. 1988 Law on Cooperation, Article 19(3).
21. Id., Article 18(2).
22. Id., Article 17(3).
23. Id., Article 18(2).
24. Article 5.
25. Id.
26. Id., Article 18(4).
27. Id., Articles 18(2), 19(3).

28. *Izvestia*, 16 Mar. 1989. Materials for these meetings are also presented in the March 17 and 18, 1989, issues of *Izvestia*.

29. Id.

30. Article 26 of the Model Statute of the Collective Farm; Article 33(4) of the 1988 Law on Cooperation.

31. *Izvestia*, 23 Mar. 1989.

32. *Kollektivnii Podriad v Sel'skom Khoziaistve*, (Saratov: 1986).

33. Article 33(4).

34. *Izvestia*, 15 Nov. 1988.

35. Id.

36. *Izvestia*, 10 Jan. 1989.

37. *Izvestia*, 15 Nov. 1988.

38. The renovations under discussion are employed in both collective farms and state farms.

39. See note 30 supra.

40. *Izvestia*, 29 July 1988.

41. Id.

42. *Izvestia*, 6 Aug. 1988.

43. Id.

44. *Izvestia*, 19 Oct. 1988.

45. Id.

46. Id.

47. *Izvestia*, 15 Oct. 1988.

48. *Izvestia*, 8 Dec. 1988.

49. Id.

50. Id.

51. Id.

52. *Izvestia*, 25 Sept. 1988.

53. Id.

54. *Izvestia*, 6 Sept. 1988.

55. Id.

56. *Izvestia*, 12 Nov. 1988.

57. Id.

58. Article 33(54).

59. *Izvestia*, 13 Nov. 1988.

60. *Izvestia*, 4 Nov. 1988.

61. *Izvestia*, 2 Nov. 1988.

62. *Izvestia*, 4 Nov. 1988.

63. *Izvestia*, 26 July 1988.

64. *Izvestia*, 8 Oct. 1988.

65. *Izvestia*, 18 Dec. 1988.

66. Id.

67. See note 55, supra.

68. *Izvestia*, 1 Oct. 1988.

69. Id.

70. "Lease Development, Reconstruction of Economic Relations in Rural areas," *Izvestia*, 14 Oct. 1988.

71. Id.

72. Id.

73. Id.

74. Id.

75. *Izvestia*, 30 Nov. 1988.

76. *Izvestia*, 15 Nov. 1988.

77. *Izvestia*, 11 Dec. 1988.

78. *Izvestia*, 4 Sept. 1988.

79. *Izvestia*, 26 July 1988.

80. *Izvestia*, 18 Feb. 1989.

81. *Izvestia*, 5 Feb. 1989.

82. *Moskovskie Novosti*, 4 Dec. 1988.

83. Id.

84. Id.

85. *Izvestia*, 14 Oct. 1988.

86. *Izvestia*, 26 July 1988.

87. There are suggestions that local executive committees made contracts of lease and collective farms imposed the appropriate tasks on individual lessees (*Izvestia*, 20 Dec. 1988). According to these suggestions, each collective farmer leasing a plot of land must be entitled to retain or to terminate his membership in a collective farm (*Izvestia*, 14 Feb. 1989).

88. *Izvestia*, 14 Oct. 1988.

89. Therefore, eventual lessees came across numerous bureaucratic obstacles. See, e.g., *Izvestia*, 5 Dec. 1988; 18 Jan., 13 Feb., 4 Mar., and 20 Mar. 1989; *Moskovskie Novosti*, 12 Mar. 1989. As a matter of course, foes of leases of land can create obstacles to the execution of these contracts even after the appropriate law is promulgated.

90. *Izvestia*, 16 May 1988.

91. *Izvestia*, 14 Oct. 1988.

92. Id. The same trend is general in the Baltic Republics (compare *Izvestia*, 17 Feb. 1989).

93. *Izvestia*, 9 Apr. 1989. As this issue of *Izvestia* reports, simultaneously the USSR Council of Ministers adopted the decree "On the Economic and Organizational Foundations of Lease Relations in the USSR."

94. Along with leases of land, the Soviet leadership resorts to other measures that must strengthen agricultural activities. See, especially, two governmental decrees of 5 Apr. 1989: "On Radical Reconstruction of Economic Relations and Administration of Agricultural/Industrial Complex of the Country" (*Izvestia*, 12 Apr. 1989) and "On the Program of Social Development of Rural Areas" (*Izvestia*, 13 Apr. 1989).

95. See note 80, supra.

Conclusion

1. *The New York Times*, 23 Nov. 1988.

2. Igor Birman, *Stroit Zanovo* (Benson, Vt.: Chalidze Publications, 1988), 66.

3. *Strana i Mir*, 1984, nos. 1-2.

4. *Izvestia*, 30 Nov. 1988.

5. See Introduction.

6. See note 2, supra, at 218.

Glossary

1961 Fundamental Principles of Civil Legislation—the supreme law of the whole system of legislation dedicated to matters of civil law. The civil codes of each of the fifteen Soviet republics and other civil legislation supplement and develop the Fundamental Principles, but they cannot contradict them.

1965 Reforms—resulted from an initiative by Aleksei Kosygin, a former chairman of the Council of Ministers. These reforms of a decentralizing character were intended to strengthen the role of contracts and to reduce the role of centralized planning of the Soviet economy. But after secret directives instigated by Brezhnev, the 1965 Reforms were abandoned soon after their adoption.

1987 Law on the State Enterprise (Association)—contains all of the important provisions of Gorbachev's economic reforms, that is, those concerning rights of enterprises and associations. This law broadens the initiatives of enterprises and associations and restricts interference by superior agencies.

1988 Law on Cooperation—one of Gorbachev's principal economic laws whose purpose is to restore trade cooperatives and to enlarge the forms of their activities. Previous trade cooperatives were dissolved in the 1950s.

Arbitrazh—a special agency to hear disputes between economic and other entities. State *arbitrazh* deals with disputes of entities of different ministries. Department *arbitrazh* (within a ministry) must resolve disputes of entities subordinate to the same ministry.

Brigades—constituent parts of workshops that in turn are constituent parts of plants or factories.

Central Committee of the Communist Party—an agency of the Communist Party of the Soviet Union (CPSU) consisting of several hundred members and elected at a Party Congress held every five years. Formally, it is subordinate to the Party Congress. In fact, it is ruled by the Politburo.

Circulating assets—materials, semi-finished goods, etc., that are consumed during one production cycle. An economic entity's rights to circulating assets are broader than its rights to fundamental assets.

Collective farms (*kolkhozi*)—rural cooperatives, based on membership, dealing only or mainly with agricultural production. They were created by Stalin through coercion in the early 1930s to liquidate individual farming.

Collectivization—mass creation of collective farms in the late 1920s and early 1930s based on the premise of abolition of individual farming.

Commercial vs. economic accountability—commercial accountability existed during NEP as a form of participation of state entities in market relations under a liberal planning scheme. The introduction of strong planning administration in the late 1920s and early 1930s transformed commercial accountability into economic accountability.

Congress of People's Deputies—the newly-formed supreme agency of Soviet power. Some members are elected by nationwide secret ballot for five-year terms. Other members are selected by Party and societal organizations. Sessions are held annually. The congress, in turn, elects the Supreme Soviet and its chairman (the Soviet President). This body deals with matters of great significance, e.g. amendments to the Soviet constitution.

Consumer cooperatives—rural cooperatives whose principle task is to provide food and other supplies to the rural population. They are also responsible for selling the agricultural produce of collective farms in urban markets.

Cooperative—a collective economic entity based on membership (for example, consumer cooperatives) and frequently based on the labor contributed by members (for example, collective farms). Cooperatives function in production, trade, and other areas of the economy.

Council of Ministers—the highest agency of executive power in the Soviet Union, headed by a chairman and consisting of deputies and ministers.

Cyclical economic development—the consistent movement of the Soviet economy from centralized administration to decentralization in order to prevent economic collapse, and the subsequent return to centralism to ameliorate the weakening of the political power of the ruling elite.

Decrees—statutory acts issued by the government, in contrast to laws adopted by legislative agencies. Decrees must not contradict laws. In cases of conflict, decrees are invalidated in a procedure provided for by Soviet legislation.

Family contracts—agreements executed between a state or cooperative entity and an entire family to perform a certain task, for instance, to cultivate a parcel of land belonging to a collective or state farm.

Fundamental assets—machines, equipment, and other means of production that can be used for a period longer than one production cycle. An economic entity's rights to fundamental assets are severely restricted.

Glasnost'—generally translated as "openness," this concept involves the broad dissemination of information about politics of the Communist Party and the state, as well as events of domestic and international life. Gorbachev has substantially enlarged public access to information, but by no means has removed censorship.

Gosagroprom—the State Committee of Agriculture and Industry, a government agency created in the mid-1980s to administer agricultural and numerous other economies connected with agriculture. Gosagroprom was abolished in 1989.

Gosplan—the State Committee of Planning, which is the government agency that plans the Soviet economy either directly or in accordance with directives of higher agencies (e.g., the Council of Ministers of the USSR).

Gossnab—the State Committee of Supply. It administers supply of most means of production (not consumer goods). Supply of the important means of production are controlled by Gosplan.

Housing cooperatives—organizations created by individuals to build and use residential apartments or other living space. All expenses are reimbursed by individual members. In form, they are governed by their own boards, but in fact, local executive committees administer the activities of housing cooperatives.

Incentive funds—created by economic entities as resources for bonuses paid to workers, enlargement of activities over the limits specified by planned indicators, etc. The creation and amount of incentive funds depend on fulfillment of principal planning tasks.

Independent work contract— an agreement between a contractor and its customer, with both parties reciprocally independent. The customer must pay for ordered work only on the condition that this work is completely performed by the contractor.

Industrial economy—that segment of the total economy represented by heavy and light industry. It is considered the principal component of the Soviet economy, and as a rule, heavy industry is developed more actively than light industry.

Khozraschet—economic accountability. Full *khozraschet* means the development of economic activities exclusively by means of an economic entity's own resources. This precludes government subsidies, but repayable bank credits can be used.

Machine and Tractor Station (MTS)—a state entity that performed machine work for collective farms and received payment in the form of agricultural produce. Khrushchev liquidated MTS entities in the late 1950s and their machinery was sold to collective farms.

May Enactments—three decrees issued by supreme soviet agencies in May 1986 and designed to combat the extraction of unearned income.

304

Ministry of Finances—administers the state budget, implements financial controls, accumulates taxes and other payments transferred to the state budget, and distributes state finances among state entities in accordance with confirmed economic plans.

Netrudovoi dokhod—unearned income, that is, income received without the labor of the acquirer. In those instances in which Soviet law precludes retention of such income (for example, inheritance) it must be withdrawn for the benefit of the Soviet state.

New cooperatives—trade cooperatives restored in the late 1980s, but in a different form than the trade cooperatives abolished in the late 1950s.

New Economic Politics (NEP)—introduced by Lenin in 1921 and abolished by Stalin in the late 1920s. NEP entailed restoration of small private enterprises, replacement of distribution in kind by a goods-money exchange, and employment of this exchange by both private enterprises and state entities.

Normativi **(normatives)**—levels of funding and other resources designated for economic entities. These amounts are centrally established and are mandatory in nature.

Operative management—a specific right of state entities with respect to property transferred to them by the state. This property belongs to the state and can be used by each state entity only in accordance with established purposes and planning tasks.

Pamiat' **(Memory)**—an informal society created by advocates of Russian chauvinism, with anti-Semitic and other similar views and purposes. The current Soviet regime neither openly supports nor prohibits this growing society and its activities.

Perestroika—literally, "reconstruction," the word employed by Gorbachev to emphasize a principal feature of his reforms. It signifies a new organization of economic and other activities to attain a higher level of social development in the Soviet Union.

Plan indicators—the amount, quality, type, and so forth of products that must be produced and sold by economic entities. Decentralizing reforms entail a decrease in the use of plan indicators. Centralization requires a corresponding increase.

Planned contracts—those specifications for production created and ordered by government planning agencies. The degree of dependence on planned contracts is an indicator of the level of centralization of the Soviet economy.

Planovoubitochnie **(plan enterprises)**—those enterprises whose products must be sold below cost. The difference between cost and revenue is reimbursed by the state.

Politburo—a collective body of twelve to fourteen members elected by the Central Committee of the Communist Party. Formally subordinate to the Central Committee, the Politburo is, in fact, the supreme ruling agency implementing unlimited political power in the USSR.

Presidium of the Supreme Soviet—the Congress of People's Deputies elects the Supreme Soviet of the USSR, which in turn elects its Presidium to handle day-to-day activities.

Primary cooperatives—the lowest links in the cooperative system, for example, *sel'po* (a society of rural consumers) is the lowest component of the system of consumer cooperatives.

Property funds—money available to economic entities for fundamental assets, circulating assets, resources earmarked for repair, etc. As a rule, it is prohibited to channel resources of one property fund to another.

RAPO—local agencies of Gosagroprom. They were eliminated along with Gosagroprom in 1989.

Raskrestianivanie—the notion of a peasant's alienation from his image of himself as master of the land resulting from the creation of collective farms. This separation from traditonal values decreases the incentive to engage in peasant or farming labor.

Republican civil codes — bodies of law in each of the fifteen Soviet republics that regulate property relations. These codes are subordinate to the 1961 Fundamental Principles of Civil Legislation of the USSR and union republics. Distinctions from one code to another are negligible.

Self-financing — funding of all investments through an enterprise's own resources or through repayable bank credits. Money in the state budget can be used only for construction projects provided for by the state plan.

Self-management — control over economic activities by the enterprise (association) itself, without interference from above. This interference can only be restricted, not abolished under the Soviet economic system.

Socialist property — tangible and intangible goods belonging to the Soviet state, collective farms and cooperative entities, trade unions, and other societal organizations. The property of individuals is called personal property, or individual labor property if a proprietor has his or her own economy.

State farms (*sovkhozi*) — state agricultural enterprises. In contrast to collective farms (*kolkhozi*), state farms are based not on membership but rather on labor contracts executed between the state farm and individual peasants.

Supreme Soviet — the Soviet legislature now elected each year by the Congress of People's Deputies.

Trade cooperatives — groups of craftsmen, dissolved by Khrushchev in the late 1950s, but restored by Gorbachev in the late 1980s.

Underground economy — unlawful economic activities of individuals or groups, implemented either secretly or under guise of lawful activities, for example, the creation of a private enterprise registered as a cooperative entity.

Vnutrenii khozraschet—the internal accountability applicable to workshops, brigades, and other constituent parts of plants and factories. These various industrial groups receive planning indicators governing the costs of their products. If actual product costs come in under the costs specified in the planning indicators, workers receive proportional bonuses.

War Communism—proclaimed in 1917 directly after the establishment of the Soviet regime and replaced by NEP in 1921. The economy was managed through distribution in kind (without the use of money), centrally-issued administrative commands addressed to state entities (without reciprocal contracts), and coercive withdrawal of agricultural produce from farmers (without monetary compensation).

Workshops—constituent parts of plants or factories.

Zakazi—mandatory state orders addressed to production entities to distribute their products among consumer entities. Because of *zakazi*, Gorbachev's reforms retain rigid centralized distribution, despite declarations of decentralized distribution.

Index

311

Update to the Second Printing: From Dilemma to Crisis

It has been less than a year since the first printing of this book. But what a year it has been! Many have said that communism died in the last year. Its flag bearer, the Soviet Union, has certainly been wounded. Putting aside for the moment the Soviet economy and its relationship to everything else that has happened, there are three developments that stand out as particularly monumental.

First of all, the Soviet bloc has ceased to be a bloc. In short order, the communists in Eastern Europe lost their dominant positions, and each country began to restructure its system itself, using Western democracy as a model.

Second, the Soviet Union has stopped looking like a union. There have been violent ethnic clashes in Azerbaijan and elsewhere, and there have been political clashes throughout the country. The secession movements in Lithuania and the other Baltic Republics have perhaps given Gorbachev his most dangerous dilemma to date, and there is growing nationalism in the form of chauvinism in the Russian Republic.

The third change has been to the Soviet government itself. The formal, constitutional recognition of the leading role of the Communist Party was abolished by the Congress of People's Deputies in March 1990. This change and the political reforms that accompanied it are more than cosmetic. They have, in fact, left a void for some other agency to fill.

Gorbachev and the Soviet leadership, faced with these three political developments and the continuing deterioration of the economy, responded in the only reasonable way they could. They filled the void left by the abolition of strong Party administration by transferring power from the summit of the Communist Party as a collective agency to the new presidency and made the President, once again Gorbachev, a personal dictator.

This book begins with a history lesson about Soviet attempts at *perestroika* through decentralization of the economy. Each of these attempts reached a point where the economic monopoly of the ruling elite became threatened and recentralization of the economy became necessary. The book proceeds to look at the economic reforms introduced by Gorbachev in his first four years of power and points out their flaws. This analysis continues to be accurate. The reforms described *are* flawed. In the current situation, however, the ruling elite is not threatened by the success of decentralization but by the continued failures of these inadequate stopgap reform measures.

This book also predicts that the cycle in administration of the economy will swing back to strong centralism unless the fundamental nature of the Soviet system is abolished. Nikolai Ryzhkov, the Chairman of the USSR Council of Ministers and one of the most outspoken reformers, suggested in December 1989 in his report to the Second Congress of the People's Deputies that centralized distribution of all products would have to be retained for at least six more years in order to create the necessary reserves of goods that will make unplanned, decentralized distribution work. He did not explain how the USSR would resolve this problem in six years, ignoring the fact that it has not been able to resolve the goods shortage during the more than seventy years of Soviet rule. Six years is clearly not enough time to reconvert the agricultural economy into one in which individual farmers have the necessary skills, incentives, and attachment to the land to increase productivity.

Update to the Second Printing:
From Dilemma to Crisis

The development of and debate over new methods of governmental administration of the Soviet economic system have been particularly active since the first printing of this book. There seems to be a consensus that the reforms of the first four years that are analyzed in this book were too little. The newer reforms may be too late.

Two new reforms are particularly significant and quite substantial: one dealing with land,[1] and the other dealing with private ownership.[2] These laws expand and strengthen the socialist economic system's combination with certain components of the capitalist economy. They introduce hereditary land ownership and the concept of private leasing of land. Moreover, private ownership in its proper Marxist-Leninist interpretation — i.e., that which is based on the labor of workers hired by individuals, previously categorically rejected by Soviet leaders as the epitome of exploitation — is now allowed with respect to small enterprises created by Soviet entrepreneurs.

These new economic phenomena, as they are expressed by the laws which open the path to their development in practice, must be examined against the thesis of this book. *What follows from this book is that Gorbachev's economic reforms do not revolutionize the Soviet economic system. They are aimed only at its improvement and are subject to the guiding principle that the economic monopoly of the ruling elite as the basis for its unlimited political power must remain intact, despite the present and eventual development of private ownership as legalized within certain limits.*

As mentioned above, the decentralization trend of Soviet economic reforms has proved not to be as consistent as it seemed initially. Planned distribution of products (except the so-called "state orders," such as means of production in the state economy) was to be replaced by non-planned, contractual distribution. The resulting shortages of almost all kinds of products, especially consumer goods, quickly revealed the impracticality of these forms of distribution, and Ryzhkov announced the need for a six-year waiting period. It is clear that the transfer to a mixed market economy, which was supposed to rescue the Soviet economy, has been postponed for at least six years.

Ryzhkov's report was followed not only by the restoration of centralized distribution for state and cooperative entities but also by the introduction of rationing in the retail trade system, which was quickly transformed from a partial to an almost all-embracing application. Nevertheless, Soviet media resumed discussion of the development of free markets in the Soviet Union, and numerous participants, including leaders such as Gorbachev himself, assess this idea as positive and even unavoidable. Such hesitation by Soviet rulers to attack one of the most important problems of their economic reforms demonstrates that to characterize these reforms simply as economic decentralization is a result of one-sided analysis. Soviet rulers resort both to centralism and decentralization, trying either to find a successful combination or to replace centralism by decentralization entirely for a time.

Gorbachev announced his economic reforms as one of the components of the comprehensive democratization of the Soviet system. The Soviet leadership ceaselessly repeats that no successful economic development is possible without establishing a genuine democracy. A certain forerunner of this democracy has already appeared in the forms of limited *glasnost'* or "openness," controlled freedom of speech, a limited principle of multiple candidates for each electoral office, etc. However, the development of democracy has also brought along anti-democratic processes. For example, the Supreme Soviet of the USSR (the Soviet parliament) is elected not directly by the whole people but by the Congress of the People's Deputies (CPSU). Members of this congress itself are not all elected by nationwide ballot; the Central Committee of the CPSU and ruling agencies of other organizations such as trade unions control 150 seats. As a result, Gorbachev became one of the deputies by means of appointment, not election. He was then elected as Chairman of the Supreme Soviet by the Congress of People's Deputies without a direct expression of the people's will.

It is strange that certain measures that seem truly democratic are frequently becoming entrapped in the channels of the new Soviet bureaucracy. For instance, a draft of new Fundamental Principles of Criminal Legislation was published before this book was begun. This draft would have outlawed capital punishment for economic crimes. Because the author is accustomed to quick transformation of drafts into laws in the USSR, the introduction to this book mentions that economic crimes would no longer carry capital punishment in 1989. However, this has not occurred because the draft remains just a draft.

In contrast, the establishment of the new presidency of the USSR was implemented in great haste, and in March 1990 both the draft and the law governing this issue were promulgated. Although the law provides that the President must be elected by the whole people, an exception was made for Gorbachev. As the first President in Soviet history, he was not elected by popular vote. He was elected by the Congress of People's Deputies, at the third, extraordinary session of the congress, summoned for the purpose of creating the office of President and choosing Gorbachev as the first President. Thus, Gorbachev managed to circumvent his own democratic institutions twice: by being appointed as a people's deputy by the Central Committee, not by general election; and through his election as President by the Congress of People's Deputies, not by popular, national vote. In other words, these two democratic initiatives introduced by Gorbachev were proclaimed powerless with respect to Gorbachev himself. Is this genuine democracy or democracy disguising dictatorship? The answer seems clear.

The Soviet President possesses powers that never belonged, at least formally, to any previous Soviet leader. He is responsible for guaranteeing the observance of rights and freedoms, as well as the Constitution and laws. He has the power to employ necessary measures to protect the sovereignty of the USSR and union republics and the safety and territorial unity of the country. He represents the USSR in domestic and international affairs and signs international treaties. He is the one who submits candidates to the Supreme Soviet for the most important governmental offices, including the post of Chairman of the Council of Ministers; and he can require the resignation of those officials and of all ministers, in conjunction with the Chairman of the Council of Ministers, and appoint new ministers. He handles military, diplomatic, and other appointments of honor and controls awards, citizenship, and political amnesty and shelter. He is responsible for mobilizing troops and forwarding requests for declaration of war to the Supreme Soviet. He can declare martial law or a state of emergency and, if necessary, introduce direct presidential administration of territories. He has the veto power over laws and has the right to initiate legislation and issue his own edicts. He is Commander-in-Chief of the military. He can resolve disputes between two legislative bodies, and he can require the Congress of People's Deputies to elect a new Supreme Soviet.[3]

The very enumeration of these powers now transferred to the President proves the view that what is happening is a consolidation of enormous power in the grasp of one person, not democratization. Is this consolidation dictated by the demands of economic reforms or by other circumstances, including Gorbachev's own cult of personality and tendency toward dictatorship? What would be Western reaction to these powers concentrated in a less attractive leader?

There is no doubt that without Gorbachev's approval or initiative all of these changes in the structure of the Soviet power system could not have occurred. The same can be said for the anti-democratic methods of implementing these changes. Thus, Gorbachev has demonstrated that he is not a democrat of the variety that has often been described by both Soviet and Western media. To what extent have the demands of economic reforms necessitated the creation of this presidency that is invested with the broadest power in Soviet history? If the reforms strive to democratize and decentralize the Soviet economy, why must the political structure be so centralized? In enumerating the purposes of the creation of the institution of the presidency of the USSR, the 1990 law also refers to "assurance of further development of deep political and economic transformations."[4] However, a look at the list of specific powers instilled in the President leaves no doubt that the establishment of this office has little to do with the implementation of economic reforms.

The development of a personal political dictatorship, putting aside Gorbachev's individual inclinations, has been engendered by the general situation in the country, predetermined by the three monumental political developments described above along with the omnipresent food shortages. Once again, the three political changes are: the breakup of the external part of the Soviet empire, i.e., Eastern Europe; the domestic, ethnic, and political clashes; and the abolition of the leading role of the CPSU that has been undisputed since Lenin proclaimed the Party to be the "vanguard of the proletariat." The consumer goods problem, and especially the food supply problem, has become more acute as a result of Gorbachev's economic reforms and experiments with decentralization. The masses certainly understand that this is a problem that cannot be resolved drastically with one stroke. But it cannot be tolerated indefinitely.

The Soviet rulers are unable to give the people these basic necessities, and therefore, they must be ready to repulse assaults stimulated by malnutrition and starvation. In order to do so, they must have strong, centralized power. Likewise, to fight back against defections and rebellion from Eastern Europe and from within the Soviet Union, they must have the power of a strong hand. Finally, there is the need to fill the gap left by the retreat of the Communist Party. All of these needs together led to the consolidation of power in President Gorbachev.

Meanwhile, the phenomena created by the economic reforms as described in this book have not remained completely stable and have contributed to the crises facing Gorbachev. For example, the new cooperatives that represent a modified form of individual ownership are now viewed by most Soviets with more hostility and disdain than ever before. Crime and corruption are rampant. The popular hostility has even affected the central government agencies, which have been forced to introduce periodic restrictions on cooperative activities. Needless to say, the requirements of local executive committee supervision over cooperatives has contributed to the problems. Judging from Soviet media, the executive committees impose all possible obstacles to the normal development of these cooperatives. Various means designed to attract private components to industry and agriculture (leases, independent work contracts, and combinations of the two) have not ensured the desired effect. Individual labor activities, though becoming more capable of satisfying the demands of the populace, still lag far behind this demand. The general growth of productivity of the Soviet economy stands between zero and two percent.

The predictions made in this book, then, that Gorbachev's economic reforms were doomed, have found corroboration in Soviet reality. This continued prospect, however, should not detract attention from the Soviet economy and the reform measures as described herein and as outlined by Soviet rulers. To understand the Soviet economy one must know the characteristics it has acquired as a result of the economic reforms proclaimed by Gorbachev during the second half of the 1980s. That analysis can be found in this book. To facilitate the study of the future development of the same phenomena, new books must be written. This author is currently working on such a book dedicated to changes in the Soviet law of ownership. It will be published by Merrill/Magnus later this year, and it will also encompass the latest economic trends in the USSR in

their legal and factual expression. Together, these two publications will give the reader an understanding of the Soviet
economy as a separate entity and as it relates to political
and other events.

Olimpiad S. Ioffe
Hartford, Connecticut
April 1990